China in the Eyes of the Japanese

The relation between China and Japan is one of the most important bilateral relationships in the world but how did the Japanese view China in ancient times? How did views change throughout the course of history? How could China's image be improved in Japanese people's eyes?

This book provides an analysis of the history of contact between China and Japan and surveys the present situation to understand general views of Japanese society toward China. Through scientific public opinion surveys as well as in-depth interviews, the book examines ordinary and elite Japanese people's views of Chinese culture, society, politics, the economy, media, and Sino-Japanese relations. In addition, it analyzes the main causes of the formation of such views, and makes suggestions on promoting positive public opinions of China. The authors hope that this title can deepen Japanese society's understanding and comprehension of China, help promote Sino-Japanese non-governmental exchange, and lay the foundation for continuous development of Sino-Japanese relations.

This title will appeal to students and scholars of cultural studies, international relations and Asian studies.

Wang Xiuli is associate professor at School of New Media, Peking University. Her research interests include social media, public opinion, and international public relations.

Wang Wei is associate professor in the School of Journalism and Communication, Hunan University. Her research interests include media convergence, social media, and international relations and media.

Liang Yunxiang is professor in the School of International Studies, Peking University. His research interests include Japan politics and diplomacy, Sino-Japan relationship, international law, and North-East Asian relations. His recent published books are *Japan Diplomacy and Sino-Japanese Relationship*, and *International Relations and International Law*.

China Perspectives

The *China Perspectives* series focuses on translating and publishing works by leading Chinese scholars, writing about both global topics and China-related themes. It covers Humanities & Social Sciences, Education, Media and Psychology, as well as many interdisciplinary themes.

This is the first time any of these books have been published in English for international readers. The series aims to put forward a Chinese perspective, give insights into cutting-edge academic thinking in China, and inspire researchers globally.

To submit proposals, please contact the Taylor & Francis Publisher for China Publishing Programme, Lian Sun (Lian.Sun@informa.com)

Recent titles in politics partly include:

Fiscal Policy and Institutional Renovation in Support of Innovative Country Building
Jia Kang

Avoiding the "Thucydides Trap"
U.S.-China Relations in Strategic Domains
Wang Dong and Travis Tanner

Syrian Civil War and Europe
Zhao Chen, Zhao Jizhou and Huang Mengmeng

Re-globalisation
When China Meets the World Again
Dong Wang and Dejun Cao

China in the Eyes of the Japanese
Wang Xiuli, Wang Wei and Liang Yunxiang

For more information, please visit https://www.routledge.com/China-Perspectives/book-series/CPH

China in the Eyes of the Japanese

Wang Xiuli, Wang Wei and
Liang Yunxiang

Routledge
Taylor & Francis Group
LONDON AND NEW YORK

First published in English 2021
by Routledge
2 Park Square, Milton Park, Abingdon, Oxon, OX14 4RN

and by Routledge
52 Vanderbilt Avenue, New York, NY 10017

Routledge is an imprint of the Taylor & Francis Group, an informa business

English Version by permission of Peking University Press.

British Library Cataloguing-in-Publication Data
A catalogue record for this book is available from the British Library

Library of Congress Cataloging-in-Publication Data
A catalog record has been requested for this book

ISBN: 978-0-367-68584-3 (hbk)
ISBN: 978-1-003-13817-4 (ebk)

Typeset in Times New Roman
by KnowledgeWorks Global Ltd.

Contents

List of Figures

List of Tables

Foreword

In modern times, three countries have had the greatest impact on China: Japan, Russia (including the Soviet Union), and the United States. Of these, Japan is most similar to China in terms of appearance and culture, and has inflicted the greatest national disasters and mental scars on China. Similarly, for contemporary Japan, China and the United States are the two most important countries. Thus, the importance how the two nations of China and Japan view each other and the complexity of their peoples' mutual feelings are second to no other bilateral relationship pairing in the world today.

This book focuses on the image of China in the eyes of the Japanese from ancient times to present times. The significance of this book is self-evident. The book is not only rich with detailed and accurate data, but also shows the authors' deep and careful observation of Sino-Japanese relations, their intentions to promote mutual understanding of the people of the two countries, and their expectation of improved bilateral relations. As one of first readers of this book, I hereby take the liberty of expressing some of my personal reflections from reading it.

What impressed me most deeply after reading the history of changes of Sino-Japanese relations is that from ancient times to the present Japan has never viewed China on terms of equality. Ancient Japan stood in awe of and worshiped China, studied China in all aspects, and imitated and accepted Chinese culture and political system. After the Meiji Restoration, and particularly after Japan defeated China in the Sino-Japanese War of 1894–1895 and seriously crippled Russia in the Russo-Japanese War, Japan became the leading power in Asia and reached an equal footing with the major European and American powers. Afterwards, in Japan and among the Japanese, the sense of intimacy with and the awe of China vanished forever, while national chauvinism belittling or even despising China and its people was rampantly spreading, till the day when Japan began to invade and enslave China.

After its victory in World War II, China became one of the five permanent members of the U.N. Security Council, and saw its international position enhanced remarkably. In contrast, Japan emerged from the World War economically crushed; following its surrender Japan yielded to American military occupation and lost the right to maintain regular armed forces. Japan after the war might have looked up to China. Unfortunately, China quickly fell into the civil war, and China's seat in the United Nations was occupied by the Republic of China in Taiwan for over two decades. As this book states, for years after the founding of the People's Republic of China, "the mainstream viewpoint on China in Japan returned to worship of and longing for China—but with the difference that the Japanese view shifted from mainly seeing China as the historical source of Japanese culture, to one of aspiration for a new country founded through revolution, as the Japanese considered the way of the People's Republic of China as one that Japan should follow. Meanwhile, facing a China worthy of worship, the Japanese naturally recognized the various crimes that Japan inflicted on China in modern times, and developed a consciousness of reflection and atonement in addition to the sense of worship."

However, the good period of Japanese views of China proved short lived. During and following the 10-year Cultural Revolution, Japan's perception of China as an ideal country collapsed, and the sense of worship and longing turned to thorough disappointment. After the normalization of Sino-Japanese diplomatic relations, Japan increasingly understood China's real social situation, and Japan's economy quickly far surpassed China's. A few Japanese people began to show sympathy for China and hoped to help China change its relatively backward situation. In other words, from looking up to China, Japan once again began looking down upon China.

After the end of the Cold War, Japan's views of China shifted yet again. This accompanied political changes in China, multiple frictions in bilateral relations since the 1990s, and the rapid rise of China's power. Japanese views of China shifted from neither *looking up to* or *down upon* China, nor *looking equally*, but rather to *aversion* and *fear*, as pointed out by the author. Though these two words may seem unpleasant and surprising, I believe the author selected them after careful consideration, and this description may be accurate and objective, and should stimulate reflection.

The supposed equality of relations between countries in contemporary times is but one variant of international law and diplomacy, rather than a reflection of real situations. In fact, inequality between countries is normal. The case where nationals of a country view and treat another country equally takes place only by chance, not as a result of effort. That the Japanese viewpoint on China has alternated between admiration and condescension, and evolved to aversion and fear today, presents a rather unique case in terms of international relations and of Japanese foreign relations. Taking the United States-Japanese relations as an example, the balance of power between the two countries has been tilted to the United States since Commodore Matthew Perry's naval expedition forcefully opened the door of Japan in 1854, and Japan has largely remained in a state of looking up to the United States except for the period of the Pacific War. In Japanese-Korean relations, Japan invaded and occupied the Korean Peninsula after the Sino-Japanese War of 1894–1895 and took possession of Korea as a colony, and Japan has remained superior to the Republic of Korea (ROK, or South Korea) in terms of major national power indexes. Therefore, Japan has never had the sense of looking up to other East-Asian countries except for South Korea and China. Japan has a sense of alienation to Russia, but can be said to view itself as an equal to major European countries. With the exception of China, Japan has no example of such changes in viewpoints of other nations. Only by understanding such particularity of Japan's attitude toward China can one understand why Sino-Japanese relations became so knotty and tortuous.

Some Chinese scholars, including those specialized in Japanese studies, have concluded that the Japanese nation lacks the consciousness of equality by its nature, and Japan only worships and gives an obedience to winners, but looks down upon and treats losers rudely. These scholars have written that when China grows sufficiently powerful, and achieves an equal footing with the United States or even exceeds its power internationally, the Japanese will be won over and submit themselves to China meekly, as it does to the United States at present.

Having never studied the characteristic of the Japanese nation, I am not qualified to comment on this view, but in terms of the images of China and other countries in Japanese eyes, the above-mentioned points of view appear paradoxical. Beyond the factual considerations, the argument rests on the idea that the essence of the international community is a kind of Social Darwinism and resting on the law of the jungle; in this view not only Japan but also other countries know only strength, rather than following any code of ethics. Neither surveys of Japanese desires and public opinion, nor the history and current situation of international relations support this argument. Recent surveys show that many Japanese people recognize that China is already a powerful state, a fact that cannot be changed. The author states that, "the best result is that China can act as a 'Gentle Giant' after it becomes powerful." I believe the analogy of Gentle Giant is vivid and proper. In the viewpoints held of China by other neighboring countries and of Mainland China by Taiwanese, we can see similar feeling and expectation.

It is only natural that power politics is main item in international politics. Nazi Germany and Militarist Japan could be destroyed only by force, rather than persuasion by words. But powerful military force and economic power can only work long under just and lawful goals, which is by no means a novel theory of international politics. In modern or ancient times, in China or elsewhere, any civilizations having developed to a certain level may leave similar proverbs and epigrams to exhort their governments. During the period of U.S. global dominance, the United States used its hard power in Vietnam during the Cold War period and in Iraq and Afghanistan later, but these wars became quagmires from which the U.S. government found it difficult to withdraw. The main problem in today's Sino-Japanese relations is not that China has insufficient hard power, but is at the spiritual and political levels, namely China's soft power is insufficient to persuade the Japanese to like or agree with China.

An opinion poll mentioned in the book shows that, of Russia, China, India, Germany, and the United States, the Japanese consider the United States as their first favorite, supported by 48.9% of respondents, followed by Germany (36%), India (9.3%), China (4.1%), and Russia in last place. The Japanese respondents preferred the United States mainly for its political democracy and developed economy, and respondents liked China for Chinese culture and rapidly growing economy.

Talking about the viewpoints on and feelings of the Japanese for the United States, I cannot help thinking about Mr. Ken Takakura, the late Japanese movie star, with whom I had some personal contacts. In a long talk with him in 2009, I asked him to name his favorite film, and without hesitation he recommended the American film *The Deer Hunter*, which won the Academy Award for Best Picture in 1978. Later, he presented to me a disk version of the film as a gift. He said he cherished the film not only because it was set against the background of the Vietnam War and condemned the war and those who triggered it, but also because it exposed how war distorts humanity and causes heartbreaking hurt to those who it touches. Mr. Ken Takakura did not mask his dislike of politics, including international politics, but showed his positive feeling for American culture and Americans; he felt that only Americans could make such touching and profound artistic works. His words made me think at that time: if our contemporary Chinese could offer spiritual products that could touch the nationals of Japan, would we need to worry about the image of China in the eyes of the Japanese?

This book arrives at a regrettable finding: "Since Japan began its modern westernization policy, Chinese culture has become much less attractive to ordinary Japanese people, who have tended to greatly prefer Western European and American cultures to Chinese culture." We can attribute this in part to the Japanese media's prejudice against China, since most Japanese people rely mainly on reports of domestic media to understand China, and for various reasons it is hard for Chinese media to reach Japanese audiences. Even more regrettable is that this preference occurs despite that "the Japanese generally report high identification with traditional Chinese values. Over half of the Japanese express agreement on the values of benevolence, righteousness, propriety and filial piety … far higher than their opinion of whether ordinary Chinese people identify with these traditional values. That is to say, the Japanese think that the Chinese have a low identification with traditional Chinese values." From this, we can further conclude that the Japanese think their recognition and practice of the values identified by both nations are higher than their Chinese counterparts. Of course, Chinese people would not agree with this Japanese view, but given the current level of morality and ethics in Chinese society, Chinese people should reflect on behaviors of ourselves, and should not merely blame this Japanese view on media. As mentioned in the book, there are distressful individual cases of unethical behavior involving citizens of China in Japan, as shown in the comments of Professor Satoshi Amako of Waseda University regarding the students he supervised.

As for how to correct the misunderstanding of and prejudice toward China in Japan and to improve the quality and impact of China's propaganda in Japan, this book makes many pertinent and useful proposals. Meanwhile, I believe that the authors will agree on my basic conclusion—namely, that the fundamental way to improve the image of China in the eyes of the Japanese is continue China's reform policy, opening-up, democracy, and rule-of-law, and thereby make Chinese citizens as a whole more civilized, polite, friendly, and trustworthy. As long as the Chinese society keeps making advances, the image of China in Japan will continue to improve. Of this we should be confident.

Wang Jisi
President, the Institute of International and Strategic Studies (IISS), Peking University
Miner Hall, Peking University
January 20, 2016

Part I

Review of history

1 The history of contacts between China and Japan

China and Japan are both culturally Asian countries, and are geographically close to each other. Geologists believe that in relatively recent glacial periods, the sea level was lower and today's Japanese Islands were connected with the Asian mainland. After the islands were separated from the continental mainland, the landmasses of China and Japan face each other across the East China Sea. The shortest linear distance from the Chinese mainland to the major islands in the Japanese Islands is about 300 nautical miles. If the small islands scattered between the countries are taken into account, the distance would be even shorter. Between China and Japan, the Korean peninsula connected to the Chinese mainland which sits only about 100 nautical miles from the Japanese islands. Therefore, even in ancient times when navigation technologies were primitive, contacts between the Chinese mainland and Japan were possible.

Their close geographical distance enabled relatively simple and frequent flows of population between the Asian continent and the Japanese islands. For this reason, the Chinese and the Japanese are genetically similar. Archeological discoveries show that the forebears of modern Japanese came from the northern Asian continent, and might have emigrated there from the mainland before Japan split off from the continental landmass, or by crossing the sea from the Korean peninsula. Some early settlers originated from today's Southeast Asia region. As peoples from different areas of the Asian continent settled in the relatively closed and isolated Japanese islands, they mutually intermixed over the centuries to form today's Japanese people. In a sense, the familial relations between the Chinese and Japanese are relatively close, as is readily apparent from casual observation.

Over 2,000 years of history, China and Japan have experienced alternating periods of gratitude or resentment, but nevertheless the two countries have maintained close ties through good or bad, and continually exerted powerful influence on each other most of the time. During most periods of ancient times, China and Japan maintained close and stable relations, albeit punctuated by short periods of conflict.

In modern times, China and Japan each joined the system of international relation initially dominated by Western countries, but the two nations responded differently to this change, leading to a reversal of their positions in the world. For a period of roughly a century, the two countries experienced a rivalry and periods of war. After World War II, when relations should have normalized, but civil war in China and then the global Cold War prevented official diplomatic relations between Japan and China, up to the 1970s when the two countries realized normalization of diplomatic relations. Since then, their relations began to develop more comprehensively, leading to over 20 years of friendly cooperation. After the end of the Cold War, and from the mid-1990s or so, China and Japan entered a new period, sometimes known among the two countries as Cold Politics, Hot Economics. This period featured close and interdependent economic ties but structural political contradictions involving tensions in all aspects related to the recognition of their historical conflicts and territorial disputes. Sino-Japanese relations today are both close and yet estranged: the two countries need each other and yet detest each other. The two countries both worship and admire yet also belittle and despise each other. Friendly cooperation coexists with fear and worry, interwoven with various historical contradictions in the long history of Sino-Japanese relations.

1.1 Contacts between China and Japan in ancient times

1.1.1 *Japan as recorded in ancient Chinese classical works*

China and Japan enjoy a long history of contact, but history does not imply the synchronous development of civilization in the two countries. Mainland China has a longer history of civilization than the Japanese islands. Indeed, even the starting point of the history of Japan has to be explored from Chinese classical works of history.

Extant Chinese ancient classical works of China have shown, and archaeological findings in Japan have confirmed, that Chinese contacts with Japan as early as in the Eastern Han Dynasty of China. For example, *The Book of the Han Dynasty (Han Shu) Geography Records (Di Li Zhi)* by Ban Gu of the Eastern Han Dynasty in the first century presented a concrete record of Japan's relations with China in this period: "In the Lelang Sea (today's Sea of Japan) are the Wa people, who live in many states and pay tribute to us annually."[1] These records provide a general sense of social development in the Japanese islands at that time. According to *The Book of the Eastern Han Dynasty (Han Shu) Records of Dongyi (Dong Yi Zhuan)*, by Fan Ye, who wrote during the Song State in 445 during the Southern Dynasty of the Southern and Northern Dynasties, in the second year of Jianwu Zhongyuan Period of Emperor Guangwu in the Eastern Han Dynasty, 57 CE: "The Wa State (Japan) paid tribute to the Han government. The envoy called himself Dafu (a senior rank of official) and described his state as the southernmost in the Islands. Emperor Guangwu bestowed his seal and its silk ribbon on him,"[2] indicating that there existed contacts between China and Japan in the Eastern Han Dynasty, and a small state on the Japanese Islands dispatched envoys to have an audience with the emperor of China. This historical case record was later verified by the discovery of a gold seal engraved with "King of Wanu State of Han," unearthed on Shiga Island, Hakata Bay, Kitakyushu, Japan in 1784. For many years, this unearthed gold seal was questioned as a fake, but eventually the seal's authenticity was accepted after various appraisals and by comparisons with other seals unearthed from Han Dynasty tombs. On the basis of this research, in 1981, the Japanese government confirmed the seal as a national treasure, and it is now kept in the City Museum in Fukuoka, Japan. Similar history records state that the king of Wa State returned to China to pay tribute to the imperial court of the Eastern Han in 107 CE.

After the late Eastern Han Dynasty, official Chinese histories began to include special records concerning Japan. For example, the *Records of the Three Kingdoms (San Guo Zhi)*, written by Chen Shou in 289, contains a special section entitled the *Records of Wei·Wa People (Wo Ren Zhuan)*, which gives a systematic account of the situation and events on the Japanese Islands, and records that in 239, the queen of small state "Yamatai," located approximately on today's Kyushu, Japan dispatched envoys to pay tribute to the Wei State, and the imperial government of Wei ruled by the Cao family conferred the title of "Pro-Wei Wa King" on her and bestowed to her a gold seal.

Over the following 300 years, when China experienced a turbulent period characterized by rule by the Western and Eastern Dynasties and the Southern and Northern Dynasties, official history books by governments of different dynasties kept records on Japan. This includes records in *The Book of Song (Song Shu): Records of Ethnic Minorities (Man Yi Zhuan)* completed in 488 and *The Book of the Southern Qi Dynasty (Nan Qi Shu): Records of Ethnic Minorities in Southeast China (Dong Nan Yi Zhuan)* completed in 514. However, due to social turbulence in the period, official contacts between China and Japan declined. These official records mentioned Japan but gave no more detailed information. Generally, the official histories provided only brief, repetitive introductions about Japan on a few words from prior historical records, and some contents derived from legends and sayings.

At the end of the third century when the Chinese society entered a turbulent period, Japan also experienced a period of social turbulence. Several small Japanese states began a series of annexation wars. The relatively powerful Yamatonokuni state rose in the region centered on Nara-ken in the west of today's Honshu Island. After a series of wars for annexation, Yamatonokuni unified the Japanese Islands at the end of the fourth century, and unity lasted to roughly the beginning of the fifth century. During this period of over 100 years, there were fewer records of exchanges between China and Japan. Chinese histories only recorded the turbulence in Japan after this period, based mainly on legendary stories. Even during the periods of relative unrest, however, cultural exchanges between China and Japan continued. Indeed, the spread to Japan of many Chinese written characters, Confucianism, *The Analects of Confucius* and Buddhism took place during this period.

1.1.2 *Japan accepted Chinese culture in an all-round manner*

In the late sixth century, after nearly three centuries years of internal strife, Chinese society entered a period of stability and unity. The Sui and Tang Dynasties, which both featured a unified China, ruled in succession during this period. The Sui Dynasty was founded in 581 and it unified China in 589, ending the long division between the South and North and bringing about a flowering of social life. At around the same time, the Japanese islands experienced political unification, with power monopolized by several aristocrat groups. The power of the Mikado as the ruler was unstable and social life subject to rapid shifts.

Against this background, the Sui and Tang Dynasties and the reunification of China served as a model for Japan. Contacts between China and Japan became more frequent during this period. In 593, after a series of palace struggles, the Japanese royal family appointed Prince Shotoku, one of the princes, as the Crown Prince and regent, and Prince Shotoku acted for the Mikado in handling government affairs. After coming into power, Prince Shotoku launched comprehensive reforms, imitating the political systems of the Sui Dynasty in China, with a view to building a centralized nation with the Mikado at its core. In 603, the new government chaired by Prince Shotoku formulated the Twelve-Level Cap and Rank System, which stipulated honorary peerages by levels of virtue, benevolence, righteousness, propriety, wisdom, and faith advocated by Confucianism, and conferred peerages in line with officials' abilities and contributions. This enabled selection of talented officials and encouraged the loyalty of officials to the Mikado, and thus helped break the power of the once despotic gentry class. In 604, the new government instituted the Seventeen-Article Constitution as the code of conduct for Japanese officials and subjects. Most of its contents referred to the hundred schools of thought such as Confucian, Fa-School, Taoist, and Buddhist thought of China, and emphasized following the tenets of Buddhism, submitting to the Mikado, serving dutifully, keeping promises, and kindness to ordinary people.

Prince Shotoku also made great efforts to popularize Buddhism in Japan by publishing Buddhist classics and constructing Buddhist temples. The famous Horyuji Temple in Nara-ken and its Five-Storied Pagoda were built in this period, and have come to symbolize Japan and its culture. Japanese histories of the period such as *Records of the Mikado* and the *National Records* make extensive use of Chinese characters. This series of measures targeted national unification through thought, by enhancing the authority and idea of the royal family and nation while strengthening the centralization of the Mikado, and by weakening the aristocratic power. These policies played a major role in the formation and consolidation of the Japanese nation.

All of the above-mentioned actions can be viewed as a result of the influence of the Sui and the subsequent Tang Dynasty of China. In 607, Prince Shotoku dispatched Ono no Imoko as the first envoy to the Sui government in Chang'an with a letter from the Mikado to the emperor of the Sui government. In 608, the Sui emperor reciprocated, sending an official envoy to Japan, Pei Shiqing. In September, that same year, Ono no Imoko returned to Chang'an accompanied by dozens of Japanese monks and students, initiating a campaign of comprehensive Japanese study of China. Over the following years, the Japanese government dispatched several such delegations of envoys, monks, and students to China. These monks and students studied returned to their country with a deeper understanding of Chinese culture and institutions, and played a role in major historical events and in promoting cultural development in Japan.

Prince Shotoku's reforms weakened the local aristocracy and laid a foundation for the Tenno System of central national government, but the reform was ultimately incomplete. After the death of Prince Shotoku in 622, aristocratic forces sought to regain lost power, leading to political instability. During this period, however, monks and students who had been dispatched to China gradually returned to Japan, bringing cultural, political, and other social influences. In 645, members of the royal family and some officials carried out a palace coup, eliminating the aristocratic forces that had intervened in government affairs, and establishing a new government. Imitating the Chinese imperial court practice, the new government declared the first year of *Taika*, and placed returned monks and students in positions to implement further reforms modeled on the Tang Dynasty.

In 646, the first year of Taika in the history of Japan began. On New Year's Day, the royal family issued the Imperial Edict on the Taika Era Reforms, imitating various systems of the Tang Dynasty. These measures included seizure of aristocratic land holdings for public use, establishing a registry of permanent residents for land allocation, collecting land rent from farmers and distributing labor to farmers based on land grants, and imposing other taxes and levies. The new system was similar to the Zuyongdiao System employed by the Tang Dynasty. To consolidate the centralized Mikado state, the new government also imitated the Tang government's Three Departments and Six Ministries System for officials, and established a central organization with Eight Departments and Officials at Various Levels, and different administrative levels of state, shire, and county for local government, with all officials appointed by the imperial court. Thus, the reforms created a relatively complete top-down ruling body known as the Tenno System of ancient Japan.

In the process of learning from and imitating the Sui and Tang government organizations, Japan dispatched envoys to the Sui and Tang capitals initiated a long practice that lasted for more than 200 years, right up to 838. This included 19 named delegations of which 12 actually traveled to China. With time, the delegations included more senior personnel and grew more diverse, growing in size from 200 in the early years to 500–600 in later periods. The members included government officials, craftsmen, doctors, artists, monks, and priests as well as students. From these delegations, notable figures in the history emerged, such as Abe no Nakamaro, Kibinomakibi, and Monk Kukai. During the period, a famous Chinese monk, Jianzhen (Ganjin), departed from Yangzhou, China to Japan intending to popularize Buddhism, but his initial voyage proved unsuccessful. Undeterred, he set out six times in 11 years, successfully arrived at the Japanese Islands in 754, interpreted the Buddhist Sutra into Japanese, delivered a sermon in Toshodaiji Temple constructed in Nara-ken in 759, and finally died in Japan, becoming a touchstone and symbol of ancient Sino-Japanese cultural exchange.

These large-scale contacts between China and Japan over nearly 300 years during the Chinese Sui and Tang Dynasties helped Japan absorb Chinese culture, science, technology, and political system, ultimately moulding ancient Japan's national governing system and social life. During this time, education in Chinese culture centered on Confucianism became an absolute requirement for senior bureaucrats and aristocrats of Japan. Driven by the Japanese imperial court and aristocrats, many Chinese collections of poems were compiled and published in Japan. Chinese culture served as the source and inspiration of Japanese culture in this and subsequent periods. Not only did Japan directly adopt Chinese written characters and classical works, but also the Japanese kana script was created by Japanese scholars based on Chinese written characters of the Sui and Tang Dynasties after the ninth century. Many works of Japanese literature were written and created by mixing Chinese characters and kana script, or in kana alone, such as *Manyoshu*, *Kokin Wakashu*, and *Genji Monogatari*.

1.1.3 *Similarities and differences in Chinese and Japanese cultures*

It is only natural that China and Japan have different historical starting points and experienced different processes of development. The starting point of the history of China was earlier than that of Japan: about 1,500 years after the Chinese Shang Dynasty developed a centralized state in the 17th century BCE did a Japanese nation began to emerge on today's Japanese Islands. Because of its relatively developed stage, China had a significant influence on Japan. Over thousands of years of historical development, the two countries have adopted many identical or similar cultural elements. In ancient times, Japan learned from China and absorbed much from Chinese civilization, including production technology, culture, and art. Japan also imitated the political systems of ancient China. Entering modern times, China absorbed many aspects of Western civilization through Japan, including modern Western thought and technologies, and numerous words and phrases to express these new thoughts and technologies.

For this reason, many think that China and Japan feature the same culture and ethnicity. That is to say, besides their close racial origins, the two countries also share similar cultures, as ancient Japanese culture originated from Chinese culture, while contemporary Chinese culture adopted certain elements of Japanese culture.

It is true that Chinese culture and Japanese culture are similar in many respects. Up to now, there are still many traces of Chinese culture in Japanese culture. For example, kanji characters, the urban design of ancient cities such as Nara-ken and Kyoto, the architectural styles of Japanese temples, historical and literary allusions, and names. Even some living habits in Japan resemble those of China. Meanwhile, many words and phrases in modern Chinese, particularly those to express new things from Europe and Americas, were first introduced from Japanese. To modern Chinese people, some symbols representing Japanese culture seem familiar.

Yet Chinese culture and Japanese culture are not identical, but rather belong to two different and independent cultures, belonging to Asian culture and featuring certain similarities and resemblances. American scholar Samuel Huntington's 1990s article proposing a coming Clash of Civilizations classified world civilizations into seven major or eight kinds, of which Chinese civilization and Japanese civilization have a coordinate rather than an inclusive relationship. This at least indicates that in eyes of one non-Asian scholar, Chinese and Japanese cultures are distinct from each other.[3]

This notwithstanding, Chinese and Japanese cultures have many similar or identical content, and some scholars look on Japanese civilization as a part of Chinese civilization, or as a sub-civilization to Chinese civilization. Despite sharing similar or identical content and origins, the cultures of the two countries have gradually differentiated via independent development. For instance, Japan introduced many elements of Chinese culture in ancient times, but the Japanese deconstructed some cultural elements and developed their own culture according to their own understanding and needs. Chinese written characters were developed into kana in Japan, which constituted today's Japanese characters together with Chinese characters (kanji).

The Japanese have also adapted some Chinese cultural elements to greater degrees than practiced in China. For example, Chinese tea drinking developed into the highly refined Japanese tea ceremony. The Chinese enjoyment of the beauty of flowers evolved into Ikebana, or flower arrangement, in Japan. Similarly, Japan adapted the Chinese art of fencing into the martial art of Kendo. Some aspects of Confucianism were accepted by the Japanese warrior class and improved and developed to become Japanese Bushido. Buddhism from China did not form a uniform denomination in Japan, but diverged into a variety of secular factions or schools. The refined aspects of all these Chinese cultural elements constitute parts of Japan's core culture, and some have become part of Japanese spiritual life.

Chinese culture and Japanese cultures are similar but not identical, and in some aspects are completely distinct. In some respects, Japanese adaptations have made a Chinese cultural tradition unrecognizable. For instance, Confucianism, after being introduced to Japan, became a pursuit of upper-level knowledge elites and officials of Japan and affected the spiritual world of the Japanese, but did not serve as an institutional power for Japanese society. As scholar Eisenstadt summarized: "In Japan, Confucianism did not change the basic structure and premise of officials or the educated classes. Some attempts were made in that direction in the eighth century, but the introduction of Confucianism into Japan did not guide institutional structures as it did in China, Korea and Vietnam. Namely, Japan never adopted the Chinese imperial examination system, and Confucianism was not concretized through implementation by the scholar class."[4]

Likewise, since modern times, China introduced and absorbed many elements of language and thought from Japan. Large groups of Chinese intellectual elites traveled to Japan for study from the end of the 19th century through the beginning of the 20th century, but China did not complete Westernization as quickly as Japan to become a capitalist country. On the contrary, China took a road completely different from Japan. Their differences led to a stage of conflict and ultimately war between the two countries over a period of nearly a century. And today there remain many sources of misunderstanding between the two.

1.1.4 *Equality and friction between China and Japan*

In the 500 years or so after the disappearance of China's Tang Dynasty in 907, Chinese society experienced frequent episodes of turbulence. During this period, Japanese society gradually perceived less urgency to study from China, reflecting also that Japanese culture and society had emerged in their own right. During the 300 years from the beginning of the 10th century to the beginning of the 13th century, Japan experienced the period known as National Culture in which the Japanese society digested Chinese culture and developed its own culture. Japanese society also underwent a period of instability in this period: the centralized Tenno System declined and was replaced by an emerging warrior class, and the first warrior government occurred in 1192. In this period, official contacts between China and Japan were almost cut off.

In 1274 and 1281, during China's Yuan Dynasty, Mongolian troops launched military expeditions to the Japanese Islands. These expeditions were brief, and the Mongolian troops returned without accomplishing anything due to typhoons, but the invasion attempts further estranged the two countries. Nevertheless, non-governmental contacts between China and Japan were never interrupted: ships and people continued to travel between

China and Japan for trade or other contacts. As such informal contact increased, they led to a period of regular, continuous contact between China and Japan.

With the inception of China's Ming Dynasty, official contacts between China and Japan were restored. In 1401, Japan's Muromachi shogunate dispatched trade envoys to Beijing, the Ming capital. The Ming emperor granted permission for commerce between two countries under the *Kanhe System* of official trade licenses. Moreover, the Ming government also offered various inducements for trade, such as tariff discounts and exemptions, subsidized room and board for traders, and mutual exchange of gifts to the Japanese shogun. Unfortunately, shortly before significant commerce between China and Japan could begin under this new arrangement, there occurred a split between the northern and southern parts of Japan, resulting in civil conflict and war. Remnants of the defeated southern Japanese army took to the sea as large pirate gangs known as the Waka, engaging in smuggling and piracy in the seas between China and Japan. Waka frequently attacked Ming-era merchants and coastal villages along the north–south route from the Japanese Islands to the Korean Peninsula and interrupted normal maritime travel and commerce on China's southeast coasts, becoming a major scourge of the Ming government. This situation persisted for over 200 years, and caused long-term disruption of China's coastal security as well as trade between China and Japan. Not until the mid-16th century did Ming forces thoroughly eliminate the Waka pirates, enabling Japan and China to resume normal trade.

Around this same period, the Portuguese began to arrive in Japan, having already occupied the island of Macao in China. The Portuguese *Nanban* trade boom in Japan led to a period of increased Japanese contact with Western science, technology, and culture. Additionally, at the end of the 16th century, China and Japan went to war over the Korean Peninsula. In 1592 and 1597, Japanese troops invaded Korea twice. During these conflicts, Japanese ruler Toyotomi Hideyoshi threatened to attack China and move Japan's capital to Beijing. Ultimately, the conflict ended when Ming troops intervened to reinforce Korean efforts to repel the Japanese invaders.

Entering the 17th century, China and Japan each experienced change of governments. In 1603, Tokugawa Ieyasu suppressed all warlord groups throughout Japan and established a new military government, known as the Edo Bakufu or Tokugawa shogunate. In 1644, Manchu forces from Northeast China beyond the Shanhai Pass occupied Beijing and established the new Qing Dynasty in place of the Ming.

From its outset, the Tokugawa shogunate adopted a relatively relaxed policy toward China, continuing trade with China and with merchants from Southeast Asia, as well with the British, Dutch, and Portuguese. Following the policy, Western religions such as Christian began to spread around Japan. Shortly after that, however, the Japanese shogun perceived risks to allowing the spreading of Western religions in Japan. The shogun particularly worried about the consequence of frequent contact between the shogunate's southwestern vassal states with Western missionaries, leading to possible disunity.

As a result of such concerns, the shogun began to institute various religious restrictions, including prohibiting foreigners from doing missionary work in Japan, demolishing churches, and suppressing followers of Western religion around Japan. Starting in the 1630s, shoguns issued a series of five edicts that completely closed the country to the outside world, prohibiting not only foreign missionaries but also foreign merchants from coming to Japan, and even barring Japanese people from going abroad.

During the 1600s, the Qing government of China adhered to the concept of the Celestial Empire, which treated surrounding countries including Japan as subservient tributaries. China adopted an informal policy of refusing admission to Western traders or missionaries who sought entry, though without any official seclusion orders resembling those of Japan.

Although China and Japan implemented similarly isolationist policies at around the same time, their economic and cultural contacts with the outside world were not entirely discontinued. China and Japan remained connected, seemingly acknowledging the existence of special ties that implied each should not treat the other as they did with other foreign countries. The Qing government viewed its neighboring countries, including Japan, as tributaries, and hence different from Western countries. Hence the Qing government did not consider its contacts with tribute-paying countries novel or risky. Similarly, for the Japanese shogunate, China was treated differently from other foreign countries. Japan continued to permit trade between its people and merchants of China, Korea, and the Netherlands, albeit under seclusion orders that restricted trade and contact to certain limitations, such as restricting trade to Nagasaki, and subjecting it to strict control by officials of the shogunate.

To sum up, beginning approximately from the early Eastern Han Dynasty when China and Japan began to have contacts and up to the middle of the 19th century when Western nations began to invade parts of East Asia, Japan, and China maintained nearly 2,000 years contact, albeit with periodic interruptions. Periods of close contact alternated with periods of estrangement. The two had close and frequent contact for hundreds of years during the Sui and Tang Dynasties, and subsequently the two underwent a period of rare contact and cold relations, punctuated by conflict such as the period of Waka piracy and the military conflicts on the Korean Peninsula in the Ming Dynasty.

For most of ancient times, China and Japan maintained normal and smooth relations, and their mutual influences had positive impacts on both countries. In Japan, China's influence had a decisive and comprehensive impact on society, and this is still a positive element in Sino-Japanese relations today. Objectively, the contacts between China and Japan in ancient times were infrequent and sporadic; instead, their relationship can be characterized as pre-modern, consisting of relatively isolated and contingent contact. Given the remoteness of these ancient contacts from modern times, their influences on Sino-Japanese relations are relatively less important than more recent experiences of contact.

1.2 Contacts between China and Japan in modern times

1.2.1 *Drastic change of the international positions of China and Japan*

In the middle of the 19th century, countries in Europe and America underwent modern industrial revolutions and completed the colonial occupation of most of Africa and Latin American regions. Subsequently, the Western powers began to expand their reach into East Asia. In 1840, China and Britain descended into war over China's ban on opium. Troops of the rotten Qing government were defeated by British forces from Europe. China, as the central country in the Sino-foreign country system[5] in East Asia, was forced to accept the punitive terms for its defeat under the unequal Treaty of Nanking in 1842. By this treaty, China agreed to cede Hong Kong to the British, and opened five coastal ports to British residency and trade. Following the treaty, other Western powers in quick succession forced the Qing government to conclude similar treaties, resulting in each of these foreign powers acquiring massive interests in China, such as leased territorial concessions, legal extraterritoriality, and tariff rights. This effectively destroyed the Sino-foreign country system of ancient East Asian international relations. As a result, all of East Asia was forced to accept the modern system of international relations dominated by Western countries.

As this impetuous wave of colonial expansion arrived in East Asia, Japan also could not escape similar misfortune. In June 1853, four American warships led by Commodore Matthew Perry entered the ports around Tokyo Bay very near to Edo, the capital city of the Tokugawa shogunate, demanding Japan accept the diplomatic credentials issued to Perry by the American president and promise to open ports to American ships. In response, the Japanese government maintained its closed-door policy, refusing Perry's demands and instead command the Americans to shift negotiation to Nagasaki, as required by existing policies. Perry refused, and threatened the shogunate with force. Taking warning from the example of the Opium War between Qing Dynasty China and the British only a decade previously, the shogunate perceived no choice but forced acquiescence, agreeing to give a reply the following year.

In 1854, Perry's fleet again sailed into Tokyo Bay and demanded negotiations, whereupon the Japanese government entered into negotiations and concluded the Kanagawa Treaty, which resembled the Treaty of Nanking except that it resulted in no cession of territory. As with China, Japan was forced to open several ports to American ships, and agreed to allow

American residence and trade in various places around Japan, as well as privileges such as legal extraterritoriality and tariff rights. Following these events, other European powers also forced the Japanese to conclude similar treaties and open more ports in Japan—effectively forcing Japan, like China, to join the modern, Western-led system of international relations.

Although the two nations confronted the same Western imperial invasion and cultural impact, China and Japan differed markedly in their responses. In being forced to open the door to Western trade and contact, China and Japan differed little: both lost materially and economically, and both experienced humiliation followed by desire to respond. At an early stage, some Japanese advocated working with China to resist Western countries, but Japan was aware that Western countries had grown more advanced than East Asian countries in technology, institutions, and culture. Hence, Japan concluded it could only safeguard its national independence and uphold its national interests in the Western manner. In contrast, the Qing government of China maintained an illusory pride in the concept of the Celestial Empire, and viewed its defeat as a result only of its lack of sophisticated modern weapons.

In 1871, China and Japan engaged in their first modern bilateral diplomatic negotiations in accordance with the Western manner, resulting in the conclusion of the *Sino-Japanese Provisions of Cordial Relations*, which stipulated that both countries would open ports for bilateral trade and grant consular jurisdiction. The document was a relatively equal treaty, but it nevertheless aroused serious discontent in Japan after its conclusion, on the grounds that Japan did not gain any special privileges in China. Consequently, Japan subsequently tried to revise the treaty, cast itself off from China, and deal with China in line with the practices of the Western powers. For its part, China wavered on the choice of upholding its own civilization or adopting Western civilization. Over subsequent decades, the paths of China and Japan gradually drifted apart.

To be sure, there are many interpretations of why China and Japan took two different roads in modern times. Chance factors may have played a role in some of their shorter-term decisions, but deeper reasons include the two countries' different views of their own cultures, as well as political and cultural differences. Specifically, Chinese culture is rich and has a long history, so the Chinese bore a heavier cultural load than the Japanese for Japanese culture. For this reason, the Chinese have been slower than the Japanese to accept new cultural influences, and tend to exhibit an unconscious negative reaction to such changes. Even when Chinese have accepted a new culture, they always express reluctance and worry about loss of the essence of Chinese culture.

Though both China and Japan confronted invasion by Western powers, Japan underwent a relatively rapid domestic political transformation, embarking on an irrevocable journey of comprehensive reforms modeled on Western practices. In contrast, China adopted the slogan of "Chinese

Learning for Fundamental Structure, Western Learning for Practical Use," and began to purchase and imitate advanced Western weapons, but did nothing to change its political system and culture.

As these changes were underway, a group of intellectuals in Japan sought to transition their own thinking from Eastern civilization to Western civilization. Fukuzawa Yukichi, a representative figure of this group, was a Confucian intellectual who confronted with the domination of Japan by Western powers and culture, adopted a modest approach that sought to learn from Westerners and understand all aspects of Western civilization. With time, he reached the conclusion that Western civilization was newer and superior to Confucianism, writing the famous book on the subject in 1885, *Datsu-A-Ron*, which argued that, "Our country must not hesitate and wait for our neighbors [China and Korea] to open its mind and join us in jointly rejuvenating Asia. Instead, it would be better for Japan to cut itself off from Asia to better track the pace of development of Western civilization. We don't need to be particularly polite to China and Korea just because they are our neighbors; instead, we must punish them for the way they allowed Westerners to deal with them."[6]

The thinking of these intellectuals was similar to the actual policy adopted by the Japanese government of this era, and was soon accepted by the general Japanese public. This thinking served as the spiritual weapon for Japan and guided its conduct in its aggression against and expansion to China.

During the 19th century, the political systems of both China and Japan were characterized by Asian authoritarian systems; as noted above, Japan's earliest national system of central government was modeled on that of China. Over more than 1,000 years, the two political systems gradually differentiated. The Chinese imperial system remained relatively unchanged, while the Japanese Mikado or imperial system continued to exist only on paper and the military shogunate held real political power. The long rule by the shogunate resembled European feudalism more than it did the highly centralized Chinese system.

In contrast, Chinese authoritarianism was directly embodied in the emperor's authority—that is, the conceptual authority almost completely coincided with real political power. In Chinese, this coincides with the saying that, *if the terminology is inaccurate, it's impossible to follow.* In China, only authorities supported by actual power could maintain and implement imperial rule. This regime featured a long-term system of imperial power, in which the leader who really controlled power should still be identified, even after the imperial system was abolished.

In Japan, the authoritarian system of the shogunate reflected a false authority: the conceptual authority did not coincide with real political power. The power of the emperor existed in name only, and the person identified as holding a position of greatest authority actually did not hold real power. This included the period of the Mikado system called the Eternal

Family by the Japanese people. The description also matches such phenomenon as short-lived prime minister and responsibility-free system in the 20th and 21st century.

These differences led to different political results when China and Japan each confronted similar Western imperial invasions. Once China was forced to open its doors to Western trade and influence, China lost many of its national rights and interests. The political authority of the emperor of the Qing government ceased to exist, but no new centralized political authority immediately replaced it: rather, the Revolution of 1911 overthrew the Qing Dynasty, but ushered in an extended period of serious social turbulence. Modern China began with the confrontation between Sun Yat-sen and Yuan Shikai, the flight of Sun, and a period of warlords engaging in tangled warfare, culminating in civil war between the Kuomintang (KMT) and the Chinese Communist Party. All these conflicts resulted from the lack of central political authority.

From the Opium War in 1840 to the founding of the People's Republic of China (PRC) in 1949, it took China over 100 years and lives of tens millions of lives to reestablished a new centralized political authority. In contrast, facing a similar crisis, Japan resurrected the prior Tenno system, a ready-made political authority that lacked real power but preserved existing forms; the speed of the adoption of a new system became the decisive factor in Japan's adaptation to the new era. In the late Edo shogunate period, the generals controlling real power resembled the weak and incapable military officials in Qing-era China who contributed to their country's humiliation and forfeited its sovereignty. When the rule of Japan's military shogunate ceased, reformers were able to swiftly adopt the Tenno system to serve as a banner of reform in Japan. Japan did not need to reestablish a new political authority, and did not undergo a long period of violent social turbulence analogous to China's. Hence the Meiji Reform, described as a revolutionary regime-change pivotal in the history of modern Japan, was achieved only in just a single year and at the price of the casualties less than 10,000.

1.2.2 *Sino-Japanese competition and the Sino-Japanese war of 1894–1895*

The differences between China and Japan in their reaction to foreign contact were quickly reflected in their bilateral relations. After the Western powers invaded East Asia starting from the mid-1800s, China and Japan took different roads when facing the historical change, and faced different destinies, different social contradictions, and different internal and external conflicts. Starting in the 1870s, on completion of the Meiji Reform, Japan began to deploy its military forces abroad, undertaking a policy of expansion. This directly brought Japan into conflict with the interests of China. In 1874, Japan invaded Taiwan on the grounds of the Ryukyu Shipwreck Incident, only agreeing to withdraw troops under conditions dictated by

Japan,[7] followed by full, forced annexation of the Ryukyu Islands in 1879 after the Qing government refused Japan's offer to partition the Ryukyus.

Around this time, Japan's attention shifted to Korea. In 1878, Japan brought military pressure to bear on Korea, forcing it to conclude the Treaty of Ganghwa, which denied Chinese suzerainty over Korea. All these actions shook the foundations of the prior Sino-Foreign Country System centered on China. After the 1880s, China and Japan experienced years of conflict over Korea continuously, including a 1882 mutiny by Korean soldiers against the Japanese known as the Imo Incident[8] and subsequent attempted coup known as the December 1884 Incident.[9] The two confrontations signaled growing conflicts between China and Japan over Korea, and impelled Japan to speed up armament, and led to the spread of an atmosphere of war across Japan. Japanese leaders had no hesitation about launching a war against China over Korea.

Clashes over Korea ultimately led to full-scale war between Japan and China. In 1894, the Tonghak Society Uprising, or Eastern Learning Society Uprising broke out in Korea.[10] Once again, both China and Japan sent troops to Korea and military clashes took place. Though Korea's internal strife abated, China and Japan disputed with Korea over conditions for troop withdraw and over domestic Korean reforms. Under such pretexts, Japanese forces suddenly occupied Korea's imperial palace, carrying out a coup and thereby forcing the newly installed Korean government to break with China's Qing government.

On July 25, Japan launched an undeclared war against China, attacking Qing naval vessels, triggering the Sino-Japanese War. The War lasted eight months and resulted in the total defeat for China. Major fighting took place in September 1894 in the Pyongyang Campaign and the Battle of the Yellow Sea; in February 1895, when Japanese troops captured Weihai and wiped out China's Northern Fleet; and in March 1895 when Japan seized China's Liaodong Peninsula and Penghu Islands.

The war ended with the Qing government's signature of the humiliating Treaty of Shimonoseki in April 1895, terms of which were dictated by Japan. The main articles of the Treaty stipulated the following Chinese obligations to Japan: Chinese admission of complete independence of Korea; cession of the Liaodong Peninsula, Taiwan, and Penghu Islands to Japan; payment of an indemnity of 200 million taels of silver; opening of Shashi, Chongqing, Suzhou, and Hangzhou as trading ports, and allowing Japanese investment in new factories in these newly opened treaty ports. Later, upon intervention of Russia, Germany, and France, the treaty was modified to remove the provision for ceding the Liaodong Peninsula to Japan, but as a result of the change, the indemnity was raised by a further 30 million taels of silver.

The Sino-Japanese War of 1894–1895 and Treaty of Shimonoseki radically changed the basic pattern of the international relations in East Asia, fundamentally altering the international positions of China and Japan, as well as their subsequent historical development. Before the West's invasion of East Asia, international relations in the region were dominated by the Sino-Foreign Country System centered on the Empire of China. The Opium War in 1840 crippled the Empire as the central country in the system: over subsequent decades, European and American powers employed gunboat diplomacy to force China to open its door to trade and diplomacy, and China suffered a dramatic loss of both dignity and material national interest. As a result, the Sino-Foreign Country System began to break up.

Nevertheless, China remained the most powerful country in East Asia and maintained the tottering Sino-Foreign Country System and suzerainty over the Korean Peninsula. Ultimately, however, the Sino-Japanese War of 1894–1895 swept away the last vestiges of the China-centered Sino-Foreign Country System, and the Empire of China lost its position as the central country in East Asia. Japan took China's former place as the top power in East Asia and began to dominate the region together with Russia and other Western powers.

Chinese scholar Song Chengyou considered the conclusion of the Treaty of Shimonoseki as a watershed in modern international relations in East Asia. The treaty marked the collapse of the coexistence of the international relation systems, and a new period of adjustment followed. After the Qing government's recognition of Korea's complete independence, the system in which Korea was subordinate to China collapsed, and the modern system of treaty relations became the only framework for international relations in the region."[11]

As Tarou Sakamoto wrote in his book, "The Sino-Japanese War of 1894–1895 exposed fragility of the Qing Empire, and the world powers of the era began to salivate at the prospect of greater intrusion into East Asia."[12] In the book *A New History of Japan*, the author wrote "According to the Treaty, Japan acquired extraterritoriality and the right to negotiate tariffs, including import tariff exemptions, gained leased territorial concessions, and the right to operate industrial and commercial companies and shipbuilding facilities in the newly opened treaty ports. Japan even gained some privileges that European and American powers had not received. Unfortunately, the European and American powers with most-favored-nation treaty guarantees were able to seize the same privileges vis-à-vis China once Japan had done so. As a result, Japan served as the vanguard of the great powers in invading China."[13]

Even historical textbooks published by right-wing Japanese writers also hold this view. The Sino-Japanese War of 1894–1895 was a fight to the finish between the Empire of China and Japan, with the latter having adopted European and American constitutionalism. The war's results came as a surprise to the world powers, which had viewed Qing-era China as a sleeping lion with immense remaining power. It's swift and easy defeat by the newly ascendant Japan ended the dominance of China's ancient diplomatic system in East Asia, and accelerated the incursions of other great powers, which sought and acquired more leased territories as springboards into China.[14]

After the war, China increasingly allowed itself to be trampled upon by Western powers. The Manchu Qing government, rotten and in rapid decline, contemplated a policy known as *restraining one foreign country by another.* Though this policy was taken with a view to continuing Qing rule, it resulted only in more loss of national interest and dignity. China's vast empire was increasingly segmented into spheres of influence by various great powers, now including Japan. These countries dumped trade goods on the Chinese market, built factories around China, and took advantage of economic, political, and military means to influence and control China.

Under these circumstances, China's nascent Westernization Movement[15] went nowhere, and the nation basically declared bankruptcy, given that China's peasant economy and just-initiated national industries were unable to cope with Western pressure. China's process of modernization was fatally interrupted. From then on, China gradually became a poor, weak, and large county, and suffered further episodes of semi-colonization. Mainstream Chinese historian Fan Wenlan view "the [Treaty of Shimonoseki) as another national betrayal, starting a new era following the Treaty of Nanking, greatly deepening China's colonization."[16] In his book, *The Modern History of China*, Fan wrote: "In the over five decades after the Opium War in 1840, the capitalist countries' aggression against China took form mainly via the export of Western goods ... At the end of the 19th century, capitalism entered the stage of imperialism, monopoly replaced free competition, and export of capital gained significance. After the Sino-Japanese War of 1894–1895, the great powers' aggression against China began to focus on export of capital ... and China fell into an unprecedented crisis of deepening colonization.[17]

Contrasting with China's dramatic decline, Japan gained greatly. As Tarou Sakamoto wrote in his book: "Contrary to the Qing Empire, the victory of Japan in the Sino-Japanese War of 1894–1895 had an immensely favorable influence on Japan. First, Japan's power as a modern country was widely recognized by the international community, and established Japan's position as an Asian power ... The victory also brought about a period of economic growth, and Japan's industry expanded by leaps and bounds."[18] Japan replaced China as the leading power in East Asia, and its new status was recognized by Western powers. Consequently, Japan became a member of the group of Western powers, and ultimately escaped China's experience of being forced to swallow unequal treaties by Western powers.

In some instances, Japan acquired privileges in China superior to those enjoyed by Western powers. The war indemnity of 230 million taels of silver imposed on China was three times greater than the annual revenue of Japan at the time. The indemnity played a major role in Japan's modernization, contributing to direct economic development, to national education, and, of course, to a further increase of military armament. The war and the treaty fundamentally distorted Sino-Japanese relations: previously reciprocal relations were transformed into an unequal relationship, and peace and friendliness were replaced by bullying, humiliation, and confrontation."[19] It is worse that the unequal relation lasted for more than half a century. The negative influences of the war even impact today's relation between China and Japan.

The Sino-Japanese War of 1894–1895 did not seriously interrupt contact between China and Japan, but rather accelerated them. Japan sought to further control and squeeze China, and rake in more material gains as a result. For its part, China began to reexamine its relationship with a neighbor it had previously considered unimportant. The war deeply shocked the Chinese: Japan, a small country China considered inferior, which had studied China for centuries, unexpectedly defeated China and its Celestial Empire.

This forced Chinese intellectual elites to reflect on prior assumptions. Many Chinese argued that Japan was a potential model for China to study. Intellectuals traveled to Japan to study, were accepted by Japanese society, and found friends among the Japanese who sought to help Chinese intellectual elites in their efforts to reform China. As a result, during this period, most Chinese intellectuals continued to hold a positive view of Japan, and hoped not only to save their country by studying Japan but also to work with Japan to jointly resist Western countries. For example, during the Russo-Japanese War, which saw fighting in Northeast China and in the Strait of Tsushima from February 1904 to September 1905, most Chinese intellectuals took the side of Japan. Japan's victory over Russia was acclaimed in China as a victory of Asians over Westerners.

1.2.3 *All-round confrontation and wars between China and Japan*

This period of good feeling by the Chinese for the Japanese proved short-lived. The Japanese government had no wish to unite with China to jointly resist European and American powers, but rather wanted only to acquire more gains in China, and potentially monopolize all spheres of interest in China by repelling the European and Americans. In January 1915, the Japanese government issued a diplomatic ultimatum to China, known as the Twenty-One Demands, which forced the Beiyang government to accept Japanese dominance of Shandong Province, Manchuria, and Mongolia, granted to Japan concessions for railways and ports in Northeast China, compelled China to accept Japanese advisors, and forced China to admit Japan's special privileges nationwide. The Beiyang government sought to be bargained with Japan, and deliberately disclosed some of the Twenty-One Demands to the media, hoping to engage the sympathy of other world powers. While there were some demonstrations against Japan's policy toward China, ultimately China's government conceded to most of the ultimatum's clauses, bowing to Japanese pressure.

For Chinese intellectuals and other elites, who previously held illusions about Japan, the Twenty-One Demands exposed the Japanese government's wild ambition to completely control China and turn it into a Japanese dependency—tantamount to destroying China as a nation. Consequently, Chinese intellectual opinion toward Japan changed to disappointment or even hatred. Regular Chinese people also experienced this emotion. From this point on, the Japanese government used its newly obtained privileges and position of strength in China to dismember China. During this period, most Chinese people became anti-Japanese and regarded Japan as a national enemy. Relations between China and Japan entered a vicious circle of interference and resistance, mutual trust evaporated, replaced by mutual hatred.

This vicious circle led to constant string of disputes between the two countries, culminating in full-scale Japanese invasion. On September 18, 1931, the Japanese Kwantung Army stationed outside Shenyang (known as Mukden to the Japanese) in Northeast China used explosives to deliberately damage a small section of railway, then placed the blame on nearby Chinese troops. On this pretext, the Kwantung Army initiated a massive retaliatory attack, going on to occupy the whole territory of Northeast China in a span of under five months. Subsequently, the Kwantung Army established a puppet regime to govern the region, which the Japanese renamed Manchukou, with its capital in Changchun.

These events directly challenged the vision of peaceful post-war international order set out at the Washington Conference of 1921. The seizure of Northeast China triggered the objection of the United States and condemnation by the newly created League of Nations followed by sanctions. The League of Nations even sent a fact-finding mission to Northeast China to conduct an on-site investigation. Japan persisted in its old ways and announced its withdrawal from the League of Nations in 1933. In China, anti-Japanese movements demanding recovery of Northeast China and calling for war against Japan became an increasing political force.

Meanwhile, the Japanese Imperial Army did not slacken in its strategy of invading China. From 1933 onwards, Japanese troops moved from Northeast China into central China through the Shanhaiguan pass, threatening the autonomy of North China and seeking to further dismember China. In 1935, Japanese troops forced Northern Hebei Province near Beijing to establish a new government, which they named the Eastern-Hebei Anti-communist Autonomous Government, effectively cutting the region off from the rule of the government of the Republic of China—and further straining Sino-Japanese relations. On July 7, 1937, a group of the Japanese troops in North China held a military exercise near the Lugou Bridge (known as the Marco Polo Bridge in the West due to its description by Marco Polo) on the outskirts of Beijing, intentionally near Chinese troops garrisoning the bridge and nearby Wanping county seat, leading to outbreak of military conflict. This became known as the Lugou Bridge Incident or Marco Polo Bridge Incident. Following the conflict, anti-Japanese sentiments in China reached the boiling point, and spread rapidly throughout the whole of China. Chinese troops ceased to exercise forbearance toward

Japanese provocations and began to resist Japanese troops. The Japanese government then initiated a massive mobilization, sending troops to China for open battle, and attacked Shanghai on August 13. Subsequently, the conflict evolved into an all-out war between China and Japan.

Stimulated by the new perception that its national power was now much greater than that of China, Japanese military officials made wild predictions that Japanese forces would destroy China within three months. In the event, China's leaders opted for a strategy of trading space for time, aiming to wear down the enemy by slow attrition with each step they took into China. Japanese troops captured Nanjing—the then capital of China—in no more than six months, but this failed to make China yield. On the contrary, the invasion further aroused the anti-Japanese resolution of the Chinese people. Total resistance by Chinese troops and the ordinary people, aided by the international assistance from the United States, the Soviet Union, and other countries, pinned down huge numbers of Japanese troops across the huge China battlefield. After the Japanese attack on Pearl Harbor and other targets in the Pacific in December 1941, China's counter-Japanese war became a part of the wider conflict of World War II. China allied with the United States, Britain, and other countries to jointly fight against Japan, ultimately defeating the Japanese fascists and winning the war in August 1945. Nevertheless, the eight-year conflict against Japan had an immense cost.

China was undoubtedly the first country to resist the invasion of Japanese fascists, and it made a substantial sacrifice and suffered great losses in the Asian theater in World War II. According to current estimates, China suffered 35 million casualties among soldiers and civilians, of whom 21 million died. As Chinese historian Xu Tianxin summarized in 1997, "China was the main battlefield in resisting the Japanese invasion, and the Chinese people undertook a tremendous sacrifice for and made outstanding historic contributions to the victory of the anti-fascist war in the world. In its eight-year fight against Japan, China sacrificed more than 21 million lives and lost property and material more than USD 100 billion."[20] That is to say, the China theater, as a part of the Asian battlefield in World War II, tied down a considerable portion of the Japanese Army, thereby greatly helping defeat the Japanese. The war was also the first instance in which China defeated Japan, after suffering decades of conflicts and wars with Japan in modern times. This showed China that the balance of power and relations between China and Japan during the modern era had the potential to reverse once again.

To summarize, modern contact between China and Japan took place amid the background of confronting Western invasion, and this invasion fundamentally changed the previous structure of international relations in East Asia. Due to different political situations in both countries and their different responses to Western incursions, China and Japan took two completely different roads. In the roughly 100 years from the middle of the 19th century to the end of World War II in 1945, and in particular during the 50 years from the Sino-Japanese War of 1894–1895 to the end of World War II, China and Japan were either in a state of friction or open war.

Although this period of history lasted far less time than the long period of positive historical contact between China and Japan in ancient times, and though the period that ended in 1945 is now long in the past, it remains strong in the memory of both China and Japan, and continues to negatively influence bilateral relations and public opinion. In particular, some wartime events such as the Nanjing Massacre—also known as the Rape of Nanking—continue to elicit intensely negative influences on Chinese public opinion about Japan. These topics are difficult to avoid in bilateral relations between the countries, even the war ended more than 70 years ago.

1.3 Postwar contacts between China and Japan

1.3.1 *The start of Sino-Japanese civil diplomacy*

After the war, China and Japan put an end to the period of invading and being invaded that characterized modern colonial times. It was now possible for the two countries to establish a new relationship in the new post-war era, and on a new basis of equality. Unfortunately, shortly after the end of World War II in 1945, new conflicts broke out among the victorious countries—namely, the Cold War between the erstwhile Eastern and Western allies of World War II, headed by the United States and the Soviet Union. The Cold War evolved into a comprehensive military and ideological confrontation. Meanwhile, China, as one of the victors in World War II, descended into the civil war between the Communist Party of China (CPC) and the Kuomintang. This civil war ended with the change of government in China, and the cross-Straits split with KMT-controlled Taiwan. The CPC government of the PRC in Mainland China became a member of the Eastern Bloc by allying with the Soviet Union, whereas the KMT government, having retreated to Taiwan, retained its alliance with the United States-dominated Western Bloc.

Japan, the defeated nation, received its deserved punishment, namely military occupation and democratic transformation of Japan by the allies after World War II. This punishment and transformation were led by the United States, which basically ceased punitive measures and democratic transformation policies in 1948. After this, American occupation authorities adopted new policies aiming to build Japan into an anti-communist fortress in East Asia as part of the Cold War with the Soviet Union, and help confront the changing situation in China. After the Korean War broke out in June 1950, the United States manipulated the peace process and, without the participation of China, convened the San Francisco Peace Conference Regarding Japan, and concluded the San Francisco Treaty of Peace with Japan, ending the formal military occupation of Japan.

Once Japan rejoined the international community, a top diplomatic priority was dealing with Sino-Japanese relations. Japan's first issue to address was whether to establish diplomatic relations with Beijing or Taiwan. This presented the Japanese government with a major dilemma: if Japan recognized Beijing and the PRC, the United States, and Taiwan would oppose the decision, and this would basically ignore the intentions of the United States and the opinions of Taiwan. If Japan recognized Taiwan as the government of China, this would be bound to worsen relations with Beijing, the legal government actually in control of most of China's territory. Establishing normal diplomatic relations with a real government was the only way for Japan to bring to a close its prior unequal or abnormal treatment of China and establish a relationship of equality between the two countries.

Prior to the ratification of the San Francisco Treaty of Peace with Japan, Yoshida Shigeru, the then Prime Minister of Japan, answered an inquiry from the Japanese diet: "Now Japan has the right to select the partners of peace talks. When exercising this right, Japan should consider the objective needs and situation in China, rather than make any rash decision on Sino-Japanese relations."[21] This quotation illustrates that the Japanese government was hesitant about which Chinese government to negotiate with. This hesitancy attracted the attention of Taiwanese and U.S. leaders, and Taiwan demanded the U.S. intervene in the case. The United States threatened Japan that the Senate would not approve the treaty. In December 1951, U.S. President Harry Truman sent John Foster Dulles to Tokyo as special envoy to pressure the Japanese government. Ultimately, the Yoshida Shigeru administration bowed to U.S. pressure and recognized Taiwan, sending an official message to the United States known as the Yoshida Letter definitively assuring the United States that Japan would establish comprehensive diplomatic relations with Taiwan and promising that Japan would never establish relations with the CPC government. The letter was published simultaneously in Washington and in Tokyo on January 16, 1952.

Soon afterwards, Japan sent a diplomatic delegation to Taiwan to conduct peace talks. After over two months of bilateral negotiations, Taiwan conceded its demands for a war indemnity in exchange for Japan's admission of its sovereignty over Mainland China. In April 1952, the two parties concluded a peace treaty between the Republic of China and Japan (the ROC-Japan Treaty). According to its terms, the two parties agreed to end the state of war between the two countries, and Japan renounced all privileges in Taiwan and the Penghu Islands seized from China in the modern era. Lastly, Japan agreed to recognize Taiwan diplomatically as the representative of China.

As one would expect, the Chinese government in Beijing issued a declaration sharply condemning Japan's decision to recognize Taiwan. However, in consideration of the importance of Sino-Japanese relations,

Beijing nevertheless hoped to keep ties with Japan. In its declaration, the Chinese government expressed the view that the Chinese people were willing to befriend the Japanese people, as would the Japanese people, and this could serve as the basis for friendly Sino-Japanese relations under the circumstances. The Chinese government therefore pursued other venues to maintain contact between the two countries—namely through civil diplomacy involving people-to-people contact with Japanese individuals friendly to China.

Civil diplomacy fell far short of official diplomatic relations confirmed by both governments, but served as an extension the various types of connections that had existed in history between China and Japan since ancient times. This had included extensive civilian contact even during periods of friction, conflicts, and war. For this reason, the Chinese government saw the possible advantage of maintaining unofficial channels to keep the relations between the two countries from total interruption during the period when the two countries had no official diplomatic relations. Unofficial contacts allowed a gradual improvement in relations through economic and cultural exchanges, and could ultimately lead to improved political relations between the two countries.

After the conclusion of the ROC-Japan Treaty, several senators in the Japanese diet attending an international economic conference in Moscow accepted an invitation of the Chinese government to China. This resulted in the first visit of nationals of Japan to China after the founding of the PRC. During their visit, the senators concluded the Sino-Japanese Non-governmental Trade Agreement with the China Council for the Promotion of International Trade (CCPIT). As the name implied, the agreement was unofficial, and specified only that the countries would carry on a limited volume of trade, but the treaty nevertheless had great significance and showed that civil diplomacy could produce concrete results. Later, in the 1950's, China and Japan concluded four additional non-governmental trade agreements in the same model.

In addition to this small-scale trade, the two countries also carried out various exchanges including in the fields of literature, art, sports, and academics. Japanese senators continued to visit, and the two countries jointly organized semi-official activities through their respective Red Cross Societies or through the China-Japan Friendship Association. Notable events included the return of nearly 40,000 Japanese nationals held in China for various reasons in the 1950s, including more than 1,000 war criminals set free by the Chinese government. In the 1960s, civil diplomacy assumed a semi-official character for a time, marked by the October 1962 visit to China of a large group of Japanese entrepreneurs led by former minister of international trade and industry Takasaki Tatsunosuke. During the visit, Takasaki signed the China-Japan Memorandum on Non-governmental Trade with Liao Chengzhi, the then vice minister of the United Front Work Department of the CPC Central Committee and the then vice director of the

Foreign Affairs Office of the State Council. The memo, known as the Long-Term Trade Memorandum, established principles for expanding bilateral trade. Both parties also agreed to establish trade representative offices in the capitals of their respective counterparts.

Given the ongoing Cold War, civil diplomacy efforts met with significant political interference. For example, the Kishi Nobusuke administration from 1957 to 1960 adopted an anti-China policy, leading to the interruption of civil diplomacy for a period. The Sato Eisaku administration from 1964 to 1972 also carried out an anti-China policy. During part of this period, China's extreme left policy halted civil diplomacy efforts between China and Japan, and planned activities were scaled back. However, civil diplomacy between China and Japan still provided a channel for exchanges between the two countries given their lack of established official diplomatic relations, kept their relations from being interrupted completely, and laid a foundation for the eventual establishment of official relations. Civil diplomacy helped foster a cohort of Japanese people friendly to China, and these individuals played an active role in the process of normalization of diplomatic relations between China and Japan, as well as developing friendly Japanese policies toward China in the subsequent decades.

1.3.2 *The normalization of the diplomatic relations between China and Japan and the overall development of bilateral relations*

At the outset of the 1970s, China's global diplomatic situation underwent a dramatic improvement. The most important development was the proclamation issued by representatives of China and the United States on July 15, 1971, after secret talks, announcing to the world that the then U.S. President Richard M. Nixon would pay an official state visit to China. In February 1972, after Nixon's visit to China took place as planned, China and the United States issued the Joint Communiqué of the United States of America and the PRC. Nixon's visit and the communique showed that the hostile relations between the two countries since the founding of the PRC had begun to thaw. In addition, at the 26th U.N. General Assembly in October 1971, Mainland China replaced Taiwan at the U.N., and also took its seat as a permanent member of the U.N. Security Council.

These events all promoted an improvement in Sino-Japanese relations. Particularly, the change of American diplomatic policy to China put the Sato administration—which had been politically hostile to China for many years—in an awkward position. Sato faced increasing domestic criticism regarding the China policy. Japanese groups formed to promote diplomatic normalization between China and Japan, and opposition political parties paid increasingly frequent visits to China to promote better Sino-Japanese relations. Under international and domestic pressure, the Sato administration was finally forced to announce its resignation in June 1972. Soon afterwards, the Tanaka Kakuei administration, which came to power in July, included normalization of diplomatic relations with China in its diplomatic agenda. Correspondingly, the Chinese government openly welcomed the advent of the Tanaka administration, and expressed appreciation of its policy promoting diplomatic normalization.

Japanese groups, and opposition political delegations having frequently visited China around the time of the establishment of the new Tanaka administration, were actively promoting diplomatic normalization. In June 1971, delegates of the Japanese Komei Party visited China and released a joint declaration with the China-Japan Friendship Association proposing conditions for the normalization. These evolved into what became known as the Three Principles of the Chinese government for resuming diplomatic relations: "(1) The People's Republic of China is the only legal government representing the whole of China. (2) Taiwan is a province of China and an inalienable part of China's territory. (3) The ROC-Japan Treaty is illegal and must be abrogated." These principles were increasingly accepted by Japanese people of various social circles, and by some political factions of the ruling Liberal Democratic Party of Japan. Tanaka Kakuei, the new prime minister, expressed full understanding of the principles at a public event.

Due to the efforts of the governments of both China and Japan, the two countries continued to progress toward diplomatic normalization. In July 1972, Yoshikatsu Takeiri, Chairman of the Central Executive Committee of the Komei Party of Japan, paid a visit to China and had talks with Zhou Enlai, the then premier of China, to preparate the ground for Prime Minister Tanaka's visit to China and a joint communiqué between both countries. After the talks, the Yoshikatsu Memorandum summarized the notes of Yoshikatsu Takeiri, which noted China's requirements for ending the official state of war and establishing diplomatic relations between both countries, anti-imperialism, concluding a treaty of peace and friendship and other agreements, and a waiver of China's earlier claims for a war indemnity to be paid by Japan. After some study, the Japanese government basically agreed to the content of the Yoshikatsu Memorandum. Shortly thereafter, Tanaka Kakuei scheduled an official state visit to China to finalize the normalization of diplomatic relations between China and Japan—after first gaining the consent of the United States and sending a special envoy to Taiwan to explain the change.

On September 25, 1972, the then Japanese Prime Minster Tanaka Kakuei and Foreign Minister Ohira Masayoshi along with other Japanese officials started for China. Japanese opposition party leaders and representatives of other social groups saw off the delegation at the airport—a rare joint ceremony crossing party boundaries that showed that the Tanaka Kakuei administration's diplomatic normalization policy had broad support across Japan. At Beijing Airport, Tanaka and his party received a similarly warm welcome. Premier Zhou Enlai personally received the Japanese leaders, and a grand welcome ceremony was held at the airport.

However, since the two countries had lacked official diplomatic relations for so many years, problems had accumulated that proved difficult to resolve completely, so some problems remained for further negotiation prior to reestablishing diplomatic relations. This included the issue of how to express the end of the state of war, whether the ROC-Japan Treaty remained valid, and whether anti-imperialism clauses should be included in treaty documents. Japan argued that the state of war between both countries had been ended upon conclusion of the ROC-Japan Treaty in 1952, and disagreed on whether to include expressions on ending the state of war or admitting the invalidity of the ROC-Japan Treaty. Japan also resisted inclusion of anti-imperialism clauses in the statement.

After difficult negotiations between the parties, the two countries agreed to a compromise statement which included a wording and approach acceptable to both parties. The statement substituted the phrase "abnormal state" to replace the "state of war," and avoided written mention of the ROC-Japan Treaty. Instead, Japan verbally announced the abrogation of the ROC-Japan Treaty after the issuance of the statement, and included anti-imperialism clauses. On September 29, the parties completed their negotiations and concluded the Sino-Japanese Joint Statement, realizing the full normalization of diplomatic relations. Soon after, the Japanese foreign minister held a news briefing and announced the abandonment of the ROC-Japan Treaty.

The normalization of diplomatic relations between China and Japan fundamentally altered the prior period of unequal and abnormal relations between Japan and China, opening a new chapter in bilateral relations. In accordance with stipulations in their Joint Statement, China and Japan concluded the Sino-Japanese Trade Agreement, the Sino-Japanese Air Agreement, the Sino-Japanese Maritime Agreement and the Sino-Japanese Fishery Agreement, with together established broad and comprehensive economic and trade relations between the countries. In August 1978, China and Japan finally concluded the Sino-Japanese Treaty of Peace and Friendship, which came about only after lengthy negotiation, in which anti-imperialism clauses had been a sticking point. Soon after the treaty's signing, China Vice Premier Deng Xiaoping paid a visit to Japan in October 1978, marking the first high-level post-war visit to Japan.

Relations between China and Japan reached a high point during this period. China's Reform and Opening policy during the 1980s saw contacts between both countries became increasingly frequent and close, and the friendly atmosphere pervaded government contacts and public opinion in the two countries. Both shared similar national interests in terms of diplomacy and national security: both faced security threats from the north, and the two countries also complemented each other economically. Namely, Japan needed China's energy supplies and access to its domestic market, and China depended on Japanese goods, investments, technology, and aid. The two countries also shared a sense of cultural intimacy. All these factors made peace and friendship between China and Japan mainstream.

Mutual visits by leaders of both countries became almost routine, and non-governmental exchanges increased as well.

While the 1980s saw overall improvement of bilateral relations, some frictions emerged. These include incidents over the historical content of Japanese textbooks in 1982 and in 1986, a dispute over Japanese official visits to the Yasukuni shrine to Japanese war dead in 1985, the Kokaryo Incident in 1987, and a dispute over civilian compensation between China and Japan that began in the 1980s. However, the extensive common interests shared by China and Japan during this time meant that such problems did not shake the foundation of Sino-Japanese relations, and governments of both countries maintained a low-key attitude and showed goodwill over how to handle such cases with as little diplomatic friction as possible.

1.3.3 *Sino-Japanese relations after the Cold War*

The political disturbances in Beijing at the end of the 1980s and the end of the Cold War between the East and the West greatly affected relations between China and Western countries as well as between China and Japan, given Japan's relation with the West. After the collapse of the Soviet Union, China, as the world's largest socialist country, began to become the object of Western efforts to change China. For a period after the political disturbance in Beijing in 1989, Western countries imposed various degrees of political and economic sanctions against China. In contrast, Japan—as a close neighbor and friendly cooperation partner with China during 1970s–1980s—expressed only certain dissatisfaction over the events in China, and as a result the major event had no serious immediate influence on Sino-Japanese relations. Japan became the first to break the diplomatic boycott against China by Western countries by arranging the visit of China's top leader to Japan, followed by the first visit of the emperor of Japan to China in 1992. As a result, bilateral relations between the two reached a new high.

The end of the Cold War deeply influenced Sino-Japanese relations in other respects starting in the mid-1990s. The collapse of the Soviet Union and the improvement of Russian relations with both China and Japan weakened the common security interest between China and Japan. Other issues raised doubts about the common security interests of the two countries: the pursuit of nuclear weapons by North Korea, Chinese nuclear testing, the Taiwan Straits crisis, and enhancements of the United States–Japan alliance. Sino-Japanese relations experienced questions about whether a Security Dilemma—in which measures to improve the security of one country inherently threatens the other—now existed between the two.

From the mid-1990s, both China and Japan experienced major changes in terms of relative economic strength. China witnessed rapid economic growth during this period, whereas Japan has proven unable to shake a long period of economic decline and stagnation following the collapse of the country's real estate bubble in the early 1990s. As a result, China rapidly narrowed the economic gap with Japan, exceeding Japan's GDP to become the world's second largest economy today. In addition, throughout this period, Sino-Japanese economic ties expanded continually, but shifted from mutual complementarity toward increased competition.

New national development goals set by the two countries in the mid- and late-1990s also aggravated mutual doubts. Having dramatically increased its position in the world through economic development and growth, China's plans sought to achieve the goal of "revitalizing the Chinese nation," reflecting thoughts of a great power. In contrast, Japan sought to reform domestic politics, enhance its influence in international politics, and realize the goal of becoming a normal country—unfettered by limitations imposed after World War II. In other words, both China and Japan sought status as major powers, leading to the situation that two countries were in parity for the first time in the history of East Asia. On the other hand, China and Japan in East Asia lacked a tradition of regionalism and regional cooperation; the two basically viewed their changed roles in terms of nationalism, and did not know how to deal with their new type of bilateral relations. The two countries seemed to lose political tolerance for each other, and harshly censured each other whenever disputes arose, often via different dialogue platforms.

Ultimately, tensions in Sino-Japanese political relations, and the domestic political and social changes in China and Japan all led to a deterioration in goodwill between the Chinese and Japanese public. Public opinion surveys in recent years show that only 10% of nationals of both countries had favorable views of the other, while 90% had a negative view. Political leaders in both countries made efforts to explore new common interests as a foundation for bilateral relations. This included the announcement in 1998 that the two countries would establish a "friendly cooperation partnership for peace and development for the 21st century." This effort failed to prevent Sino-Japanese relations from seriously deteriorating for a period of over five years after the visits starting in 2001 of the Japanese prime minister visits to the Yasukuni Shrine. This visits also triggered frictions over other historical issues, as well as over the East China Sea. In 2006, both countries announced the establishment of a Strategic Relationship of Mutual Benefit and exchanged mutual visits of national leaders, reported in mainstream Chinese media with words such as "Ice Breaking," "Thawing," "Ushering in Spring," and "Warm Spring," as a way to enrich official relations. In 2008, the heads of both countries signed the China-Japan Joint Statement on Overall Promotion of a Strategic Relationship for Mutual Benefit. But these efforts were limited to proposing mutual goals and principles, and lacked a solid foundation of specific, common interest as a basis for bilateral relations—unlike the period of shared interest that served as the basis for warm relations in the 1980s.

Against the general backdrop these contradictions, Sino-Japanese relations seemed fragile and were affected by crises. This included long-running disputes such as over recognition of history, territorial disputes over the

Diaoyu Islands, and Taiwan, which became sharper. There were also new crises, such as disputes over maritime border demarcation and the strengthening and expansion of the United States–Japan alliance. Of these, territorial and maritime disputes have served as the main focal points that influence Sino-Japanese relations up to the present time—for instance, the ongoing dispute over the Diaoyu Islands. These problems involve the most sensitive issues of security and real interests of both parties, and differ from disputes about the recognition of historical events. While the issue of recognition of historical events appears unresolvable and frequently affects public opinion in both countries, this is unlikely to lead directly to armed conflict.

During the roughly two years after a diplomatic crisis broke out between China and Japan over the Diaoyu Islands in September 2012, Sino-Japanese relations entered a period of crisis. Each refused to give in to the other, and there were tense confrontations at sea and in the air. The issue remained prominent, and in both countries, government officials and regular people continued to issue provocative words and demonstrations. The outside world grew increasingly concerned that military conflict might occur over the Diaoyu Island waters. During the crisis, China and Japan broke off any attempt to hold diplomatic summits, and the dispute also hurt non-governmental exchanges in the economic, cultural, and other fields.

Fortunately, both countries are no longer in the colonial or Cold War eras. They share common needs in terms of peace and development, and have different strengths which enables them to avoid descending into armed conflict. The dispute over the Diaoyu Islands has not affected all of the many links between China and Japan. The countries continue to share many common or similar interests, such as economic and cultural exchanges, joint efforts on environmental protection and climate change, and joint approaches to regional and global issues.

For these reasons, the trend of deteriorating Sino-Japanese relations remained limited, and in November 2014, China and Japan reached a negotiated agreement that established four points of consensus: (1) Both parties confirm they will observe all principles and the spirit of the four political documents previously signed between China and Japan, and they two will continue to develop their strategic and mutually beneficial relationship. (2) Both parties, in the spirit of facing history squarely and working together for the future, will reach agreement to resolve political barriers to bilateral relations. (3) Both parties recognize that there exist different claims over the Diaoyu Islands waters and other waters in the East China Sea, and agree to prevent the situation from worsening by engaging in dialogue and consultation, and to establish a crisis management and control mechanism to avoid unexpected incidents. (4) Both parties agree to restart political, diplomatic, and security dialogues through multilateral and bilateral channels and strive to build political mutual trust.

Of the four points, the crisis management and control mechanism greatly decreases the probability of any armed conflict between China and Japan.

This alone should prevent Sino-Japanese relations from further deterioration. Of course, full resolution of all outstanding disputes and removing all difficulties in Sino-Japanese relations would require elimination of structural contradictions between the countries, identification and expansion of mutual interests, and undertaking more joint regional responsibilities given their power status.

To summarize, post-war Sino-Japanese relations have undergone wide fluctuations, alternating between warming and cooling, and between good periods and bad. The countries increasingly shared mutual interests and wished to cooperate, but were often hindered by difficult-to-overcome contradictions and conflicts. To realize their national interests, governments and the public in both countries must take Sino-Japanese relations seriously and jointly explore ways of casting off present difficulties.

Notes

1. Teng, Jun, et al. *The History of Sino-Japanese Cultural Exchanges*. Peking University Press, 2011: 24. Lelang was one of the four shires established in the northern Korean Peninsula by Emperor Wudi of the Han Dynasty after destroying Wei-family-ruled Korea. Lelang Sea should mean the Yellow Sea and the East China Sea area. In late Eastern Han Dynasty, Liaodong Governor Gongsun Du implemented separatist rule and controlled former Yan State and Lelang Shire. In 204 (Jian'an Year 9), Gongsun Kang, son of Gongsun Du, established Daifang Shire to the south of Lelang Shire, to centrally administrate affairs of contacts between China and Japan and Korea.
2. Teng Jun, et al. From the *History of Sino-Japanese Cultural Exchanges*. Peking University Press, 2011: 24.
3. Huntington, Samuel. *The Clash of Civilizations and the Remaking of World Order* (translated by Zhou Qi, et al.). Xinhua Publishing House, 2002: 29–32. The civilizations currently existing and affecting the world mainly include Chinese civilization, Japanese civilization, Indian civilization, Islamic civilization, Western civilization, Latin American civilization, African civilization, and Orthodox Christianity civilization.
4. Eisenstadt, S.N. *Japanese Civilization: A Comparative View* (Translated by Wang Xiaoshan, et al.). The Commercial Press, 2008: 266.
5. There are different views on whether this order in fact existed, whether it always centered on China, and whether it consisted primarily of trade and tribute between China and surrounding countries. Most hold that the order existed, and that the Empire of China held a central position most of the time.
6. Fukuzawa, Yukichi. *Datsu-A-Ron*. The Complete Works of Fukuzawa Yukichi (Vol. 10). Iwanami Shoten, 1962: 240.
7. Japan dispatched troops to Taiwan on the ground of the incident that some Ryukyu fishermen drifted to and were killed in Taiwan. It did not overwhelm the Qing government militarily, but finally forced officials of the Qing government to admit Japan's military operation as a "chivalrous deed" and reaped the indemnity of 500,000 taels of silver, occupying a dominant position in the issue about Ryukyu.
8. The "Incident d'lmo" means the incident that some Korean soldiers and people attacked the Legation of Japan to oppose Japan's interference in Korea's internal affairs. After the incident broke out, China and Japan dispatched

their troops to Korea and intensified the contradictions between them. Finally the indent was ended by the conclusion of the Jiwupo Treaty and Japan's acquisition of the indemnity and the right to station troops in the Legation.

9. The December Incident of 1884 refers to a coup carried out by Japanese forces in support of the reform-oriented Civilized Party of Korea. The coup was later suppressed by the troops of the Qing government, which were invited in by Korea, further worsening the conflict between China and Japan. The conflict ended with the Treaty of Tianjin between China and Japan, which stipulated that China and Japan would withdraw their troops from Korea and would keep each other informed of relevant actions before dispatching troops.
10. Qi, Qizhang. "Korean Tonghak Society and Tonghak Society Uprising [chaoyan dongxuedang yu dongxuedang qiyi]." History Teaching, 3 (1989): 16–21.
11. Song, Chengyou. *A New Modern History of Japan*. Peking University Press, 2006: 237.
12. Tarou, Sakamoto. *The History of Japan* (Translated by Wang Xiangrong, etc.). China Social Sciences Press, 2008: 422.
13. Bitou, Masahide. *A New History of Japan*. 1995: 183.
14. Nishio, Kanji. *New History Textbook*. Fusosha Publishing Company, 2001: 219.
15. A massive campaign of learning from Western technologies and establishing government-run factories that some bureaucrats sought and advocated to implement in more than 60 years from the beginning of the 1860s to the end of the Sino-Japanese War of 1894–1895.
16. Fan, Wenlan. *The Modern History of China, Vol. 1 of Book I*. People's Publishing House, 1951: 336.
17. Fan, Wenlan. *The Modern History of China, Vol. 1 of Book I*. People's Publishing House, 1951: 297–300.
18. Tarou, Sakamoto. *The History of Japan* (Translated by Wang Xiangrong, et al.). China Social Sciences Press, 2008: 422–424.
19. Song, Chengyou. *A New Modern History of Japan*. Peking University Press, 2006: 237.
20. Xu, Tianxin et al. *The General History of the World (Modern Times)*. People's Publishing House, 1997: 605.
21. Wu, Wenxue, et al. *Contemporary Sino-Japanese Relations*. Current Affairs Press, 1995: 11.

2 The views of China of the Japanese

As the foregoing chapter has shown, Japan and China have a history of more than 2,000 years of contact, alternating between periods of warm and active relations and periods of conflict. Each alternation between good and bad periods had its own historical reasons, but the perceptions each country held of the other played an extremely important role in shaping their relations. Japan in particular faced the question of how to view relations with China has remained a central topic, and the Japanese view of China has influenced the destiny of both countries. For this reason, this chapter focused on how the Japanese view China and the Chinese people—namely, on determining Japanese views of China, and how and why these viewpoints have changed over time.

Japanese society, like any society, is not a simple two-dimensional plane, but rather a diverse, three-dimensional structure with multiple levels. Every individual Japanese person may have a unique viewpoint on China. This chapter discusses only the conception of China held by selected mainstream groups within Japanese society—namely, among those classes that had contact with China or held a leadership position in Japan in each period of interest. Due to the immense span of time between ancient and modern eras and the post-war period, and given the remoteness in time, it is difficult to capture Japanese views of China in ancient periods. Therefore, in this chapter, descriptions of Japanese views of China in ancient times or in the 1800s are relatively basic and broad, whereas it is possible to be more meticulous, specific, and rigorous on the Japanese view of China since World War II.

2.1 The views of China of the Japanese in ancient times

When considering the Japanese views of China in ancient times, it is necessary to focus on perceptions of the ruling Chinese dynasties, given that there was little concept of nation or nationality at that time. The different dynasties in China naturally created different impressions on the different dynasties of Japan, as well. Ancient times also saw relatively little personal exchange between China and Japan, so it is probably out of the question to summarize any overall view of the Japanese public about China in those times. The Japanese perception of China was mainly embodied by the views of Japanese officials and intellectual elites.

In the earliest days of historical contact between China and Japan, the two countries differed greatly in terms of their level of civilization. The earliest historical starting point of Japanese civilization was far behind that of contemporary Chinese civilization. For this reason, prior to the Sui (581–619) and Tang (618–907) Dynasties in China, the Japanese records indicate a sense of worship and awe of China.

During these times, there was unquestionably little personal exchange, and those few who had any contact with China or could travel to Mainland China were limited to upper-class personages hailing from different Japanese minor states during the long period prior to Japanese unification. Japanese elites often traveled to China to receive ceremonial grants and titles, which could help accumulate fortune and power back in Japan. As the mentioned previously, in the Jianwu Zhongyuan period during the reign of Emperor Guangwu of the Eastern Han Dynasty in China, officials from a small Japanese state paid tribute to the Han Government and received in return a gold seal. Similarly, the queen of small Japanese state Yamatai—approximately on today's Kyushu—dispatched envoys to pay tribute to the Chinese state of Wei, receiving in return a gold seal and the title of "Pro-Wei Wa King" from the imperial government of Wei, which was then ruled by the Cao family. These records support the general view that Japan, during the period of national unification, held a worshipful view of China. Due to this worship and awe, Japanese elites sought to absorb elements of Chinese civilization, and adopted China as a model for the initial shape of ancient Japanese civilization. Even today, this is recognized in Japan, and some present-day Japanese people with unfriendly views of China nevertheless express deep respect for ancient Chinese civilization, notwithstanding their dislike of today's China, for the reason that much of ancient Japanese civilization had its origins in ancient China.

During the Sui and Tang Dynasties, Japan became a unified country, but remained relatively backwards in terms of social and technological development. Japanese scholars and elites began to travel to China to study both intellectual knowledge and technology. Those who were sent to China for study included officials, scholars, monks, and craftsmen—together the backbone of Japanese society in that day. During their studies in China, these visitors reached a peak in terms of their worship and awe of China: they could see both the immense power and openness of the Sui and Tang Dynasty China, as well as its great prosperity. During this century-long period, Japanese visitors studied and imitated China, ultimately to shaping the eventual Japanese central government system, known as the Mikado to resemble the Sui and Tang Dynasties. Chinese culture also influenced Japan in all other aspects of written characters, literary and artistic style, architecture, Confucianism and other aspects of religion.

During the period when Japanese elites worshiped, studied, and imitated China, some Japanese leaders held a mentality of admiration, covetousness, or rivalry toward China, possibly typical of political figures seeking greater political power. For example, a letter from the then Japanese emperor to the emperor of the Chinese Sui Dynasty employed the phrases "from the Emperor of the Sunrise State to the Emperor of the Sunset State" and "from the Eastern Emperor to the Western Emperor." It was said that these expressions made the Sui emperor dissatisfied, though he had no recourse. Those in power in Japan were well aware that China was much more advanced and powerful than Japan, but nevertheless they spared no effort to shake off the yoke of the Sino-Foreign Country System, centered on the emperor of China, while still enjoying various honors and benefices held over from the times of the Sui and Tang Dynasties. The geographical characteristics of Japan, and its separation from the Asian continental landmass, further enabled Japan to adopt a middle position neither close nor distant from the powerful Chinese Empire.

After the end of the Tang Dynasty, China experienced a long period of turbulence, essentially lasting until modern times, and Chinese civilization never recovered the degree of openness and splendor of the Sui and Tang Dynasties. Meanwhile, the gap between Chinese civilization and Japanese civilization narrowed, as Japan completed the overall process of national unification, and gradually adapted the Chinese elements it had absorbed into its own civilization. As a result, Japanese views of China changed subtly, and Japan continued to view China through a lens of worship and appreciation, but no longer with the same level of reverence. Japanese scholars saw it as less imperative to learn from and imitate China as had been the case during the Sui and Tang Dynasties. Elements of Chinese civilization such as Confucianism still served as important ideology for high officials and intellectual elites to cultivate their moral qualities and administer the state for the benefit of the people and society. But by this time Japan had thoroughly absorbed and digested these elements of Chinese civilization, gradually localized them as Japanese, and developed some Chinese cultural elements independently if they had disappeared in China. Thus, these elements formed the core of Japanese culture. Japanese scholars even began to compose criticism of Confucianism or develop new doctrines or ideas about Confucianism and other Chinese learning.

Politically, Japan had grown stronger, and in any conflict between Japan and China, Japanese leaders had lost their sense of awe, and would not submit to China. There were two reasons for this change: first, the relative gap in civilization and strength between China and Japan was narrower than before the Sui and Tang Dynasties. Second, after Mongolian troops from the Yuan Dynasty wiped out the Southern Dong regime in the 1279 naval battle of Yashan, many Japanese viewed China in a different light. "There is no China after the Yashan Sea Battle," it was said, and many Japanese felt that China was not the same country that the Japanese had worshiped and studied. The ethnically Mongolian Yuan Dynasty government did not appear to the Japanese as a successor of the previous Chinese Dynasties. Later, the advent of the Ming Dynasty returned Dynastic control to ethnically Chinese leaders, but during this time, Japan's social development had converged with that of China, and there was no longer any obvious gap between them. As a result, the Japanese lost their previous sense of awe toward China.

Generally, across the centuries of ancient times, the Japanese view of China basically consisted of admiration, worshipping, standing in awe of, studying, and imitating China. This was particularly so among Japan's intellectual elite. The sense of Japanese admiration for China reached its peak during the Sui and Tang Dynasties. Any powerful political figure will have the impulse to challenge those powers higher his, but ancient history records only a few successful challenges by powerful Japanese figures to the imperial power of China. Indeed, those few Japanese political elites who tried to challenge China in fact showed a worshipful or admiring view of China. However, with the gradual social changes that narrowed the gap between China and Japan after the Sui and Tang Dynasties, the Japanese sense of worship was declined and eventually faded.

2.2 The views of China of the Japanese in modern times

The history of modern Japan since the mid-19th century was a period of both splendor and shame for the Japanese. This contrast relates particularly to how the Japanese treated China. That is to say, tracing the Japanese view of China since modern times effectively amounts to tracing the history of Japan in modern times.

Up until modern times, Japan's history of contact with China was one in which Japan occupied a relatively inferior position. Prior to the arrival of Western colonial powers in East Asia, China occupied a central position in the region. For Japan viewed China as the country it worshiped or admired, and most to study and imitate. However, once Western colonial powers began a series of massive incursions of East Asia, a new model of international relations emerged, and the influence of Western civilization had a major impact on the region. As a result, China's international position began to slip, and eventually nearly collapse. As a result, the Japanese view of China changed gradually.

After China was forced to open its door in the aftermath of the Opium War, Japan, as a neighbor of China, underwent similar experiences and changes. Indeed, Japanese officials and intellectual elites worried that Western powers would treat Japan in the same manner as they did China, and essentially had sympathy with the Chinese experience. Not long after, Western powers used their more sophisticated military technology to force Japan to open its doors—but this happened without the devastating war China suffered. In the unprecedented process of cultural collision and resulting social instability, Japan bore firsthand witness to the defeats suffered by China, its humiliation, and the forfeiture of its sovereignty. This outcome presented a sharp contrast with the image of China that Japanese previously had held. At the same time, the Japanese came into closer contact with new civilization. These circumstances forced the Japanese to rethink their views of different civilizations, and Japan prepared to accept this change. So as a result, Japan gradually lost the sense of worship toward China, and quickly began to despise China notwithstanding former feelings of sympathy.

As noted above, during the Edo shogunate, Japan adhered to a closed-door policy and banned all contact with the outside world except for opening Nagasaki to allow limited trade by Chinese, Korean, and Dutch merchant ships. Japan deliberately maintained contact with China and the Dutch as window for information on Western countries. Through such contacts, Japanese shogunate officials quickly learned of the Sino-British Opium War and its outcome. The downfall of China's position in the Japanese mind as the Celestial Empire had an immense impact on Japanese society.

Events in China were much discussed by officials of the military shogunate, provincial officials, and intellectuals, all of whom sought to analyze the reasons for China's defeat and draw lessons from its fall. Kaishu, a major official under the shogunate, thought that "affairs of the neighboring country can serve as a warning to us."[1] Tokugawa Nariaki, head of the State of Mito, a domain directly under jurisdiction of the shogun, advocated military preparedness. Such people argued, "The Qing Empire calls itself Huaxia and considers Western countries as beasts. Yet Western countries are resourceful and agile, and equipped with advanced machinery, while the Qing government made no preparation [for conflict with the West]. So the foreigners sweep through the Qing Empire through attacks from the sea, and as a result, the Qing Empire is humiliated by them."[2]

To investigate actual situation in China, in 1862, the shogun sent Takasugi Shinsaku and others to Shanghai by the *Chitose Maru*. Takasugi and his party stayed in Shanghai for more than two months, carrying out field investigations and keeping detailed records of what they found. After return to Japan, they reported to the Bakufu government. The records contain descriptions such as, "There are thousands of merchant ships and warships in the docks of Shanghai, their masts as dense as a forest."[3] At the same time, "the Chinese residents we visited were mostly poor, with squalid and filthy homes."[4] "The urban environment of Shanghai is poor, and the Chinese people show a servile attitude toward foreigners. If a Chinese person meets British or French people on the road, the Chinese often make way and by stand off to the side of the road."[5] In a word, the *Chitose Maru* delegation, on its return to Japan, depicted China as a weak country of extreme poverty, submitting under the oppression of Western powers. This new viewpoint completely overturned the previous image of China held by the Japanese, and led Japanese society to experience a sense of national crisis. Japanese elites worried that Japan would be another China when it faced a coming invasion by Western countries.

After the Meiji Restoration, when Emperor Meiji took the throne in 1867 following the defeat of the shogunate by the anti-shogunate forces, Japanese government underwent a complete transformation and a new political power system was established. Under the new system, Japan set out a basic national policy of opening to the West and studying the West, with the aim of enriching the nation and strengthening its military power. On the issue of China, there occurred divergence of views: some thought China's national power had been badly weakened, and Japan should join the invasion of China by Western powers. Others maintained the traditional view of China and sympathized with its plight, proposing that China and Japan ally to resist invasion by Western countries. For example, in 1881, the Japanese freedom and civil rights parties published Contemporary Commentary, and Japanese Liberty News firmly objected to Japan undertaking the hostile actions against China, arguing that Japan and China should form an alliance to jointly resist Western powers. However, as time went on, and as China was too slow in its modernization, Japanese scholars gradually cast aside the idea of an alliance with China, instead arguing for discarding the relationship with China or promoting internal change within China. Even proponents of such views gradually came to despise China, and increasingly agreed that Japanese invasion of China alongside Western countries would bring benefits to Japan.

In terms of illustrating this shift in thinking from sympathy to despising China, the most representative Japanese scholar was Fukuzawa Yukichi and his *Datsu-A-Ron*. At the end of the Edo shogunate, young Fukuzawa Yukichi visited Europe and explored aspects of Western civilization. His published writings in the early days of the Meiji period, such as the *Gakumon No Susume* and the *Bunmeiron No Gairyaku,* argued Japan should abolish its old cultural traditions and institutions and introduce new Western forms. He also thought it is imperative for Japan to thoroughly reform society; without such reform, he thought Japan would be unable to exist in the modern world. Like most Japanese intellectuals at that time, as a child Fukuzawa had studied Sinology and the theories of Chinese philosopher Zhuzi, and developed a sense of kindness and of worship toward China. Fukuzawa held such views up to the Meiji Restoration in the 1860s. With the success of the Meiji Reform, Japan's opening to the West, and the new Japanese government policies aimed at enriching the country, strengthening the military, and developing industry, Fukuzawa's thought changed accordingly. From the 1870s, Fukuzawa's *An Outline of the Theory of Civilization*, *Common National Rights* and *Common Civil Rights* as well other influential works were published in rapid succession. In these works, Fukuzawa took Western civilization as a reference point to compare China with Japan on various aspects of society, history, national identity, culture, customs, and habits. By these measures, Fukuzawa found much to praise about Japan, but belittled China, and he advocated for divorcing Japanese civilization from Chinese civilization. After the 1880s, Fukuzawa wrote that, "Today, the Japanese are no longer in awe of China," adding that, "the idea that the relationship between Japan and China is like that between the lips and the teeth—sharing a common destiny and interdependence—is nothing but an unrealistic fancy." "Hostility to China is not to be feared, and it is not useful to consider China as a spiritual friend ... rather, the only thing to fear is Western countries, and these are the only powers with which we should maintain exchange."[6]

In March 1885, Fukuzawa published an editorial entitled *Datsu-A-Ron* in the *Current News*, a publication he directed. In the famous editorial, he expressed the view that if Japan "follows Western civilization and casts off long-settled social forms, this will bring a favorable turn to all of Asia. The main idea is to divorce Japan from Asia."[7] Following the editorial, a group of Japanese intellectual elites represented by Fukuzawa began to advocate wholesale westernization, abandoning their prior focus on Chinese learnings, and increasingly despised China, advocating that Japan treat Asian countries such as China and Korea in the same manner as Western countries did. At first, such arguments remained only a marginal trend among intellectuals, and its main significance was only cultural. Not long after, however, the ideas came to be tied to the Meiji administration's political and military policies to "expand national rights overseas," and Fukuzawa's arguments became the spiritual tools for Japan's invasion of neighboring countries.

It was through this process that Japanese views of China shifted from adoration to sympathy and ultimately toward contempt. As a result of this shift, the Japanese government could take advantage of intellectual contempt for China and the Chinese to incite nationalist feelings and justify aggression against China and neighboring countries. From the late 1870s, Japan launched its strategy to penetrate into and invade the Ryukyus, Taiwan, and Korea, all of which were either Chinese territories or had long-standing connections to China. In diplomatic negotiations or other dealings with the Qing government of China concerning smaller countries or territories, Japanese officials came to the view that Chinese officials were ignorant, decadent, and unfamiliar with the new rules of international relations. This further heightened the contempt for China among Japan's official elite.

The Sino-Japanese War of 1894–1895 was the first full-scale war by Japan against China following the shift in Japanese views on China from worship to contempt, and following Japan's own internal reforms and diplomacy. Public opinions in Japan described the war as a "just war," and a war "by the civilized against the savage." At the war's outset, Japan feared war in China given its vast land area. But the course of the war and its outcome further persuaded the Japanese in their superiority over the Chinese, and Japan's self-confidence and contempt for China grew accordingly. For this reason, the Japanese gave little consideration to Chinese feelings after China's defeat, and the resulting Treaty of Shimonoseki forced China to cede territory and pay oppressive indemnities. Even after a common Japanese man tried to assassinate and seriously wounded Li Hongzhang, the Qing government's chief representative in the negotiation, Japan did not alter its demands territorial cessions and indemnities. As one Japanese scholar wrote after World War II, "In the Sino-Japanese War of 1894–1895, Japan's unexpected victory made the Japanese wild with joy and wonder at the weakness of China.

After that, an earth-shaking change occurred in the attitude of the Japanese toward its neighbor, and feelings of contempt overwhelmed respect. We should have been vigilant against such conceit, as this was the source of all tragedies."[8] It is a pity that such recognition came too late.

After the Sino-Japanese War of 1894–1895, contempt for the Chinese among the Japanese reached its zenith. Just as Song Chengyou said: "The greatest influence of the Sino-Japanese War of 1894–1895 on Japanese society was the sharp increase in Japanese awareness of its great power status, and the resulting unchecked spread of militarism. The sense of intimacy with and the awe toward China in Japan disappeared forever, while national chauvinism and the belittling and despising of China caused great clamor."[9]

Subsequently, Japan started the Russo-Japanese War on Chinese territory and defeated Russia. The victory in turn made the Japanese government and ordinary Japanese people still more arrogant and tyrannous. Japan began to bully China and the Chinese people with ever-increasing intensity. For example, Japanese intellectual elites who sought freedom and civil rights in Japan also unanimously expressed support for the Japanese invasion of China. Some Japanese residing in China under the terms of the unequal treaties also showed an extreme sense of superiority over ordinary Chinese. The Japanese government not only stationed troops in China on the grounds of protecting the Japanese people or guarding railway facilities, but also fabricated an endless string of disputes aimed at dismembering China.

As already mentioned, Japan's Twenty-One Demands in 1915 were designed to transform China into a Japanese dependency. In the view of the Japanese, China and the Chinese people were incapable of properly administering the country, so China should instead be administered by Japan. This idea led inexorably toward Japan's continuous string of actions aimed at invading and dismembering China, culminating in the September 18 Incident in 1931 and the Lugou Bridge Incident in 1937, which marked Japan's full-scale invasion of China. In 1941, Japan put forward the concept of the Greater East Asia Co-Prosperity Sphere, in which Japan would dominate East Asia including China and other countries in the region, and attain "co-prosperity" by transforming the countries in Japan's orbit. These ideas, including the spite toward China and bullying and invasion of China, were thoroughly smashed by Japan's total defeat in 1945.

Overall, Japanese views on China in modern times basically have consisted of looking down on China, starting from sympathy, then shifting to contempt, bullying, and efforts at transforming China from the outside. To be sure, this discussion focuses on the views of the Japanese government and intellectual elites in leading positions in Japan. We do not deny that there were many Japanese people who opposed the war and remained friendly to China and the Chinese people. However, at that time, these individuals did not play a leading role in Japan, and their views on China did not serve as the mainstream Japanese view of China in this period.

2.3 The views of China of the Japanese after World War II

After World War II, as a vanquished country Japan's national confidence was hit hard. Japanese views of China in this period included various contradictory ideas. Japan had previously worshipped and been in awe of China, imitated and studied it, and then later showed sympathy for China, despised it, bullied it, and sought to transform it. However, given the new positions of Japan and China after World War II, Japanese views of China underwent various changes, and featured different ideas and viewpoints in succeeding periods.

Generally, from the beginning of the 1950s, when Japan resumed independence and the CPC-KMT civil war ended, up until today, Japanese views of China have experienced four stages: (1) From the beginning of the 1950s to the mid-1960s, Japanese worship of the People's Republic of China was the mainstream view, due to Japanese consciousness of responsibility for the war and desire to atoning for Japanese crimes. (2) From the mid-1960s to the end of the 1970s, Japanese worship of China turned to disappointment, tinged with sympathy. (3) From the beginning of the 1980s to the mid-1990s, Japanese mainly showed sympathy for China, and gradually came to consider China as an equal partner. Japan mainly sought cooperation with China during this period. (4) After the 1990s, Japanese people began to detest and fear China, and sought to be vigilant against China. The four stages are detailed below.

2.3.1 *From the beginning of the 1950s to the mid-1960s*

Through the San Francisco Treaty, signed at the San Francisco peace conference in September 1951, Japan obtained independence, and in April 1952 when the treaty entered into force, Japan rejoined the international community as a country with full sovereignty. Meanwhile, the civil war in China ended resulting in a change in government, leaving unresolved the cross-straits confrontation with Taiwan. Given that China was split, Japan bowed to U.S. Cold War pressure and granted diplomatic relations to Taiwan. Thus, Japan isolated itself from the government of Mainland China, and a state of hostility existed between the two. However, official isolation did not determine the views of ordinary Japanese toward China. Due to ongoing civil diplomacy links between China and Japan, non-governmental exchanges continued, including small-scale trade, cultural exchanges, visits by political party leaders, as well as other activities. These exchanges reflected general Japanese views of China in mainstream Japanese public opinion at that time. The views of China described here doubtless refer mainly to the ideas held by Japanese intellectuals, rather than of the Japanese government. The governments of the two countries remained in a state of mutual political opposition, and given the East–West confrontation of the Cold War, it was impossible establish good official relations.

After its occupation and transformation by the United States, Japan submitted diplomatically to the Western Bloc, which was unacceptable to the Chinese side. After the occupation, however, Japan's system of Fascist dictatorship was broken and replaced by a Western democratic system. Under the new system, Japanese society gradually lost the previous top-down direction of public opinion. Public opinion on many matters diversified, and the ruling party or government in power exercised less control over public opinion. Instead, left-wing intellectuals from the academic and media circles played a leading role in public opinion formation at that time. As a result, though China and Japan lacked official relations and were even officially hostile, the non-governmental relations between the two continued and remained relatively friendly. In this period, Japanese society obtained information and formed opinions on China mainly through the left-wing intellectuals or opposition parties with contacts with China.

The Japanese society's views of China immediately following the War were based on mainstream Japanese intellectuals' comparison of China with Japanese society since modern times and on the basis of intellectual criticism of this period of history. Due to Japan's defeat, mainstream Japanese intellectuals began to rethink the whole history of modern Japan leading up to war, which inevitably involved the issue of how to view China. According to this school of thought, the modernization of Japan had failed, whereas China was on a successful path toward modernity, since social reform in Japan in modern times was not a top-down one. Japan's modernization had been based on a highly centralized system centered on the emperor. This form of modernization had enabled Japan to undergo reform and grow stronger in a short period, but had led Japan down the road of imperialism, and, ultimately, to total defeat. In contrast, through its anti-imperial and anti-feudal social revolution, China had achieved unification more gradually than Japan, but had ultimately established the People's Republic of China, and embarked on the wholly new course of development. China's process of modernization took longer than Japan's, but followed a more normal path of development, and would guide China to prosperity and power. Thus, according to this view, Japan should study China's path of modernization.

Moreover, by comparing post-war China and Japan, Japanese intellectuals noted the superiority of China: China had cast off its poverty, weakness, and divisions, and it had unified and increased its influence in the international community. China's campaign of national reconstruction also attracted Japanese attention, as China surpassed the United Kingdom and began catching up with the United States, as did the Great Leap Forward. In today's view, these social movements and mass campaigns had their defects, but few Japanese people thought so at the time. To the contrary, many Japanese people were moved by scenes of mass support for the government, and of stirring social movements. At this time, Japanese people saw China as constructing a new society in which all people lived happily.

During the period, Japanese who were friendly to China visited the country, and on their return to Japan, they wrote articles conveying their impressions, and giving wide publicity to what they had seen and heard in China. These accounts gave the Japanese public a wholly new image of China, one in which China seemed like a paradise—thriving, full of life, with people working together. In this image, China had no poor, and all showed high morality—regular people would leave their doors open all night without fear, no one would even pocket items lost by others on the road. China was seen as healthy and clean, lacking even flies. For example, one Japanese scholar who visited China wrote, "China boasts a huge population and immense resources, is constantly developing new technologies, and under the new system the masses are able to achieve their full potentials ... China advances by long strides in this environment ... Those who respect the People's Republic of China are usually jealous when they realize they are Japanese."[10] In contrast, Japan remained under the shadow of its recent defeat and occupation by American troops. Japan's economy had not only recovered and begun to take off, but also Japan's economy had not surpassed China's. Therefore, Japan appeared inferior to China in all these aspects. Hence, many left-wing Japanese intellectuals worshiped China to extremes, and advocated Japan again study China as a model.

Japanese intellectuals of this period also severely criticized Japan's past aggression against China, and condemned the disastrous crimes by Japanese militarists against China and Chinese people. As Japanese people, these intellectuals expressed words of reflection and apology, and sought to atone for Japan's crimes against China. Japanese intellectuals also expressed appreciation for China's tolerance of Japan and for the Chinese government's policy of distinguishing regular Japanese people from the Japanese militarists, and recognition that the Japanese people had also been victims of the militarists. They transformed their appreciation and thanks into friendship toward China. For example, Tomoji Abe stated that "the existence of China and the progress of the People's Republic of China are great events for Japan. We should at least recognize and respect these facts, repent our sins, thoroughly rectify our errors, and resolutely maintain our friendship with China."[11] And Uchiyama Kanzo said that "The Chinese people oppose policies of the Japanese government and Japan, but are not hostile to the Japanese people. No matter what happens, the nationals of the two countries should stay closely connected and work together for peace, which is a basic principle followed by the Chinese people."[12]

Such examples clearly illustrate that during this period the Japanese intellectual view that Japan should reflect, apologize to China, and atone for crimes was due to several reasons. The first was Japan's military defeat. Since the advent of the modern era, Japan had begun invading and expanding into neighboring countries, and its initial victories affected the whole of Japanese society, causing Japanese to go mad with the notion that the Japanese nation, due to its superiority, should rule over other nations. The outcome of World War II dealt a crushing blow to the Japanese militarists, and Japan's defeat fully exposed the brutal and inhuman nature of Japanese militarism both at home and abroad. Militarism had not only caused disaster for China and other neighboring countries, but also led Japan itself suffer. Given the destruction to Japan, the Japanese view on the way—as represented by intellectual opinion—began to undergo a rethinking. While intellectuals condemned the war, they also realized that the Japanese nation bore responsibility for committing a major crime of history, necessitating reflection and atonement for Japan's crimes.

A second reason for Japan's changed view of China was the increasing openness of Japanese society, and the fact that left-wing intellectuals began to occupy key positions in education and public opinion. With the post-war democratic transformation, the Japanese society became increasingly open. Books and periodicals from China were available in Japan, introducing China to Japanese readers. Even books about socialist theory could be published in Japan. At the same time, prominent Japanese opponents of the war or of the wartime government were discharge from prison or returned to Japan from other countries. These were mainly intellectuals, so they found positions in education and public opinion circles. The relatively open and tolerant society, and the willingness of these Japanese intellectuals to reflect on the war, worked together to promote wider introspection on the war by the whole Japanese society.

Third, China's tolerance of Japan. After the end of the war, China, as the victim suffered most in the aggressive war by Japan, should have demanded severe punishment of and claimed the war indemnity against Japan in accordance with general logic, but it did not send its troops to directly station at Japan and make any requirements for dismembering Japan. On the contrary, China stuck to the principle of education first for the Japanese war criminals, and would give lenient treatment to them as long as they gave up evil and expressed repenting and mending their ways. For some other reasons, China also waived the war indemnity against Japan. Without doubt, such tolerance of Japan may be denounced by some people today, but really touched a very big batch of Japanese people at that time, even some former Japanese soldiers having invaded China and borne blood debt. Facing so open-minded Chinese people, Japanese intellectuals at that time became more willing to rethink the war and more pious to make atonement for their sins before China. In addition, only such reflection and atonement could make them feel confident with justice on their side and free from too much censure in the Japanese society.

In a word, during this period, the mainstream views of China in the Japanese society were full of worshiping and longing for China once again, and the worship and long for was different from that the Japanese held for Chinese culture as the source of Japanese culture historically, but a yearning for establishing a new country through revolution. Meanwhile, when facing such a country as China worthy of worshiping, they naturally recognized various crimes they committed to China, and thus had some consciousness of reflection and atonement in addition to the sense of worship.

2.3.2 *From the mid-1960s to the end of the 1970s*

In May 1966, under the Left ideological trend emerging from the mid-1950s, the Cultural Revolution broke out in China finally. The social movement causing all-round turbulence of the Chinese society brought impacts to the international community including Japan, and changed the views of China gradually formed in the Japanese society since the 1950s.

At first, Japanese mainstream society admired the Cultural Revolution, as the Japanese had again grown accustomed to admiration of China and longing for China. However, as the Cultural Revolution deepened, and in particular after the Red Guards began their campaign of rooting out and destroying traditional China culture, setting off waves of violence, Japanese intellectual circles split into two parties for and against the Cultural Revolution. Japanese intellectuals engaged in a long-running debate over issues connected to China, and those opposed ultimately prevailed. Subsequently the prior trend of worship of and longing for China gradually disappeared, replaced by disappointment with China.

Among those Japanese favorable to the Cultural Revolution, there were essentially two groups. Those in the first group firmly adhered to Mao Zedong Thought and the writings of Chinese revolutionary intellectuals. Their worship of, longing for, and love of China had developed to the level of faith. These intellectuals had followed the socialist movement in Japan or in other countries or regions in the world when they were young, and opposed the conservative Japanese government and tried to institute socialism in Japan after the war. Thus they felt strong ties with socialist China, and argued that China served as the hope of socialism and the model for Japan's future development To this group, everything China did would form an essential part of the development course of socialism. Therefore, these Japanese were elated at the outbreak of the Cultural Revolution, and applauded openly. For example, Kiyoshi Inoue, a famous Left Japanese historian at Kyoto University, considered the Cultural Revolution as part of the development of Marxism in China. He had Marxism when he was young, and after the war he considered the founding of the People's Republic of China as a victory for Marxism in Asia. In his view, China's Cultural Revolution was designed to maintain the purity of Marxism, and a great contribution to socialism.

Other famous left-wing intellectuals also admired the Cultural Revolution. Kozai Yoshishige and others had wrote: "I think the Cultural Revolution acts as a spring, and will promote a leap forward in development of the 3rd Five-Year Plan starting this year … and China's socialist drive will take a significant step forward."[13] Bai Shifan also wrote: "In any case, a central aspect of the Cultural Revolution is the cultivation of the socialist spirit of selflessness for the public good. In particular, those who had experienced the prior eras still retain subconscious capitalist thinking, though they know how to behave in theory. This even includes those who have made contributions to the revolution. To remove such contaminants, there is no other approach except self-criticism."[14] Kyouichi Saionji and Shunichi Matsumoto stated that "I think the most important point of the Cultural Revolution lies in national consolidation and public education. National reconstruction means thorough implementation of the goals and ideals of the socialist campaign led by Chairman Mao, without any distortion. To achieve these goals, the most important point is to educate the people and sharpen their thinking."[15]

The second group of Japanese supporters of the Cultural Revolution consisted of those dissatisfied with the contemporary living conditions in Japanese society. This group supported some of the most extreme practices of the Cultural Revolution, because they supported criticism and transformation of the old systems, as well as the novel approach of the campaign. For example, observing that during the Cultural Revolution the Chinese education system was broken up, and young students from cities were sent down to rural areas to establish a completely new system of education. This group considered this movement as contributing to the training of a healthy and bright younger generation, whereas they believed Japan's educational system made young people slack and undisciplined. In their view, Japan's young were unable to strive toward progress, lacked vigor, and preferred to abandon themselves to vice.

In addition, there were some in Japan who favored China's Cultural Revolution without any specific reason other than as a means to opportunistically benefit their own private interests or expand their personal influence through their contact with China. For example, at this time a group announced the establishment of a Labor Party of Japan, and issued a statement of firm support for the Cultural Revolution in the Chinese newspaper *People's Daily*. It emerged that this Labor Party of Japan was in fact an organization provisionally established by just six to seven individuals, in imitation of Cultural Revolution mass combat organizations, and intended only to satisfy Chinese officials who sought voices of support for the Cultural Revolution in other countries. People with these motivations doubtless had little influence, and had little effect on mainstream Japanese views of China. Indeed, these voices were known through Chinese media reports on their support of the Cultural Revolution.

Similarly, the Cultural Revolution's opponents in Japan fell into two categories. The first group of people were scholars or intellectuals who were fascinated by traditional Chinese culture, and did not understand scenes from the Cultural Revolution showing how the Chinese had begun to criticize and attack traditional Chinese culture. This group felt nothing but revulsion toward such attacks, particularly toward attacks on ancient Chinese philosophers and sages such as Confucius and Mencius. Many in Japan saw these figures as the embodiment of traditional Chinese culture, and deeply respected them. Accordingly, a large number of those Japanese intellectuals who held a good feeling for even worshiped the People's Republic of China came instead to have an aversion toward China, and grew disappointed with China due to the long-lasting turbulence of the Cultural Revolution.

The second category comprised Japanese intellectuals who focused on general laws of social development and the history of China, and observed the events in China during the Cultural Revolution in this more rational and objective context. Intellectuals in this group remained friendly to China, but from its very beginning they viewed the Cultural Revolution as a movement of political persecution masquerading as a cultural reform. The movement began by targeting cultural celebrities and high-level officials, and continued with little regard for legal procedures. These intellectuals worried that social turbulence would cause long-term problems for Chinese society. For example, Minoru Takeuti, professor with Kyoto University, once said: "What I wonder at is, if the Red Guards wanted to beat down the bourgeoisie, but why did they physically wipe out scholars like Jian Bozan, a well-known Chinese historian and educationalist, who were loyal to the Chinese nation?" Professor Minoru Takeuti also wrote "The Red Guards around China are in a state of total disorder, each supported by a different faction. I am concerned that China will witness an internal disruption as in the times of Beiyang Warlords."[16]

Hikotaro Ando and other scholars also pointed out: "in my view, events in China are completely absurd. China is heading in a very dangerous direction."[17] These more rational Japanese intellectuals were naturally disappointed with China under the Cultural Revolution. Moreover, they and other intellectual opponents of the Cultural Revolution maintained a long record of criticism of the campaign, increasing the influence of their opposition and overcoming the voices of those who supported the Cultural Revolution. By the end of the Cultural Revolution, mainstream Japanese views of China had shifted to disappointment.

Certainly, there were those who opposed the Cultural Revolution who were never friendly toward China from the beginning, and maintained an attitude of opposition toward everything related to China. Some even believed that the Cultural Revolution and its promotion of social violence would ultimately pose a threat to Japan itself. However, there were few who held this opinion and it had little impact on mainstream Japanese views.

The period of the Cultural Revolution coincided with a fundamental change in the economic status of Japan relative to China. After the war, Japan witnessed a sustained period of rapid economic growth starting in the late 1950s and lasting through the 1960s. By the 1970s, Japan had become the second largest economy in the world and the Japanese living standard reached developed-country levels. In contrast, given the mass political movement of the Cultural Revolution, China verged on economic collapse, and the country faced real material shortages, leading living standards to fluctuating around the level of the least developed countries.

After 1972, when China and Japan normalized diplomatic relations, more Japanese people visited China and began to understand the Cultural Revolution from first-hand accounts, and were also able to witness the huge economic and social gap that had emerged between China and Japan. This pushed Japanese intellectuals to gradually shift their thinking on China due to the change in their relative positions. Many intellectuals came to have a stance on China completely opposite to that of the 1950s, affirming Japan's post-war social progress and economic success, while noting that China had stagnated economically and failed at social progress, instead falling into social chaos. Hence, these intellectuals saw China no longer as a country worthy of Japanese admiration, but rather as a country that should study Japan as a model.

At the same time, China and Japan had improved their official relations, and signed the Sino-Japanese Treaty of Peace and Friendship in 1978. Evidently, Japanese disappointment with China had little impact on official relations. Indeed, in short order disappointment changed to sympathy, as Japanese leaders sought to help the Chinese economy shed its difficulties and contribute to the stabilization of Chinese society. After the end of the Cultural Revolution in October 1976, China underwent a hesitant transitional period. By the end of the 1970s, China had thoroughly put an end to influence of the Cultural Revolution. Chinese figures disavowed the campaigns of the Cultural Revolution, and the illegal and inhuman acts of the movement were made public. This change in the Chinese view of the Cultural Revolution discredited those Japanese intellectuals that had previously supported it, and this group lost any say in issues concerning China. Mainstream Japanese views on China shifted toward disappointment and sympathy for its plight.

In short, the decade of the Cultural Revolution and the transition years after its end was a period in which an idealized Japanese view of China collapsed, replaced by disappointment with China across all aspects, even though Japan had previously viewed China through a lens of worship and longing. During this period, China and Japan normalized diplomatic relations and concluded the Treaty of Peace and Friendship, and their official relations and political relations improved, but the Japanese view of China and the Chinese people lost its hold on Japanese imaginations. On fully understanding the facts of the Cultural Revolution, Japanese disappointment in China intensified. Nevertheless, improved political relations compelled those Japanese who had once admired China to feel sympathy for it and hope to help China recover from its relatively backward position.

2.3.3 *From the beginning of the 1980s to the mid-1990s*

After the Cultural Revolution, China embarked on the journey of Reform and Opening, a policy that began officially in the 1980s. During the Reform and Opening period, the guiding principle of policy and government shifted from that of class struggle to one centering on economic development. Meanwhile, China opened its door to the world, fostering friendly relationships with a wide variety of countries and embracing political, economic, and cultural exchanges, ushering in a period when China fully integrated into the international community. Sino-Japanese official relations had already developed in the 1970s, and given the changes in China during the

1980s, space opened up for wider development of relations. Japanese views of China changed accordingly.

The opening of China led to a major increase in the number of Chinese and Japanese traveling between the countries. Japanese went to China for work, study, and sightseeing, and Chinese traveled to Japan for work and study, giving nationals of each country immensely greater opportunities for understanding each other. Through direct contact, Japanese views of developed in new directions. On one hand, Japanese visitors to China bore witness to the country's progress in opening up and casting off its previous social and economic fetters. They viewed Chinese society as vigorous and rapidly changing. Construction was everywhere, and though most Chinese remained poor, they seemed to have zeal for life. Chinese who went to Japan for work or study also left a good impression on Japanese society, and were generally viewed as hardworking, thrifty, and industrious.

On the other hand, actual contact between people and greater understanding of China's real situation led more Japanese to see the economic and social gap that remained between China and Japan. In this environment of good official relations and increasing contact, Japanese society developed empathy for China, and Japanese support rose for official assistance to China and its economic modernization under the Reform and Opening policy. Both the Japanese government and the public sought increased aid to China and economic exchanges with it. Starting in 1980, the Japanese government launched a major policy of overseas development assistance (ODA) to China. By 1995, Japan had provided a total of 1.6149 trillion yen in low-interest loans to China over 15 years, plus a significant amount of grant-based assistance. These funds went mainly for infrastructure construction at the beginning of the Reform and Opening, when China had an urgent need for funds, and therefore played a significant role in catalyzing China's economic growth. Japanese private companies also entered the Chinese market, importing and exporting trade goods, making capital investments, and initiating business cooperation, all of which promoted China's economic development and integration with the outside world.

Given increasingly close Sino-Japanese economic relations, Japanese society once again saw a wave of interest in Chinese culture. Closer political and economic relations between the two countries enabled Japanese to see their two cultures as more intimately connected. Japanese culture had originated with many elements of Chinese culture, and the new situation encouraged Japanese people to visit China in search of local cultural elements which they were familiar with and loved, such as the history of ancient China, natural landscapes, local customs, and Chinese cuisine. This movement set off a wave of China Fever in Japan. Contacts with China and knowledge of China became fashionable, contributing to the honeymoon period in bilateral relations. Japanese views of China included many friendly elements, including sympathy for its economic situation as well as willingness to provide aid and other assistance. During this period, China and Japan jointly established nearly 300 sister city pairings, leading to local cultural exchanges across various themes, further enhancing and intensifying the friendly feelings between nationals of the two countries.

Japanese sympathy and aid for China and friendly cooperation were not only driven by Japan, but also encouraged by China. China needed Japan's economic aid and cooperation, and Chinese leaders were interested in how postwar Japan had achieved economic success. Chinese society maintained an attitude of appreciation toward Japan during this period. In addition, the introduction of some modern Japanese mass culture shaped the Chinese image of Japanese culture. Many Chinese people began to view Japan mainly through the prism of Japanese products and culture. This new Chinese love of Japan and friendliness toward it in turn promoted a reciprocal friendly Japanese view of the Chinese. The Japanese government and people were both willing to actively support this China friendship toward Japan, and Japan hoped that by supporting China's Reform and Opening, it would help Chinese society become peaceful, stable, and well-off, which would in turn make China more favorable to Japan, enabling complementary economic ties and a friendly, long-term Sino-Japanese diplomatic relationship, on the basis of friendly opinion among nationals of both countries.

With China's rapid economic development, the economic gap between China and Japan narrowed, and China's dependency on Japan in the economic field declined apace. During this period, troubles began to arise in the political relationship between China and Japan. Instances of conflict included Japan's revisions of its history textbooks in 1982 and 1986, the 1985 visit of the Japanese prime minister to the Yasukuni shrine to Japan's war dead, and the Kokaryo decision in 1987. However, these troubles were quickly dealt with, and they did not change Japanese views of China.

The political disturbances in Beijing in 1989 caused a significant change in Japanese views of China, leading to significant deterioration in China's image among the Japanese public. But the shift in public opinion took time to develop, given the friendly relations and solidification of close political and economic ties between China and Japan since the 1970s. Though unpleasant incidents occurred between both countries, they sought to maintain friendly cooperation. Japanese public opinion continued to show sympathy for China and seek cooperation with it, and hoped for a continuation of China's policy of Reform and Opening. Japan remained willing to help China, though the degree of Japanese friendliness toward China began to slip.

To summarize, during this period Japanese mainstream views on China were dominated by sympathy and friendliness. There were frictions in terms of Japan's recognition of history, the Taiwan issue, and ideological differences, but mutual interests generally prevailed over these frictions. Japan was stronger than China, and inertia worked to prop up friendly Sino-Japanese relations worked, essentially helping mainstream Japanese public opinion on China continue in the path of friendship and sympathy.

2.3.4 *After the mid-1990s*

The end of the Cold War between the East and the West at the beginning of the 1990s was a turning point in post-war international relations, and constituted the most important factor that influenced multilateral relations among the major countries of the world in this period. The event also deeply influenced Sino-Japanese relations and Japanese views of China. The political disturbance in Beijing in 1989 began this transition, and Japanese feelings of friendliness and sympathy began to fade at least from that time, though this trend only became obvious starting in the mid-1990s, due to shifts in their relative strengths, diplomatic policies, and domestic social changes.

From the mid-1990s, there occurred a series of major events that were sufficiently serious to change the basic structure of Sino-Japanese relations. Fragile bilateral relations worsened due to decrease in common security interests between China and Japan after the end of the Cold War. Multiple Chinese nuclear tests conducted by China in 1995 caused public opposition in Japan and resulted in an official protest of the Japanese government. The Taiwan Straits crisis in 1995–1996 heightened Japanese alarm over the armed threat posed by China, as well as generating sympathy for democratization in Taiwan. The reconfirmation and intensification of the alliance between the United States and Japan in 1996 affected views of China.

The continuous growth of China's military capabilities also enhanced the Japanese sense that China posed a threat. This was heightened by a series of conflicts and disputes. One such dispute was triggered by oil and gas field development in the East China Sea in 2005. Another was the entry of Chinese vessels ships into the waters of the Diaoyu Islands and China's establishment of the East China Sea Air Defense Identification Zone (ADIZ) after the Diaoyu Islands crisis in 2012. These events highlighted the issue of security in Japanese society, leading to greater perception of China as a threat to Japan. According to public opinion surveys performed by the Japanese cabinet as well as public media outlet recently, over 80% of the Japanese felt increased dislike of China and fear of China.

Throughout this period, China maintained high rates of economic growth; in contrast, Japan experienced a prolonged economic depression after the collapse of the country's over-inflated real estate market. As a result, the economic gap between China and Japan narrowed rapidly. In 2010, China's GDP surpassed that of Japan, reversing the world economic rank of China and Japan. On the one hand, this changed Chinese views of Japan, and many Chinese began to feel superiority to Japan in some respects, and Chinese public opinion became more conscious of China's growing great power status. Given this new situation, anti-Japan demonstrations occurred in China over various issues. For example, in 2005, public demonstrations opposed Japan's application for qualification as a permanent member of the United Nations Security Council, and more recently protestors rallied against the Japanese government's nationalization of the Diaoyu Islands. Japanese media aggravated tensions by prominently covering Chinese demonstrations and various anti-Japanese incidents that accompanied them, heightening any Japanese sense of dislike and fear of China and Chinese people. On the other hand, the change in the countries' relative economic positions also affected Japanese mentality, eliminating any remaining Japanese sense of superiority to China. On the contrary, in many respects Japan felt itself pressured by China, exacerbating Japanese sense of fear of China.

Aside from these problems in bilateral relations, contemporary domestic troubles in China and Japan also promoted changes in public opinion toward the other in each country. After the 1990s, Japan's politics shifted toward right-wing, conservative leaders. Left-wing political forces that had historically been friendly to China lost their ability to block conservative forces in the Japanese society. Accompanying this trend, there occurred political changes that China viewed as unacceptable, such as Japan's revision of the pacifist article of the national constitution, Japan's denying or glossing over the history of its various aggressions in Asia, and Japan's expansion and upgrading of its independent defense forces. These intensified China's official criticism of Japan.

For the Japanese, China's economic development produced dissatisfaction or even disgust in Japan, because economic development made the Chinese rich, but without bringing about the peaceful Chinese society favorable for Japan that many Japanese had anticipated. On the contrary, driven by the economic growth, China not only developed a strong degree of anti-Japanese nationalism, but also encountered new social issues that affected its image in Japan. These included environmental damage, reports of official corruption, an increasing gap between the rich and the poor and between social classes, disclosure of poor quality food and drug products, and exposure of cases of social fraud. In addition, with more and more Chinese people working and studying in Japan, crime committed by Chinese natives in Japan became an increasingly prominent topic in the Japanese society.

All these problems had a negative influence on Japanese views of China. Many Japanese viewed China as a much stronger country, but also as a socially backward country that posed a possible threat to Japan. These problems were interwoven with the political and security issues between both countries, such as recognition of Japan's historical aggressions, territory disputes, and Taiwan, further worsening the sense of dislike and fear of China in the minds of the Japanese people.

To sum up, due to changes in the international environment and the domestic situations of China and Japan, after the mid-1990s Japanese views of China changed from sympathy and friendship toward China to dislike and fear of China. To avoid doubt, it is important to clarify that Japanese views of China described here refer to mainstream views. Currently, Sino-Japanese relations have become more complex and changeable, and are a mixture of various contradictions and close connections. Present Sino-Japanese political and security relations are based on the same structure as in prior decades, but non-governmental contacts between the two countries have experienced an upswing. Since 2014, Chinese travel to Japan for tourism and shopping have increased rapidly. In 2015, Japan sent a 3,000-person group to China called the Japan-China Delegation of Sightseeing and Cultural Exchange. Given the new situation, future changes in Japanese views of China will differ not only according to shifts in bilateral political relations and changes in society, but also differ by social class. With this in mind, study of Japanese views of China should be based on more detailed surveys and public opinion analysis of various segments of Japanese society.

Notes

1. Katsu, Kaishū. *The Origin of Japan*. Vol. 2 of the Complete Works of Katsu Kaishū, Kodansha, 1973: 4331.
2. Masahiro, Fujima. *Formation of the Modern East Asia World*. Nippon Bunka Publishing, 1977: 60.
3. Takasugi, Shinsaku. Records of the Tour Around the Qing-ruled China, The Posthumous Work of Mr. Takasugi Shinsaku by the Committee in Memory of the 50th Anniversary of Mr. Takasugi Shinsaku. Kotobank, 1961: 76.
4. Takasugi, Shinsaku. Records of the Tour Around the Qing-ruled China, The Posthumous Work of Mr. Takasugi Shinsaku by the Committee in Memory of the 50th Anniversary of Mr. Takasugi Shinsaku. Kotobank, 1961: 104.
5. Takasugi, Shinsaku. Records of the Tour Around the Qing-ruled China, The Posthumous Work of Mr. Takasugi Shinsaku by the Committee in Memory of the 50th Anniversary of Mr. Takasugi Shinsaku. Kotobank, 1961: 109.
6. Song, Chengyou. *Taking History as a Mirror: the Views of China under the Perspective of Fukuzawa Yukichi's Theory of Civilization*. Li, Yu, et al. *Sino-Japanese Relations under the Perspective of Civilization*. Hong Kong Social Sciences Press, 2006: 81.
7. Fukuzawa, Yukichi. *Datsu-A-Ron*. Vol. 10, The Complete Works of Fukuzawa Yukichi. Iwanami Shoten, 1960: 239.
8. Sakuzo, Yoshino. *On Sino-Japanese Relations*. Vol. 6, Works of Dr. Sakuzo Yoshino on Democracy. Shinkigensha, 1947: 10.
9. Song, Chengyou. *A New Modern History of Japan*. Peking University Press, 2006: 238.
10. Ikutaro, Shimizu. "Peaceful coexistence between Japan and China." Top Travel 11(1959).
11. Tomoji, Abe. "Culture and Society." Top Travel 1(1955).
12. Uchiyama, Kanzo. "Returning from China." Top Travel 5(1953).
13. Kozai, Yoshishige, Shiro Nohara, and Nomura Koichi. "Discussion on 'What is Mao Zedong Thought on the Proletarian Cultural Revolution.'" Top Travel 11(1966).
14. Bai, Shifan. "Second Revolution to Build a Socialist Country." Chuokoron Shinsha 4(1967).
15. Kyouichi, Saionji, and Matsumoto Shunichi. "China? Japan? Asia." Chuokoron Shinsha 10(1970).
16. Yan, Shaodang. "The Japanese View on China in the Post-War 60 Years." In Li, Yu et al. (Eds.), *Sino-Japanese Relations under the Perspective of Civilization*, Hong Kong Social Sciences Press, 2006: 37.
17. Hikotaro, Ando, Muramatsu Akira, and Takeuchi Minoru. "Is the Cultural Revolution destruction or construction?" Chuokoron Shinsha 11(1966).

Part II

Current situation survey

In Part II of this book, using data from survey questionnaire and in-depth interviews, we analyze Japanese respondents' knowledge and evaluation of China, Chinese culture, Chinese media, Chinese people and Sino-Japanese relations. Through this survey and analysis, we find that, on the one hand, Japanese maintain a degree of contact with Chinese politics, economics and culture, identify highly with traditional Chinese culture and values, and are willing to have Chinese people as close friends, neighbors and co-workers. On the other hand, some Japanese people do not understand China's political system, have little contact with China's media and cultural products, and hold a negative evaluation of relations between China and Japan. We conclude that to enhance inter-governmental dialogue and cooperation, China and Japan should further strengthen non-governmental exchange and cooperation, particularly economic and trade cooperation in the fields of environmental protection and technology, to promote common development of the two countries and friendly relations between their nationals.

3 Research methods

This book combines questionnaire-based surveys and in-depth interviews to develop a more accurate portray of China's image in the eyes of the Japanese. Through the questionnaires, we sought to understand the Japanese citizens' overall impression of China, their understanding and recognition of Chinese culture, the main channels they use to access to Chinese culture, and their perception of Sino-Japanese relations. In-depth interviews are designed to investigate the causes for various perceptions, and find effective ways of improving Japanese perceptions of China and Sino-Japanese relations.

3.1 Questionnaire survey

The data mainly came from the three rounds of questionnaire surveys that were conducted among the Japanese public in 2010, 2011, and 2013, respectively. The three questionnaire surveys are different, in terms of their target groups, research methods and focuses, but complementary, which to some extent remedies the deficiency of reliability and validity that exist in single questionnaire survey. Their results, though with some similarities, bear many differences, which have provided plenty of inspirations.

3.1.1 *First round survey questionnaires*

Due to budget and resource limitations, the first round of questionnaires employed non-probability convenience sampling instead of probability sampling. For small-scale trial questionnaire surveys, this method can provide a general perspective in understanding the Japanese citizens' attitudes toward China and their perception and recognition of Chinese culture, though its results are less reliable. This initial round served as preparation for a second round of questionnaires.

3.1.1.1 *Content and structure*

The first round of questionnaires focused on Japanese respondents' understanding, recognition of, and means of accessing information about China and Chinese culture. The survey consisted of five sections: The first section consisted of respondents' personal details: gender, age, educational background, and income. The second section was designed to investigate respondents' understanding and recognition of the surface aspects of Chinese culture, such as the Great Wall, pandas, and the Chinese dragon. The third and the fourth sections focused on respondents' understanding and recognition of Chinese cultural institutions and values. The fifth section concerned the media or channels used by respondents to obtain information about Chinese culture. The questionnaire used the Likert scale to measure respondents' like or dislike of Chinese culture, ranging from 1 (dislike) to 5 (like).

3.1.1.2 *Survey dissemination and collection*

The first round of questionnaires was distributed simultaneously in Beijing, China, and Tokyo, Japan between September 2010 and October 2010 with the help of friends and Japanese students, who distributed surveys among friends and acquaintances, targeting Japanese students and workers studying or working in China, as well as Japanese students and ordinary Japanese people in Japan. A total of 300 questionnaires were distributed in the two locations, and 225 valid responses returned, or 75% of the total distributed. Among those received, 156 questionnaires, 69% of responses, came from Japanese students and corporate employees living in China. Sixty-nine responses, or around 31% of all responses, were from Japanese college students and ordinary Japanese people living in Tokyo.

3.1.1.3 *Sample characteristics*

Among the 225 respondents, 58% were male, and 42% female. In terms of age, 28% were between 18 and 20, 58% between 21 and 30, 9% between 31 and 40, and 6% between 41 or older. The respondents were therefore on the younger side. By occupation, around 73% were undergraduate college students, 6% graduate students, and the remaining 20% corporate employees, housewives, teachers, journalists or photographers. By income, 20% had an annual income less than 3 million yen, 25% ranged between 3.01 and 6 million yen, 25% ranged between 6.01 and 9 million yen, 17% ranged between 9.01 and 12 million yen, and 12% had an annual income over 12 million yen.

3.1.2 *Second round survey questionnaires*

Based on analysis of the first round of questionnaires, a second round of questionnaires was developed, revising the proportions of questions regarding gender and age, as well as question technique and structure. The second round questionnaire also consisted of five sections: The first section focused on respondents' understanding of Chinese cultural expression forms. The second section centered on respondents' understanding and recognition of Chinese cultural institutions and values. The third section was designed to explore the channels through which respondents obtained information on Chinese culture, as well as respondents' opinions of Chinese media. The fourth section concerned respondents' opinions on China and Sino-Japanese relations. The fifth section concerned respondents' personal details, such as age, gender, educational background, and income.

3.1.2.1 *Dissemination*

As mentioned above, the first round of questionnaires partly targeted Japanese living in Beijing; this group would tend to have high knowledge about China, and is likely unrepresentative of Japanese opinion of China. For this reason, the sampling and survey distribution process for the second round of questionnaires was conducted via an online panel using the Sample Survey International, performed by the Beijing E-panel Market Research Co. Ltd. The process took around one month. In November 2011, the survey company randomly sent 35,130 e-mail invitations to a sample pool consisting of 456,980 Japanese people, representative of the gender, age, income, and marriage status of the overall Japanese population. Among email questionnaires sent, recipients opened 3,923, and 1,038 valid responses were collected. To ensure sample quality, the questionnaire collection system employed IP address and PC physical address recognition, eliminating responses from duplicate accounts, computers, and IP addresses.

3.1.2.2 *Sample characteristics*

In this round, a total of 1,038 valid responses were collected, of which 311 (30%) were from women and 272 (around 70%) from men. The gender balance of responses relates to the differences in political status between men and women within Japanese society. Despite the large difference in responses from the actual gender ratio of Japanese society, this structure nevertheless can accurately reflect the voices and opinions on social, economic and political issues across the Japanese population.

The second round of questionnaires covered the population aged 18 and above in a representative fashion. Among all respondents, 70 (7%) were students between 18 and 24; 212 (20%) were between 25 and 34; 687 (66%) were between 35 and 54; 69 (6.7%) were older than 55. This age structure was in line with the study design aimed at evaluating the views and perception of younger and middle-aged Japanese people. This group has more say in economic and political issues and policies than those in the elderly population. Compared with the first survey round, the second round had a more balanced age structure and broader coverage of age groups.

In terms of the educational background, 60% of the second survey's respondents held a junior college degree, bachelor degree or post-graduate degree; 32 (3%) held just a middle school degree; the remainder (37%) possess a high-school degree or occupational degree. In terms of occupation, 25% were ordinary office workers; just under 20% were managers or middle-level management; 20% were civil servants, technical workers or college students; and the remainder were housewives, labor workers, design workers or artistic workers. In terms of income, around one-third of respondents reported an annual income lower than 2 million yen; one-third reported incomes between 2 and 5 million yen; and the remainder reported incomes higher than 5 million yen.

In terms of religious affiliation, nearly 70% reported no religious belief. Twenty-five percent identified as Buddhist, 2.8% as Christian, and 3.4% as Taoist. The proportion identifying as Shinto was lower than expected. This may be explained by the fact that Japanese may consider Shintoism as a part of daily life instead of as a religion.

Nearly 70% of respondents claimed no party affiliation or support for any party. A number of 139, or 13.3%, supported the Liberal Democratic Party of Japan. A number of 114, or 10.9%, expressed support for the Democratic Party of Japan. Fewer than 3% expressed support for the New Komeito or the Communist Party of Japan.

For this round, 16.6% of respondents had visited China previously. About 30.2% had Chinese friends or acquaintances, and 4.8% reported Chinese language ability.

3.1.3 *Third round questionnaires*

The data source for the third round of questionnaires came from a research project of Ministry of Culture called the Assessment of the International Influence of Chinese Culture in the New Era. The questionnaire mainly focused on assessing the recognition, reputation, and cultural influence in Japanese society of Chinese cultural symbols, products, activities, and values.

3.1.3.1 *Questionnaire distribution*

Same with the second-round survey, the third round was conducted online, using an online panel via Sample Survey International, implemented by the Beijing e-Panel Market Research Co. Ltd. In December 2013, a national-level online questionnaire-based survey was carried out among the Japanese population. The recipient group was an SSI-owned sampling pool with 235,145 Japanese individuals selected on the basis of representative gender, age, income, ethnicity, and place of residence. Invitation emails were sent to respondents randomly sampled within representative sub-populations. Recipients of the email survey can opt to respond or not. To ensure sample quality, the SSI Verify System was employed to eliminate duplicate IP addresses, devices, and accounts. The company excludes invalid data through strict data cleaning using response-time records and comprehensive logic inspection. In this survey round, a total of 1,497 responses were received. After review, a total of 1,225 valid responses were obtained, accounting for 81.8% of responses received.

3.1.3.2 *Sample characteristics*

In the third round of the survey, samples were set to match a gender ratio of 6:4, which generally matches with the structure of discursive power in the Japanese society. The average age of respondents was 41.6; the youngest was 15, and the oldest 75. Over 50% of respondents were between 19 and 44; 7.4% were between 19 and 24; 22.2% between 22 and 34; 23.8% between 25 and 44; and 27% were between 45 and 54. The remainder were either high school-age students between 15 and 18 (2.8% of respondents) and respondents older than 55 (16.8%).

The survey responses were balanced across income categories. Those with an annual income less than 1 million yen and those with an annual income between land 2.99 million yen each accounted for a sixth of the total. Roughly a third earned between 3 and 5.99 million yen. About 20% reported an income between 6 and 8.99 million yen. The remainder reported income above 9 million yen.

Geographically, 44.25% of respondents resided in the Kanto region, and 17.8% in the Kansai region, with some in the Kyushu region, the central region and the northeast regions. These proportions are generally in line with Japan's geographic population distribution. In terms of education, nearly 60% held a tertiary education degree (bachelor's, master's, or doctorate). Nearly a third have a high school degree or a junior college degree. Only 6.4% had only a middle-school degree. This survey round emphasized those with a mid-to-high level of education relative to the educational structure of the population reported by 2010 Japanese government data.

In terms of occupation, the largest portion (24.2%) were office workers, followed by housewives (13.3%), other workers (11.7%), middle management (11.1%), technical workers (8.2%), owners of businesses with fewer than ten employees (6.6%), and professionals (6.3%). The remainder accounted for only a minor portion.

About 54% of respondents were married, 37.5% were unmarried, 8.6% were married but living separately, divorced, or in pre-marital cohabitation. In terms of political affiliation, over 60% reported no partisan affiliation. Self-reported supporters of the Liberal Democratic Party of Japan accounted for 21.6%, supporters of the Communist Party of Japan for 3.4%, and supporters of the Democratic Party of Japan for 3.3%. Supporters of other parties accounted for only a minor portion.

3.1.4 *Use of data*

Because the sample of the first survey round were unrepresentative, given most respondents were Japanese citizens studying or working in China, the analysis in the following sections focuses on data obtained from the second and the third rounds. In particular, the third round deals with the Japanese opinions on Chinese cultural symbols, cultural products, and cultural activities. The second round includes elements relating to familiarity with various different forms of Chinese culture and the media channels respondents used to access Chinese culture, and also includes topics regarding the Japanese economy, politics, society, and culture, which make the second round survey more comprehensive. Therefore, most of the data analysis results in this book are derived from the second round of survey questionnaires. To help readers identify sources, data used have been identified in the notes.

3.2 In-depth interview

Although analysis of survey-based questionnaires can help understand Japanese general impressions of China or opinions about China, this method cannot enable deep exploration of causes of negative perceptions or corresponding remedies. Based on survey results, we found that among all sources of information on China, Japanese media have had the greatest influence on Japanese impressions of China. Based on this finding, we interviewed several China-based journalists from major Japanese media outlets, in an effort to understand the standards journalists used for selecting topics for China-related news reports, Japanese journalist perceptions of China, media opinions on Sino-Japanese relations, and the sources of or reasons for these opinions. We also interviewed two Japanese scholars on Chinese issues to gain understanding of how Japanese intellectuals perceive China, Chinese culture, and Sino-Japanese relations.

3.2.1 *Selection of interviewees*

The interviews were mainly conducted over two months, from December 2014 to January 2015. All were carried out face-to-face, and each interview lasted around 1 to 2 hours. To protect their privacy, and considering sensitivity of Sino-Japanese relations, interviewees requested anonymity. Table 3.1 provides general information about the interview subjects.

3.2.2 *Interview questions*

In the interview, we mainly focus on the following questions:

1 Do you like Chinese culture? Do you have frequent contact with Chinese culture? How do you see Chinese culture? Is it possible for you to convert the recognition and love for Chinese culture into the love for China as a nation?
2 How do you perceive the traditional Chinese values of being benevolent, being righteous, being honest, having courtesy, and having wisdom? Do

Table 3.1 List of interviewees

No.	*Occupation*	*Position*	*Understand Chinese language or not*	*Proficiency*	*Length of life, study, or work in China*	*Venue*	*Duration*
A	Journalist	A China-based reporter of a Japanese TV media	Yes	High	9 years	Cafe	1 hour
B	Scholar	An associate professor of political science in a Japanese University	Yes	Ordinary	1 year	Office	1.5 hours
C	Journalist	A China-based reporter of a Japanese news agency	Yes	Ordinary	2 years	Cafe	1 hour
D	Journalist	A China-based reporter of a Japanese newspaper	Yes	Ordinary	6 months	Cafe	1 hour
E	Scholar	A professor of political science in a Japanese University, and an expert on Chinese issues	Yes	High	3 years	Office	2 hours
F	Journalist	A China-based reporter of a Japanese news agency	Yes	Ordinary	2 years	Office	45 minutes
G	Journalist	A visiting scholar of a Japanese newspaper	No	NA	6 months	Office	1.5 hours
H	Journalist	A China-based reporter of a Japanese newspaper	Yes	Ordinary	1 year	Office	1.5 hours

you think that Chinese people still hold these values? What influences do you think have these values brought to the Japanese?

3 How do you see the political system of China? Do you think the difference of political systems between the two countries is the cause of their distrust toward each other?
4 What influences has China's economic development brought to Japan? Which one do you agree with: China's economic develop can bring more benefits to Japan than harms, or harms more than benefits? Why?
5 How has China's development influenced the world? In a positive way or a negative way? What about its influence on Japan?
6 What are the channels through which you know about China?
7 What's your view on Chinese media? Do you have often contact with China' media of Chinese language, English language, or Japanese language?
8 Which topics do Japanese media focus on about China? Do you think the Japanese reports on China are objective? Why?
9 What's your view on the Chinese, including those living in Japan? Do you have a close Chinese friend?
10 What's your view on the current Sino-Japanese relations? What are the most important influencing factors? Are there any methods to improve the relations?

During the interview, our conversations about the above questions have been mostly frank, though some of them were hesitant in answering sensitive topics for fear of causing misunderstandings. With repeated explanation of our desires for their true feelings, they were finally willing to express their opinions, though in a reserved manner. We will present our analysis on specific topics in the following sections.

4 The image of China in the eyes of the Japanese

National image consists of the cognitive impressions and emotional attitudes of the people of one nation toward another nation. Such impressions or attitudes might come from media reports, interpersonal communication, or personal experiences. With the rapid development of science and technology, as well as economic globalization, most countries have witnessed increasingly frequent exchanges and cooperation in political, economic, cultural, and other spheres. The image of a nation has an increasingly profound impact on the security and economic prosperity of nations: national image affects the evaluation of the nation's exports by foreign consumers and their intention to purchase such exported goods, and can influence the formulation and implementation of foreign countries' political, economic, or diplomatic policies. In the 1990s, American scholar Joseph Nye proposed the idea of "soft power," which he defined as the ability of a nation to gain popularity among people of other countries by appealing to them through its culture, policies, and values rather than through means such as economic sanctions and coercion.[1] The importance of soft power is increasingly accepted by governments and people with an interest in international relations and related topics.

In recent years, especially following the September 11 attacks, the United States-led western countries have begun to pay increasing attention to their national images and work to improve them through activities such as cultural exchanges, tourism promotion, business expansion, and media planning. The Chinese government, facing the rampant China Threat, has also taken many steps in this direction, such as establishing Confucius Institutes overseas to promote Chinese culture, and setting up scholarships to attract overseas students to study in China. In doing so, China is attempting to improve its national image by enhancing its cultural soft power.

China and Japan, the two most important countries in Asia, are not only close neighbors across a narrow sea, but also close economic and trade partners. However, the two have experienced constant friction and frustrations in their relations, for reasons such as historical issues and territorial disputes, resulting in a steady decline in the sense of familiarity and trust between the two peoples. This not only affects political and diplomatic ties between the two, but also exerts adverse influence on their economic development. What is the image of China in the eyes of the Japanese in today's Sino-Japanese exchanges? What factors affect the Japanese awareness of China's image? This chapter will deal with these questions in combination with the data from survey questionnaires and in-depth interviews, and thereby seek to uncover methods and strategies for improving China's image.

4.1 Studies on the image of nation

National image is a combination of the general evaluations and understandings of a country, of the actions taken by a country, and of various activities of the country and their results by the internal and external publics of that country.[2] National image is an integral part of a country's soft power. It consists of "material, spiritual and institutional elements,"[3] and specifically covers "social institutions, national culture, comprehensive national power, the political situation, international relations, leadership, citizen quality, social civilization" and other aspects.[4] The China National Image Global Survey 2012 evaluates China's national image on the basis of China's diplomatic attitude, international political exchanges, international economic exchanges, image of the Chinese people, Chinese culture, and Chinese brands. A good national image can not only promote economic development and cultural exchanges, and enhance national self-confidence and sense of pride, but also improve a country's position amid the complex international environment. There are quite a few domestic and overseas studies on national image, but few deals with the image of China in Japan using survey questionnaires. This section briefly reviews existing literature on the topic.

4.1.1 *Studies on national image*

In China, academic studies on national image date back to the 1990s. Examples are *On National Image in International News Communication* by Xu Xiaoge[5] and *International Consciousness and National Image in External Publicity* by Huang Qing.[6] These studies, though few in quantity, aroused the attention of the media and communication community in China.

In the 21st century, national image has become a hot topic for Chinese academic studies, resulting in many papers and books. Studies such as *Shallow Views on National Image* by Zhang Yuqiang[7] and *Connotation and Functions of National Image* by Sun Youzhong[8] focus on the definition and connotation of national image, and discuss the relationship between news media and national image from a broad and macro perspective. *The Image of China in World Mainstream Media*, a book written by Liu Jinan et al., explores the image of China in world media by analyzing the content of reports on China in mainstream media in countries such as the United States, the United Kingdom and Japan.[9]

In recent years, an increasing number of studies on national image seek to bring forward policy proposals for improving national image from a public relations perspective. *The Building and Communication of China's National Image*, a monograph of Wu Youfu, elaborates on how to build and communicate the image of China from the perspective of government image, public relations, media communication and Chinese brands.[10] *The Construction and Communication of National Image in the New Media Environment*, a book by He Hui and Liu Peng, analyzes the effects of developments of new media such as Internet and mobile phones on the construction and communication of national image, and puts forward ways and tactics to improve China's image.[11] Cheng Manli's *On National Image Building and Mass Communication* expounds on the key role of mass media in forming the national image.[12] Other studies have probed the topic of national image building through case studies. For example, *Crisis Public Relations: The Role of the Media in Restoring National Image* by Li Zhengguo[13] and *Agenda-Building during the Beijing Olympics and National Image Communication* by Tu Guangjin and Gong He.[14]

Overseas studies on national image are represented by Michael Kunczik's *Images of Nations and International Public Relations*,[15] Michael Morley's *How to Manage Your Global Reputation: A Guide to the Dynamics of International Public Relations*[16] and Simon Anholt's *Competitive Identity: The New Brand Management for Nations, Cities and Regions*,[17] among others. Of these, the idea of national branding initiated by Anholt is quite influential: as in the case with the brand image of products, countries may also build their own brand images in six ways, including tourism promotion, export product branding, government decisions, foreign investment, cultural exchanges, and public communication.[18]

4.1.2 *Studies on the image of China in Japan*

Most studies on Japan's perception of China have been conducted by Chinese and Japanese scholars. With closer economic ties between China and Japan and the evolution of bilateral relations, studies on Japan's perception of China have grown in both quantity and scope. They involve Japan's understanding of China's international status, Japan's understanding of the Chinese people and the image of China in Japanese media. The studies cover a number of disciplines such as history, literature, international relations, and cross-cultural communication. Existing research literature have the following different research perspectives:

4.1.2.1 *Perspective of representative figures*

Representative figures from different fields in Japan dominate Japan's overall understanding of China during a specific historical period. Therefore, some studies directly analyze how Japanese historical figures in politics, military, literature, and other fields have viewed China, as well as looking at the historical backgrounds and root causes of such views, which are then taken to represent Japan's understanding of China at that specific time. Some journal articles focus on specific historical figures such as Fukuzawa Yukichi, Naito Konan, Natsume Soseki, Ryunosuke Akutagawa, and Haruki Murakami. Other literature depicts specific groups' perceptions of China. For example, in his book *How Japanese Modern Intellectuals View China*, Liu Jiaxin analyzes the views of Japanese intellectuals such as Asatarou Gotou and Nagano Akira on Chinese society, Chinese people, and Sino-Japanese relations.[19]

4.1.2.2 *Perspective of historical changes*

Much of the literature compares Japan's views of China in different historical periods vertically, from the perspective of the history of Sino-Japanese relations, and analyzes the tendencies and characteristics of changes in Japanese views. For example, Wang Ping's *On the Historical Changes of the Japanese Perception of China* analyzes four changes in Japan's view of China by reviewing major historical events in Sino-Japanese relations.[20] *The Japanese View of China in the 20th Century*[21] and *The Japanese View of China in the Post-War 60 Years*[22], the two representative articles written by Yan Shaodang, both divide a long historical period into several historical stages based on the characteristics of Japan's view of China and the course of China's social development, and then analyzes these changes from the perspective of cultural comparison.

4.1.2.3 *Perspective of specific historical events*

Apart from studies that span a longer time of period, some literature focuses on specific historical events and analyze Japan's views of China reflected by these events. For example, Shen Haitao analyzes modern Japan's view of China by studying historical materials concerning the September 18 Incident,[23] and Zhang Yajing explores into how Japanese media and intellectuals have viewed the Cultural Revolution in China.[24]

4.1.2.4 *Perspective of cultural exchanges*

Literature that deals with research on the issue as it relates to Sino-Japanese cultural exchanges can be divided mainly into three categories. The first category focuses on the image of China in Japanese literature, including novels, travelogues, and other forms of literature. For example, in a doctoral thesis entitled, *The "Image of China" in Modern Japanese Literature*, Li Yannan analyzes the image of China in modern Japanese novels, diaries, documentary literature, and other forms of literature.[25] The second category focuses on the image of China in Japanese media reports on China, such as Zhao Xinli's paper entitled *The Image of China in Japanese Documentaries*,[26] Zhang Ning's monograph entitled *China in Japanese Media: Reporting Framework and National Image*,[27] Ruan Suqian's thesis entitled, *Study on China-Japan Mutual Reporting and the National Image of the Two Countries*,[28] and Liu Linli's *The Image of China in Japanese Mass Media*.[29] The third category analyzes China's image in Japanese textbooks, for instance, Tan Jianchuan's *The Image of China in Japanese Textbooks*.[30]

4.1.2.5 *Perspective of personal experiences*

Some scholars explore the Japanese image of China based on their own personal feelings and experiences rather than rigorous academic research methods, and depict Japanese views of China's social development, daily life, mass culture, Sino-Japanese relations, and other related issues. In contrast, studies by Japanese scholars in this respect, which are represented by Satoshi Amako's *China in the Eyes of the Japanese*[31] and Kato Shuichi's *The 21st Century and Chinese Culture*,[32] better reflect Japan's understanding of China. For example, the book *China in the Eyes of the Japanese* not only contains objective discussions and clear views, but also addresses serious and academic issues such as the rise of China, Sino-Japanese relations, and historical issues in simple terms through his personal experiences, providing some reference for better understanding the Japanese view of China. In his book, professor Satoshi Amako argues that the biggest problem between China and Japan is "misunderstandings on both sides" and expects the Japanese to view China and Sino-Japanese relations in a rational, peaceful, and factual manner.

4.1.2.6 *Perspective of cause analysis*

Apart from cataloging and describing Japan's view of China from the different perspectives described above, some scholars also probe the underlying causes of the formation and variation of Japan's view of China. Most of these studies underline the significant influence of western modernity on the formation and development of Japan's image of China and analyze present conditions and causes in view of changes in Japans' relations with Asia and western countries. For example, by analyzing the intrinsic links between "breaking away from Asia" and "reviving Asia" and motives of "de-orientalism" and "mutual orientalism," Zhou Ning in *"A Giant Other"—"China" in Japan's Modernity Self-Imagination* states that the reason why China's image in the view of Japan is "stigmatized" is that Japan, which is forced by western modernity to be caught in modern anxiety over its identity, has to identify itself constantly from the "cultural snobbery" of affirming the image of the West and negating the image of China.[33] Wu Guanghui also argues that "the knowledge system and value position of western modernity acts as the benchmark for Japan to understand and explore the image of 'China.' The Chinese history depicted by Japan is a geographically and culturally incomplete image of China."[34]

4.1.2.7 *Comprehensive works*

In addition to studies above, some other academic studies address Japan's view of China in a relatively comprehensive manner from various perspectives. One example is Japanese scholar Nomura Koichi's *Comprehension of China in Modern Japan*, which explores Japan's view of China in different periods with different methods and includes both comprehensive description of specific historical periods and analysis of the views of key figures.[35] Among domestic studies, Wu Guanghui's monograph *The Image of China in Japan* analyzes and expounds on China's image in Japan from the perspective of cross-cultural image analysis, history, and philosophy.[36] *Japan's View of China since Modern Times*, edited by Yang Dongliang, sums up the characteristics of various stages in Japan's view of China from 1840 to 2010, and focuses on the understanding of China held by Japanese people from all walks of life, including political and economic circles, as well as ordinary Japanese people. The book is more comprehensive and wide-ranging than any topical study or analysis of Japan's view of China during specific historical periods.[37]

Generally speaking, existing studies on Japan's understanding of China are comprehensive and cover many different perspectives, though each has limitations. Studies from the first three perspectives are limited in that they are based on information and data mainly from historical records of major events and focus on political and intellectual elites. These figures are representative to some extent, but analyzing their views may ignore the views of China held by ordinary Japanese people and the image of China in Japan's mass culture. In the light of the definition of national image, Japan's understanding of China's image should be holistic, meaning that it should include both elites and ordinary people, and both macro aspects reflected by major historical events, such as China's international status and level of economic development, and micro aspects such as mass culture and the image of Chinese people held by ordinary people. Studies from the perspective of cultural exchange are mostly based on readily available data within a particular scope—for example, confined to certain type of media reports or literary works. Such analysis can fail to fully integrate historical context and cultural foundations, and thus lack a deeper understanding of Japan's view of China. Descriptions based on personal experiences can serve as supplements to academic studies, but these are inevitably subjective, reflecting their authors' personal experiences. They can hardly form a systematic basis for analysis. Studies probing into the underlying causes of Japanese views, for their part, are mostly theoretical, and employ analysis so abstract that it seldom includes specific examples or representative figures. These studies are difficult to apply to external manifestations of Japan's understanding of China.

4.2 The image of China in the eyes of the Japanese

4.2.1 *The first impression China makes on Japanese people*

In the first survey, when asking Japanese people that "what first comes to your mind at the mention of China," Chinese food was ranked first, receiving 67 mentions. In addition to a general reference to Chinese food, specific food or cuisines were also mentioned, such as dumpling (15 mentions), mapo tofu (6 mentions), Peking duck (4 mentions), steamed stuffed buns (3 mentions), steamed buns (2 mentions), almond junket (2 mentions), fried rice (2 mentions), and Chinese egg pancakes/jianbing (1 mention). The phrase "large population" received 58 mentions, ranking second only to "Chinese food," followed by panda (48 mentions), the Great Wall (46 mentions), CPC/Communism (30 mentions), long history (29 mentions), Mao Zedong (29 mentions), vast territory (26 mentions), and red (24 mentions).

Figure 4.1 lists impressions of China mentioned more than ten times. It can be seen that Japanese people are deeply impressed by cultural symbols of China (such as the Great Wall and panda), political party/political system characteristics (CPC/Communism, Mao Zedong, red, Tian'anmen), and historical elements (History of the Three Kingdoms). Beyond these, Chinese cultural elements such as Confucius, calligraphy, the Imperial Palace, Tang suit, Tai Chi, Hutong, and Li Bai were also mentioned, together with China's family planning policy, wealth gap, human rights, and food safety, among others.

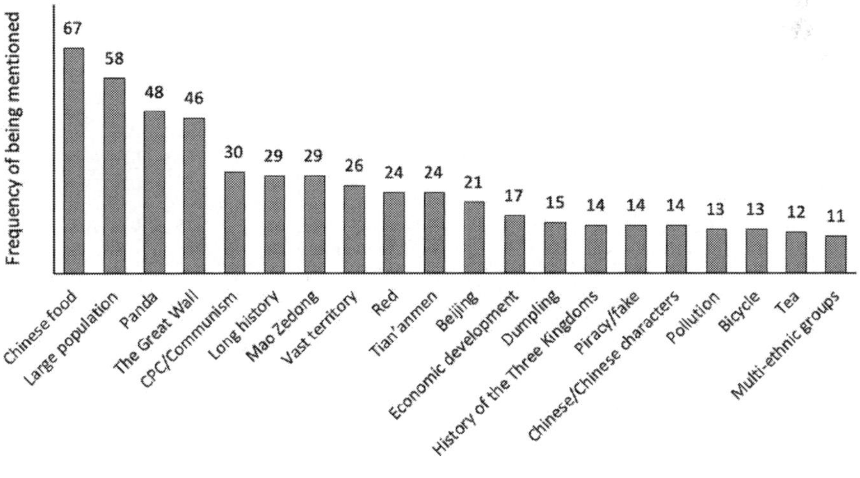

Figure 4.1 The first impression China makes on the Japanese people

Source: The first survey.

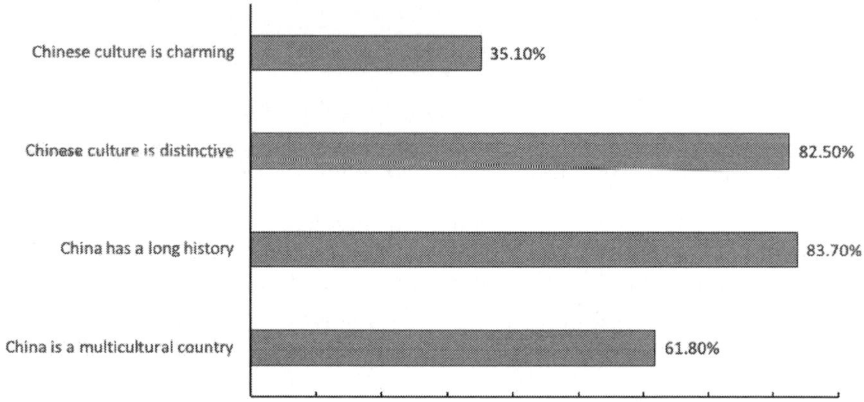

Figure 4.2 Proportions of the Japanese respondents who agree with the statements concerning China and Chinese culture

Source: The second survey.

4.2.2 *Japanese people's overall impression of and evaluation on China*

When it comes to respondents' overall impression of China and Chinese culture, excluding those answering "unclear," more than 80% of Japanese interviewees agreed that China has a long history and distinctive culture. Over 60% of respondents considered that China is a multicultural country while only 30% considered Chinese culture appealing. Figure 4.2 lists specific statistics.

A regression analysis indicates that the degree to which the interviewees agreed with the statements "China is a multicultural country," and "China has a long history," was significantly correlated with age and education. Interviewees who were older and more educated were more inclined to consider China as having a long history and diverse culture. Meanwhile, more education correlated with agreement with the statement that "Chinese culture is appealing."

In the survey questionnaire, we surveyed attitudes toward China using the eight adjectives given by Brand Asset Valuator (BAV) in 2004–2006 in Joshua Ramo's book *Brand China*: *dependable*, *pleasant*, *original*, *leading edge*, *glamourous*, *on the move*, *steadfast* and *dynamic*. Respondents were asked to rate China on a scale of 0 to 10, with 0 representing strong disagreement and 10 representing strong agreement. In general, respondents held a low rating of China's image based on these adjectives: the average response on each item was below 5, indicating disagreement. To put it another way, Japanese people generally disagree with these descriptions. Relatively speaking, "dynamic," "steadfast," and "on the move" scored the

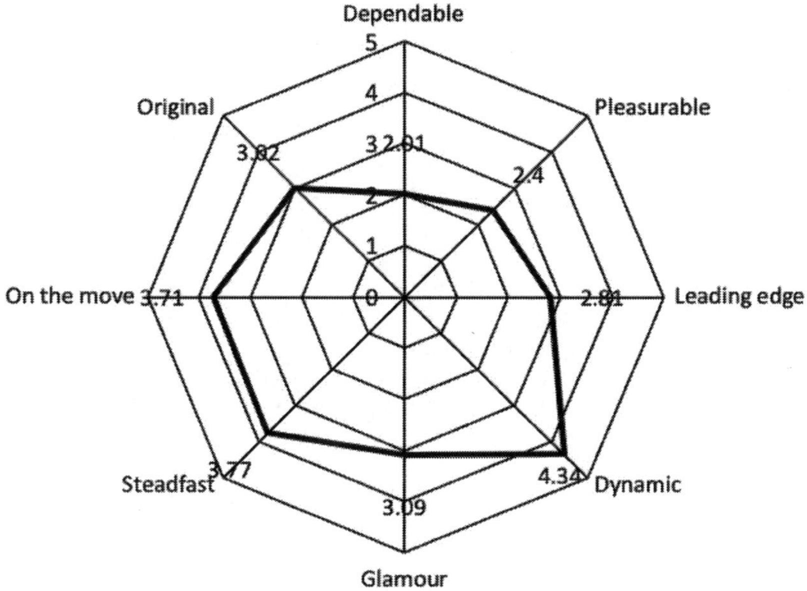

Figure 4.3 Overall evaluation on China

Source: The third survey.

highest while "dependable" and "pleasant" scored especially low. Figure 4.3 displays the average response for each adjective.

In terms of China's influence on world peace and development, only 12.6% of the respondents considered that China has an positive impact on world peace and development, while nearly 60% took a negative view, and nearly 30% were neutral or unaware (as shown in Figure 4.4). Regarding the statement that "China has a positive impact on world peace and development over the past five years," responses were significantly correlated with the age and political affiliation of respondents. Older Japanese were more inclined to support the view that "China has had a positive impact on world peace and development over the past five years." Those with no political party affiliation were more likely to see China as having a positive impact on world peace and development.

In the research interviews undertaken in the study, Japanese journalists in China expressed the view that recent Chinese political actions, such as the naval buildup, the sending of the Chinese navy to the Western Pacific, and China's getting tough on the South China Sea issue, were the most important reasons why Japanese people feel threatened by China. These were also the explanation for why Japanese people disagreed with the survey statements regarding China's positive influence on world peace and development.

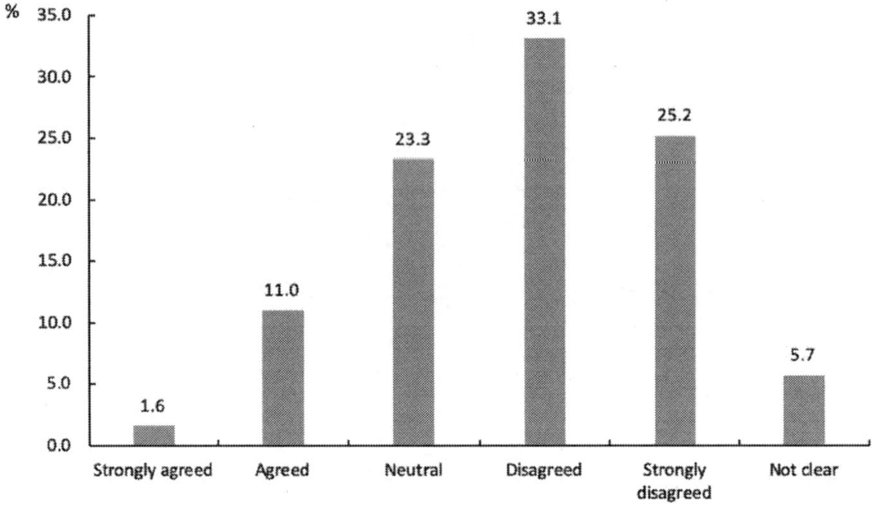

Figure 4.4 Does China positively influence world peace and development

Source: The second survey.

Japanese scholars interviewed for this study expressed relatively neutral views about the causes. With respect of China's contribution to world peace and development, one Japanese scholar and expert on China pointed out that "development is a condition for peace and China has contributed a lot to development, which has been well proven by Africa. Recent economic development in Africa owes largely to China's assistance. Therefore, on the economic development front, China is a major contributor to world development. On the security front, China has added to frictions, although China has also made positive contributions. For example, in the Gulf of Aden, the Chinese and Japanese navies have cooperated successfully. After natural disasters that have struck Southeast Asia, Chinese troops have also helped. Generally, non-traditional security cooperation between the countries seems successful. With respect to traditional national security issues, China's desire to exclude U.S. forces from the East China Sea and the South China Sea is growing. If this desire comes to dominate Chinese thinking, then conflict is unavoidable."

Another Japanese scholar stated that "given China's present pace of development, if China can be a responsible great power, it definitely will make great contributions to world peace and development. However, it is unclear which direction China will take when it becomes strong. It would be wonderful if China could become a responsible great power, but we cannot rule out the possibility that China may become an irresponsible power."

In the survey, most respondents replied negatively or neutral about "whether China's development is positive or negative for Japan," with only

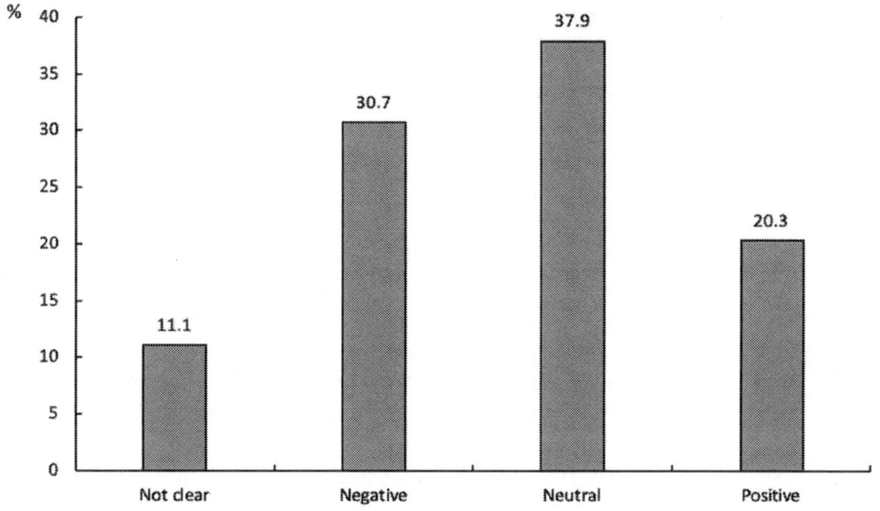

Figure 4.5 Is China's development positive or negative for Japan

Source: The second survey.

20% expressing a positive view (see Figure 4.5). The attitudes of respondents were significantly correlated with education levels and whether respondents reported having Chinese friends. More educated respondents tended to give neutral responses on this question, and those reporting having Chinese friends were more inclined to consider China's development positive for Japan.

In the interviews conducted for this study, most Japanese journalists and scholars argued that China's development had both advantages and disadvantages for Japan—ultimately offering more advantages than disadvantages. The growth of China's military power is viewed by most Japanese as a threat to Japan; while economically, an increase in consumption brought about by a large number of Chinese people traveling to and shopping in Japan is favorable to Japan's economic development. Based on data released by Japan Tourism Agency on July 30, 2015, the number of Chinese tourists to Japan during the first half of 2015 reached 2.17 million, allowing China to overtake Korea to become the largest source of tourist visits to Japan, and reversing Japan's tourism deficit.[38]

One Japanese scholar interviewed for the book noted that "the odds of economic cooperation between China and Japan are pretty high. Although China and Japan are now less economically complementary than in the 1970s and 1980s,[39] and compete with each other in many fields, there is ample room for cooperation. For example, the two may cooperate to improve air pollution in China, given that Japan has also undergone a period of high air pollution and therefore has experience in this regard."

4.2.3 *Japanese people's sense of familiarity with and affinity for China*

To examine the familiarity of Japanese respondents with China, the survey questionnaire listed five specific forms of contacts with China: doing business with China, traveling to China, studying in China, working in China, and emigrating to China. Familiarity with China was tested by respondents' expressed willingness to engage in the five forms of contact. Using a five-point scale, "strongly unwilling" was rated as 1 and "strongly willing" as 5. Higher the values correspond to greater willingness. Generally, average responses on all five items fell below the middle value of 3, indicating respondents were less than willing to engage in the five forms of contact. Only willingness to travel to China scored above 2 at 2.27. In other words, Japanese people surveyed were generally unwilling to work, study, do business in, or travel to China (see Figure 4.6). Given that our survey questionnaire targeted people living in Japan, and such respondents differ from Chinese in language, living habits, and other aspects, it is unsurprising that respondents gave such answers to this question.

Among the five countries named in the survey—namely Russia, China, India, Germany, and the United States—48.9% of Japanese respondents reported the greatest affinity for the United States, followed by Germany (36%), India (9.3%), China (4.1%), and Russia (only 1.5%) (see Figure 4.7). Figures above indicate that the experience of Japan in learning from western countries such as the Europe and America since modern times has resulted in Japan's sense of familiarity with these countries.

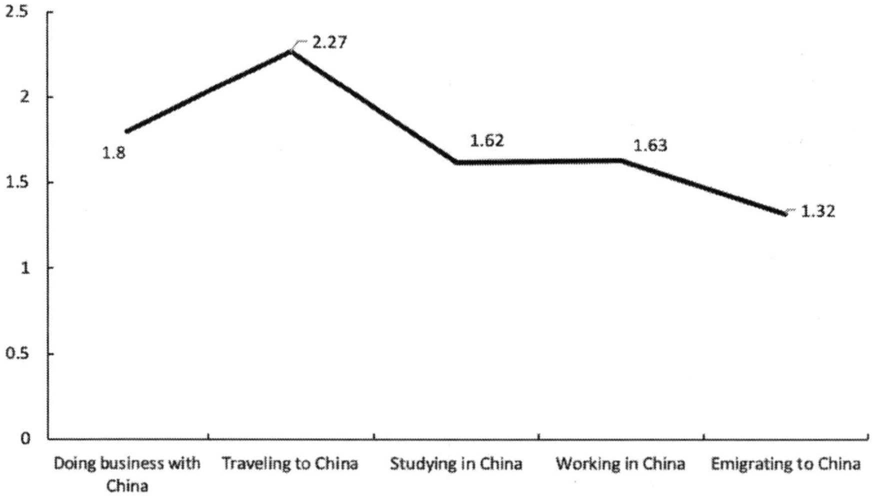

Figure 4.6 The willingness of Japanese people to have contacts with China

Source: The third survey.

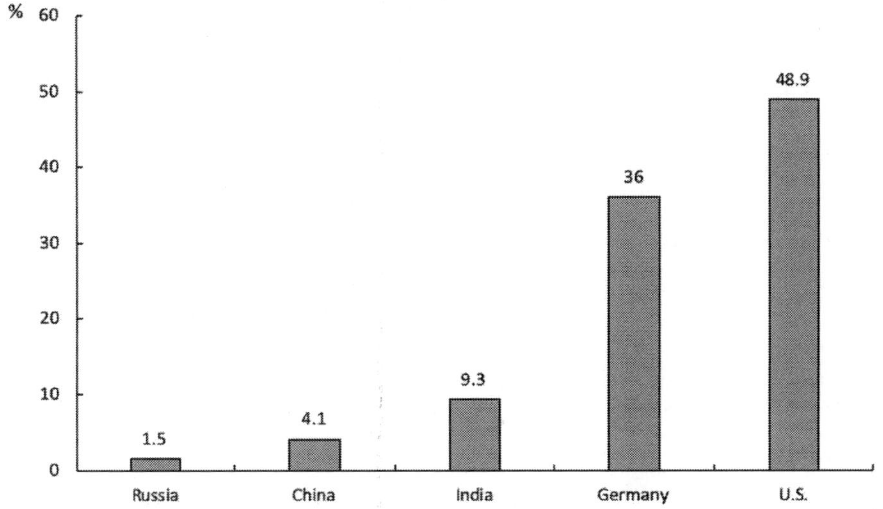

Figure 4.7 Percentage of Japanese who like China, the United States, Germany, Russia, and India the best

Source: The second survey.

In the interviews, several Japanese journalists and scholars mentioned that Japanese people have greater day-to-day exposure to American and European culture, including through films, books, and news media. This can partly explain why Japanese people like the United States and Germany more. Japanese people like Russia least, and a quite important explanation for this is the ongoing modern territorial disputes between Japan and Russia. The mutual dislike between Japanese and Chinese people is largely linked to historical issues and territorial disputes between the two countries.

The 508 survey respondents who expressed liking the United States stated that the main reason for such affinity is democratic politics and developed economy in the United States. The 374 respondents who liked Germany stated that the main reason is the high quality of citizens, beautiful environment, and stable society in Germany. The 97 respondents who liked India stated that the main reason was the high quality of citizens and the splendor of Indian culture. The 43 respondents who like China stated that the main reason is China's cultural splendor and rapid economic development. The 16 Japanese people who liked Russia expressed liking Russia's culture and stable society. It can be seen that China's long and splendid culture and fast-growing economy have a certain appeal for Japanese people. The difficulty is in determining how to interest more Japanese people in Chinese culture and rapid economic development, to increase the number of China-friendly people in Japan. Table 4.1 lists different reasons expressed by Japanese respondents for liking each specific country.

Table 4.1 Percentages of different reasons why the Japanese people like each country

	United States *N = 508*	*Germany* *N = 374*	*India* *N = 97*	*China* *N = 43*	*Russia* *N = 16*
Social stability	14.0%	30.2%	4.1%	7.0%	25.0%
Beautiful environment	8.5%	34.0%	10.3%	25.6%	12.5%
Splendid culture	11.2%	17.1%	26.8%	53.5%	50.0%
Democratic politics	42.1%	27.3%	12.4%	4.1%	6.3%
Developed economy	29.7%	23.5%	19.6%	20.9%	0
Peaceful diplomacy	8.3%	13.9%	18.6%	2.3%	6.3%
High citizen quality	13.2%	50.3%	39.2%	7.0%	18.8%

Source: The second survey

4.3 Survey analysis

4.3.1 *Japan wants China to be a "gentle giant"*

Our survey data show that only 10% of Japanese people consider China's impact on world peace and development positive, and only 20% consider the effects of China's development on Japan positive. This likely represents the overall view of ordinary Japanese people. Meanwhile, in the interviews, all interviewees affirmed the importance to Japan of a stable and developing China. A stronger China has brought more trade income to Japan, enabled more Chinese to travel to and invest in Japan, and advanced other forms of exchange between the two countries, all of which have benefitted Japan. If China's money flows mainly to technology innovation, projects that benefit people, and economic cooperation, China will be vital to Japan, Southeast Asia, and even the entire world. In the interviews, a scholar stated that the current problem was that "the more developed China is, the more worried its neighbors will be, so peaceful development must stay at the top of the agenda. If we do not stress peaceful development, other countries will be worried. Our stance is to favor stable development of China, since economic stagnation will definitely lead to social instability, which will then affect neighboring countries including Japan."

In recent years, despite China's commitment to peaceful development, the concerns of neighboring countries about the rise of China have not diminished. The main reason is China's increasing military power and its territorial disputes with neighboring countries. This, in turn, relates to China's economic development. One interviewee indicated that China's recent demands to restore historical claims, including claims to the Diaoyu Islands and some South China Sea islands, was an important factor driving the fears of neighboring countries, and also drove negative Japanese attitudes toward the effect of China's development on world peace and on Japan's development, as indicated by the survey data.

From the viewpoint of Japan's real national interests, neither a turbulent China nor an especially strong China benefits Japan. Hence, it might be best for Japan's interests if China does not become strong enough to pose a threat to Japan, yet can maintain domestic social stability and steady economic development, without surpassing Japan. However, as one interviewee put it, "China is already a great power and the best result is that it can be a gentle giant. When choosing between a turbulent China and a strong China, a gentle giant is the best and the only choice for Japan."

4.3.2 *Main reasons for Japanese people's unwillingness to come to China*

The survey data show that the Japanese are less willing to travel to and study or work in China. Interviewees also mentioned that the number of Japanese people willing to study in and travel to China has declined in recent years.

In the 1980s and 1990s, many Japanese people traveled to China for tourism and study. Of the journalists and scholars interviewed, four had been to China for travel or study in the 1980s or 1990s. Why are many Japanese less interested in travel to China in recent years? Environmental pollution is a key reason. One Japanese scholar stated that Japan suffered severe air pollution in the past, and Japanese people are aware of the harm to human health of environmental pollution. Due to media reports about haze in China, and the frequent occurrence of various environmental incidents, Japanese parents are unwilling to send their children to study in China. The decline in the number of Japanese tourists to China is also closely related to environmental pollution.

Another important reason behind declining Japanese travel to China is the deterioration of Sino-Japanese relations, especially the anti-Japanese protest demonstrations that took place in a number of Chinese cities in 2005 and 2012, which raises personal safety concerns for Japanese visitors in China. In an interview, one Japanese journalist who had been in China for less than half a year stated that he was worried about the risk of being beaten up before he came to China, but after coming to China, he found such worries completely unjustified, and that the Chinese he met were quite friendly. Another scholar pointed out, "the naval expansion strategy of the Chinese government has raised fears about China among the Japanese, negatively influencing Sino-Japanese relations. If the relations between China and Japan can be improved, the Japanese people will also change their feelings and understanding of China, and will be more willing to visit

China." It is fair to interpret this evidence as showing that the worsening of Sino-Japanese relations has reduced the willingness of Japanese people to approach China, so declining to travel to or study in China becomes a rational choice, which in turn could exacerbate mutual misunderstandings.

4.3.3 *Reasons for a decline in Japan's sense of affinity with China*

The survey questionnaires showed that, compared to the United States, Germany, India, and Russia, only 4% of the Japanese liked China. When interviewees were asked about this, one scholar pointed out that Japanese people's feelings toward China were closely tied to the frequent crises between the two countries in recent years. The Japanese people's sense of affinity with China decreases every time a crisis occurs, and goes up after the crisis is addressed. This appears clearly indicated by the data from opinion polls conducted by the Cabinet Office of Japan since 1978. The solid line in Figure 4.8 represents the proportion of the Japanese reporting a sense of affinity with China, while the dotted line stands for the proportion of those having no sense of affinity.

The past few years indeed show the lowest sense of affinity for China reported by Japanese. The 1980s marked the period of time when Japanese people felt closest to China, and this was also when a large number of Japanese visited China. In the 1990s, in the wake of the economic bubble in Japan, the rise of China, and changes in Sino-Japanese relations, the

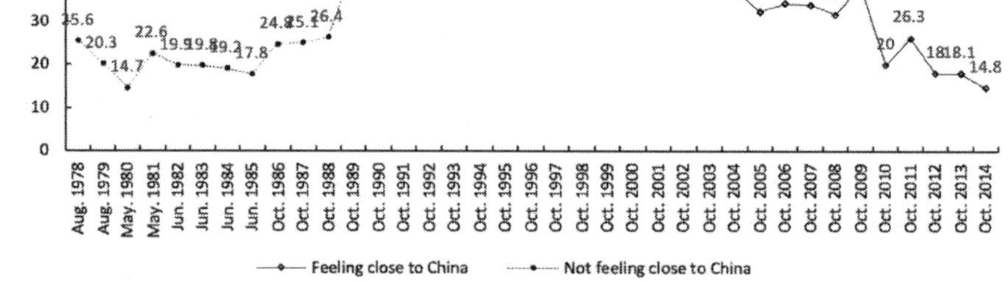

Figure 4.8 Opinion polls on the familiarity of the Cabinet Office of Japan to China (October 2014)

Source: The Cabinet Office of Japan: Opinion Polls on Diplomatic Relations, http://survey.gov-online.go.jp/h26/h26-gaiko/zh/z08.html.

Japanese sense of affinity with China began to decline. In 2000 and beyond, as events such as the Japanese history textbook controversy, disputes over the official visits to the Yasukuni Shrine, and the Diaoyu Islands disputes intensified, Sino-Japanese relations further deteriorated and the proportion of the Japanese people reporting close feelings for China continued to fall. According to the poll by the Cabinet Office of Japan in October 2014, only 14.8% of Japanese people had a sense of affinity for China, while 83.1% reported no such affinity.

As several Japanese scholars interviewed put it, correlating the results of opinion polls by the Cabinet Office of Japan with some important events indicates that every time a significant event takes place, Japanese affinity for China declines. In 1978, the Japanese people felt quite close to China, with more than 70% of respondents reporting such feelings. A sudden decline was observed in 1989, following the political turmoil in Beijing. The year 1996 saw near-record lows, for which an important reason was the Chinese military exercises directed at Taiwan that year. This was followed by some slight ups and downs. A large downward inflection point took place in 2004, after Chinese fans booed Japanese athletes during the AFC Asian Cup match, which was provoked violence. The proportion of Japanese expressing affinity for China was relatively low in 2005 given the large-scale anti-Japanese demonstrations in China; and the same case occurred in 2012. The incident of poisoned dumplings in 2008 caused a downward turn of public opinion in Japan, and another the sudden fall took place in 2010 arising mainly from the collision of Chinese and Japanese ships near the Diaoyu Islands waters. Consequently, Figure 4.8 clearly shows that the sense of affinity with China as indicated by Japanese opinion polls declines whenever a major event takes place between the two countries, and recovers when situation is relatively eased.

Why do Japanese people feel less close to and have worse impressions of China in recent years? Figure 4.9 lists various possible reasons mentioned in opinions polls conducted by the Cabinet Office of Japan and proportions of the Japanese people agreeing with these reasons. Dark-colored columns represent the data in 2014 and light-colored columns represent the data in 2013. As indicated by the data in 2014, more than half of Japanese people attribute the decline in their sense of affinity with China to four main reasons, including acts of China that are inconsistent with international rules (55.1%); China's self-centered policies aimed at securing resources, energy, and food (52.8%); China's criticism of Japan due to historical issues (52.2%); and continuous antagonism between China and Japan on the issue of the Diaoyu Islands (50.4%). Other reasons given included continuous anti-Japanese propaganda and reporting in China's media, growth and opacity of China's military power, China's hegemonic actions, lack of understanding of the Chinese patriotic behaviors, and ways of thinking and differences in the political system accounting respectively for 41.1%, 31.2%, 29.4%, 28.7%, and 25.7% of responses. Other reasons that were given by under one-fourth

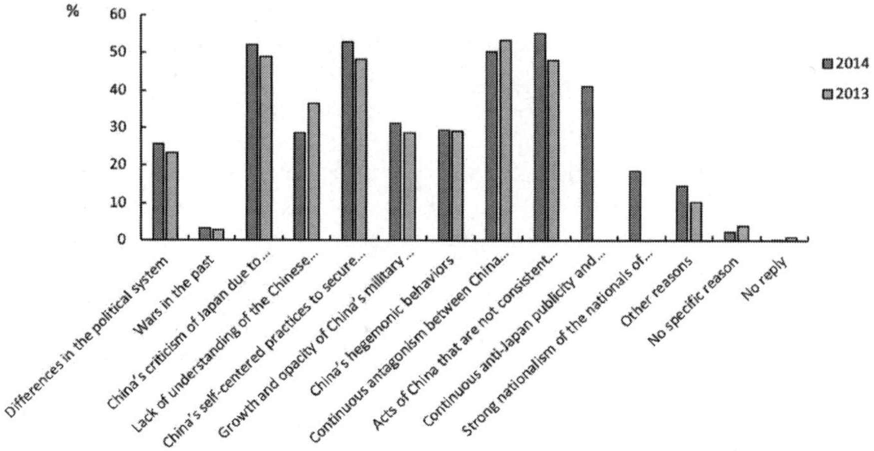

Figure 4.9 Reasons for a decline in Japanese people's sense of familiarity with China

Source: Genron NPO-China Daily: The 10th China-Japan Joint Opinion Poll, http://www.genron-npo.net/world/genre.

of respondents were the nationalism of the Chinese people (18.4%) and past wars (3.3%). The above-mentioned reasons listed by Japanese people indicate that the competition between China and Japan for practical interests and emotional considerations are main reasons for the decline in Japanese people's sense of affinity for China.

4.4 Policy proposals

In order to improve Japanese people's sense of affinity for China or improve the impressions Chinese and Japanese people have on each other, it is essential to strengthen exchanges and communication between China and Japan. In the interviews, one Japanese scholar pointed out that people built their knowledge of something through the information they obtain through daily life, so he was not worried about Chinese people's impressions of Japan, but about Japanese people's impressions of China. Nowadays, in addition to personal experiences in Japan, many Chinese people acquire information on Japan mainly from media reports, which contain a lot of negative information. This, together with the historical issue of Japan's invasion of China, has resulted in negative Chinese impressions of Japan. As more Chinese people travel to Japan and get to know the actual situation in Japan, Chinese people will improve their sentiment for Japan. The key now is how to change Japanese people's attitude toward China. Today, Japanese media are also inundated with a large amount of negative information on China, but fewer and fewer Japanese people are willing to visit China and experience the real China. Since they can only get to know China through the negative information in the media, therefore they can hardly form a full and accurate understanding of China. Given this, the scholar stated that he was worried more about Japanese people's impressions of China, which, once formed around certain stereotypes, is difficult to change.

We basically agree with the Japanese scholar on this. Many Chinese people dislike Japan on the macro level, but like it on the micro level. After reading media reports about Japan's invasion of China, Japanese leaders' visits to the Yasukuni Shrine, and the whitewashing of the Japanese invasion of China in Japanese textbooks, no Chinese will have a favorable overall view of Japan. However, the Chinese who have visited Japan and truly know the country admire it for its society, public security, consumer goods, and culture. Hence, we often see media reports of Chinese tourists snapping up electric appliances and daily necessities in Japan. It is because of such affinity at the micro level that Chinese people's negative impressions of Japan due to macro-level media reports will improved quickly if Sino-Japanese political relations improve and the direction of media reports changes for the better.

In contrast, the Japanese look at China more at a micro level, although also at a macro level. At the overall level, with more reports on China Threat in Japanese media, those who have never been to China might be affected by the media and come to dislike China. Nevertheless, this can change quickly if there are improvements in Sino-Japanese relations and changes in the direction of media reports. Microscopically, Japanese people dislike China for problems such as food safety, environmental pollution, and official corruption. These problems are mainly Chinese domestic issues that cannot be addressed overnight. As long as no improvements are made at the micro level, Japanese people's impressions of China will not change. In this sense, it is harder to change Japanese attitudes toward China.

Notes

1. Nye, Joseph. *Soft Power: The Means to Success in World Politics*. New York: Public Affairs, 2004, p. x.
2. Guan, Wenhu (Ed.). *On National Image* [guojia Xingxiang lun]. University of Electronic Science and Technology of China Press, 2000.
3. Zhang, Kun, and Qiong Xu. "On the Inscape of the Nation Image [guojia xingxiang chuyi]." Chinese Journal of Journalism & Communication 3(2007): 11–16.
4. Liu, Xiaoyan. "Thinking on Shaping of State Images by the Media [guanyu chuanmei suzao guojia xingxiang de sikao]." Chinese Journal of Journalism & Communication 2(2002): 61–66.
5. Xu, Xiaoge. "On National Image in International News Communication [guoji xinwen chuanbo zhong de guojia xingxiang wenti]." Journalism & Communication 2(1996): 36–46.
6. Huang, Qing. "International Consciousness and National Image in External Publicity [duiwai xuanchuan Zhong de guojia yishi yu guojia xingxiang]." Chinese Journalist 9(1998): 54.

7. Zhang, Yuqiang. "Shallow Views on National Image [guojia xingxiang chuyi]." Modern Communication 2(2002): 27–31.
8. Sun, Youzhong. "Connotation and Functions of National Image [guojia xingxiang de neihan jiqi gongneng]." International Forum 3(2002):14–21.
9. Liu, Jinan, and Hui He, et al. *Image of China in World Mainstream Media* [jingxiang zhongguo: shijie zhuliu meiti zhong de zhongguo xingxiang]. Communication University of China Press, 2006.
10. Wu, Youfu. *The Building and Communication of China's National Image* [zhongguo guojia xingxiang de suzao he chuanbo]. Fudan University Press, 2009.
11. He, Hui, et al. *Construction and Communication of National Image in New Media Environment* [xinmeiti huanjingzhong guojia xingxiang de goujian he chuanbo]. Foreign Languages Press, 2008.
12. Cheng, Manli. "On Nation Image Building and Mass Communication [dazhong chuanbo yu guojia xingxiang suzao]." Chinese Journal of Journalism & Communication 3(2007): 5–10.
13. Li, Zhengguo. "Crisis Communication, Role of the Media and Restoration of State Image [weiji gongguan, meiti juese yu guojia xingxiang de xiufu]." China Radio & TV Academic Journal 3(2006): 25–27.
14. Tu, Guangjin, and He Gong. "Agenda Building in Beijing Olympics and National Image Communication [Beijing aoyun yu guojia xingxiang chuanbo Zhong de yicheng jiangou]." China Radio & TV Academic Journal 7(2008): 5–7.
15. Kunczik, Michael. Images of Nations and International Public Relations. Mahwah: Lawrence Erlbaum, 1997.
16. Morley, Michael. *How to Manage Your Global Reputation: A Guide to the Dynamics of International Public Relations*. New York: New York University Press, 1998.
17. Anholt, Simon. *Competitive Identity: The New Brand Management for Nations, Cities and Regions*. New York: Palgrave Macmillan, 2007.
18. Ibid.
19. Liu, Jiaxin. *How Japanese Modern Intellectuals View China* [riben jindai zhishifenzi de zhongguoguan]. Nankai University Press, 2007.
20. Wang, Ping. "On the Historical Changes of the Japanese 'China Perception' [lun ribenren de zhongguoguan de lishi bianqian]." Mutual Understandings between China and Japan—Proceedings of the Fourth Japan Youth Studies Forum. World Affairs Press, 2003. 19.
21. Yan, Shaodang. "The Japanese View of China in the 20th Century [20 shiji ribenren de zhongguoguan]." Daizong Journal of the Journal of Taian Institute of Education 2(1999): 37–46.
22. Yan, Shaodang. "The Japanese View of China in the Post-War 60 Years [zhanhou 60nian ribenren de zhongguoguan]." Japan Studies 3(2005): 1–11.
23. Shen, Haitao. "Japan's Perception of China and the September 18 Incident [riben de zhongguo renshi yu jiuyiba shibian]." Northeast China History and Geography (Dong Bei Shi Di) 4(2011): 10–15.
24. Zhang, Yajing. "The Japanese View of China: During the Period of the Cultural Revolution in China [ribenren de zhongguoguan: yi wenhua dageming shiqi wei zhongxin]." Historical Journal of Fu Jen Catholic University 12(2001).
25. Li, Yannan. "The 'Image of China' in Modern Japanese Literature [jindai riben wenxuezhong de zhongguo xingxiang." Doctoral Thesis of Jinan University, May 2005.
26. Zhao, Xinli. "The Image of China in Japanese Documentaries [riben jilupianzhong de zhongguo xingxiang]." Youth Journalist 10-1(2009): 15–17.
27. Zhang, Ning. *China in Japanese Media: News Frames and National Image* [riben meiti shang de zhongguo: baodao kuangjia yu guojia xingxiang]. Jilin People's Publishing House, 2006.

28. Ruan, Suqian. "Study on China-Japan Mutual Reporting and the National Image of the Two Countries [zhongri xianghu baodao yu liangguo xingxiang yanjiu]." Master's Thesis of Nanchang University, June 2007.
29. Liu, Linli. *The Image of China in Japanese Mass Media* [riben dazhongmeiti zhong de zhongguo xingxiang]. Communication University of China Press, 2007.
30. Tan, Jianchuan. *The Image of China in Japanese Textbooks* [riben jiaokeshu de zhongguo xingxiang yanjiu]. Peking University Press, 2014.
31. Satoshi, Amako. *China in the Eyes of the Japanese* (Trans. Fan Li). Social Sciences Academic Press, 2006.
32. Kato, Shuichi. *The 21st Century and Chinese Culture* (Trans. Peng Jiahong). Zhonghua Book Company, 2007.
33. Zhou, Ning. "'A Giant Other': 'China' in Japan's Modernity Self-Imagination [juda de tazhe: riben xiandaixing ziwo xiangxiangzhong de zhongguo]." Tianjin Social Sciences 5(2011): 101–113.
34. Wu, Guanghui. "Research on Japanese Images of China—Exploration of Theories and Methods [riben de zhongguo xingxiang yanjiu: lilun yu fangfa tansuo]." Japanese Language Education and Japanese Studies 1(2011): 151.
35. Nomura, Koichi. *Comprehension of China in Modern Japan* (Trans. Zhang Xuefeng). Central Compilation & Translation Press, 1999.
36. Wu, Guanghui. *The Image of China in Japan* [riben de zhongguo xingxiang]. People's Publishing House, 2010.
37. Yang, Dongliang (Ed.). *Japan's View of China since Modern Times* [jindai yilai riben de zhongguoguan]. Jiangsu People's Publishing House, 2012.
38. Save the Economy: China Becomes the Largest Source of Tourists to Japan. Reference News, August 2, 2015. Retrieved from http://tech.huanqiu.com/news/2015-08/7165749.html
39. In the 1970s and 1980s, China and Japan were economically complementary, in that Japan needed China's energy and market, while China desired Japan's technology and capital.

5 Chinese culture in the eyes of the Japanese

Culture plays a decisive role in shaping the national image of a country. Culture can help people communicate intellectually and exchange deeper levels of thought, and thereby enhance people-to-people understanding and mutual reliance, and develop deeper impressions of another country in the minds of the whole people. Cultural factors usually take root in the hearts of people, in their innermost soul, so cultural exchange exerts an invisible, long-lasting, and far-reaching influence, which regular political dialog or economic and trade activities cannot replace.

The history of cultural exchanges between China and Japan goes back to ancient times, including exchange in traditional literature, music, dance, calligraphy, and religion, as well as mutual development of institutional culture in the political and economic fields. Part I of this book has presented a description of the history of cultural exchange between China and Japan. Here we explore the following questions: How does cultural exchange influence the image of China in the eyes of the Japanese? How do the Japanese view traditional Chinese culture today? To what extent do Japanese people understand China's contemporary political and economic systems? How can cultural exchange serve as a bridge to enhance mutual understanding between the people of the two countries and to improve Sino-Japanese relations? This chapter will probe these questions based on the results of the survey questionnaire and in-depth interviews.

5.1 Culture and national image

5.1.1 *Literature*

Many studies have demonstrated the active role of cultural factors in shaping the national image of a country, mainly focusing on international communication and relations. Studies of international communication mainly highlight culture as the content of communication, showing the role of cultural communication, what factors cultural communications influence, what problems it can cause, and the potential solutions for these problems. Namely, these studies show how culture shapes the national image of a country in international and bilateral cultural exchanges through books, newspapers, periodicals, broadcasting, film, TV, Internet, and mobile phones. Simon Anholt, writing from the perspective of national branding, proposes six channels to improve the image of a country, one of which is cultural exchange.[1]

Scholars of international relations mainly focus on how cultural factors drive and promote the diplomatic and national interests of a country, and usually use the term of "cultural diplomacy" to designate this influence. To be specific, *cultural diplomacy* means various cultural exchange activities undertaken by the government of a country to achieve the goals of its diplomatic policy, such as enhancing mutual understanding, realizing national interests, changing national stereotypes and impressions, and improving the national image.[2] Many cultural activities fall into the domain of cultural diplomacy, including literature and art, language teaching, book publishing, artistic performances, painting and calligraphy exhibitions, sporting events, film and animation, news media, personnel exchange, trade in cultural products, and protection of cultural heritage. Compared with political and military diplomacy, cultural diplomacy is more nuanced and flexible, and often influences the masses of foreign countries without any visible display of power. The goal of cultural diplomacy is to strengthen a county's soft power: through cultural diplomacy, a country enhances others' views of its policies, values, and cultural appeal in order to achieve its national interests.[3] For example, Hollywood movies broadcast seeds of American views of freedom and democracy and the nature of the American Dream to all corners of the world while spreading its mass culture around the world. The powerful appeal and artistic charm of French literature and culture have fueled a fever for the study of the French language worldwide and attracted soaring numbers of inbound tourists for decades. The "Hallyu" triggered by Korean films and TV programs has swept Asia and shaped a positive image of South Korean society and country, and also driven rapid growth in the Korean tourism, clothing, and cosmetics industries. Japanese animation has become so popular worldwide that the Ministry of Foreign Affairs has appointed the cartoon character Doraemon—known worldwide—as the first Ambassador of Animation Culture in the history of Japan, with responsibility for propagating Japanese animation culture around the world and thereby raising the international image of Japan.

Western scholars were the first to seriously study cultural diplomacy. *The Cultural Approach: Another Way in International Relations*, written by American diplomats Ruth McMurray and Muna Lee, summarizes the cultural exchange programs of France, Germany, the United Kingdom, the United States, Japan, as well as of other countries since 1900. The authors advances the viewpoint that cultural exchange can enhance the sense of trust between different countries.[4] In his book *Cultural Internationalism and World Order*, professor Akira Iriye points out that cross-country cultural and intellectual exchange between peoples can build an atmosphere of mutual benefit, enhancing mutual trust, and cooperation and thereby serving as a stabilizing factor in international relations, helping to resolve the vagaries of international politics. He argues that where there is no cross-border exchange of thoughts, there can be no stable international order.[5]

In China, studies of cultural diplomacy, such as *American Cultural Diplomacy and Its Practice in China* by Hu Wentao,[6] *Cultural Diplomacy: An Interpretation as a Mode of Communication* by Li Zhi,[7] *Cultural Diplomacy and China's Soft Power: A Globalized Perspective* by Peng Xinliang[8] and *American Culture and Diplomacy* by Wang Xiaode, have emerged in large numbers in recent years.[9] In addition, many journal articles, theses and dissertations have focused on cultural diplomacy and the relations between culture and national interest.

Multiple hierarchies of cultural meaning imply that there also exist multiple hierarchies in cultural diplomacy. Generally speaking, culture can be understood from three levels: (1) superficial material culture, namely, cultural aspects with a physical form, including cuisine and clothing styles and related accessories; (2) mid-level institutional culture, meaning the political, economic, social, and legal systems established by human societies; (3) and deep cultural values, namely cultural values of thought, belief, and morality.

From this, the forms of cultural diplomacy can also be divided into three levels, from the elementary to the profound, and from the outside to the inside: superficial exchange of material culture, mid-level output of institutional culture and deep-level communication of core cultural values.[10]

5.1.2 *China's practice of cultural diplomacy*

In recent years, in order to improve its image and enhance the soft power of Chinese culture, China has undertaken a variety of cultural exchange activities, all of which can be considered as cultural diplomacy. These include: (1) organizing a Year of Chinese Culture in various countries—that is, a national public relations activity agreed by two countries concerned, taking place in a specific time and region and with cultural activities performances as the carriers. Examples have included holding a Year of Chinese Culture in the United Kingdom, France, and Italy, and holding a Year of Chinese Language in Russia. These activities can help the public of participating countries have contact and personal experience with Chinese culture over a sustained period, thereby helping spread Chinese culture abroad; (2) holding various large-scale sports events, cultural exhibitions, theatrical performances, and other cultural exchange activities to demonstrate Chinese culture and enhance mutual exchange and understanding internationally. Examples have included the Beijing Olympic Games in 2008, Expo 2010 Shanghai, the Xi'an Garden Expo, and the upcoming Beijing-Zhangjiakou Winter Olympic Games in 2022; (3) founding Confucius Institutes worldwide to popularize Chinese language and Chinese culture. The spreading of the language of a country not only improves the appeal and influence of the country's culture, but also plays an important role in enhancing international understanding and communication. European countries have exemplified this practice through institutes such as Alliance Francaise, the Goethe Institute of Germany, the Instituto Cervantes of Spain, and the Istituto Dante of Italy, all of which serve as educational institutions that can spread language and culture around the world; (4) establishing Chinese government scholarships, the HSK Winner Scholarship, and Confucius Institute Scholarship to attract overseas students to study in China, explore Chinese culture, understand Chinese society and gain familiarity with China.

China's practices of cultural diplomacy in recent years, with the exception of the above-mentioned Year of Culture and Confucius Institutes, mostly take the form of unilateral cultural demonstration and cultural promotion. These have focused on the level of exchange of superficial culture. Relatively speaking, such activities do not include deep exchange over institutional culture, spreading of cultural values, enabling people-to-people contact, or fostering academic exchange and cooperation. Michael Kahn-Ackermann, former General Director of Goethe-Institute China and current Senior Advisor at the headquarters of Confucius Institute, pointed out at a forum entitled How should Chinese culture go abroad?: There are three stages in cultural exchange: first, contact, to contact the culture of a country due to curiosity; second, exchange, both parties enhance understanding through mutual communication and learning; finally, cooperation, namely both parties cooperate with each other for a common goal, so as to enhance their mutual feelings and understanding.[11] China's practice of cultural diplomacy is basically at the stage of contact and exchange and has not really developed to the stage of two-way cooperation.

5.2 Traditional Chinese culture in the eyes of the Japanese

5.2.1 *Japanese people's awareness of and affinity for Chinese cultural symbols*

The survey data show that Japanese people are highly aware of Chinese cultural symbols. Over 99% of interviewees knew of the Great Wall, Chinese cuisine, traditional Chinese medicine (TCM), and the panda, and could recognize Chinese characters and calligraphy concerning 28 Chinese cultural symbols, particularly the Great Wall. As shown in Figure 5.1, a total of 14 Chinese cultural symbols enjoy 90% recognition among Japanese people, and have become the popular cultural symbols representing China. In addition to the above-mentioned six cultural symbols, the cheongsam/Tang suit, Fengshui (geomancy), Chinese Kongfu (martial arts), Confucian thought, Chinese silk, verses and musical tunes, the Spring Festival, and the Dragon Boat Festival are also considered as Chinese cultural symbols by Japanese people. Indeed, Japanese interviewees have a high overall awareness of

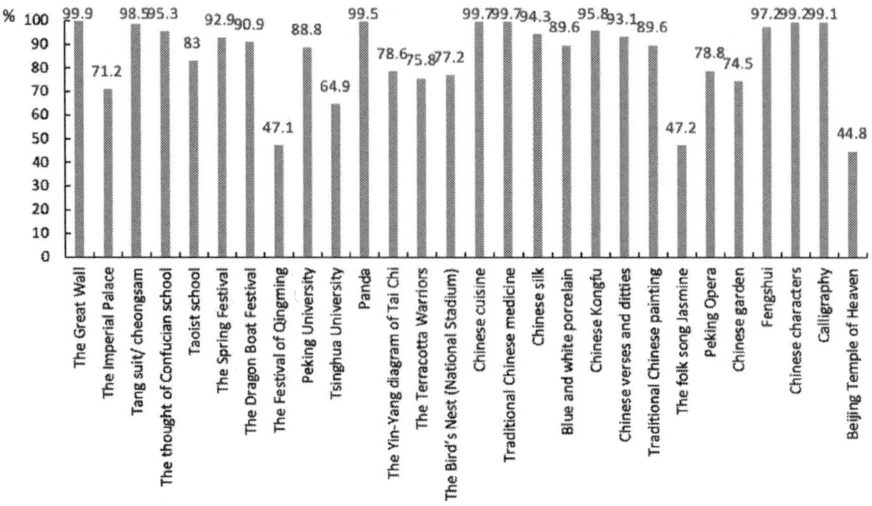

Figure 5.1 Japanese people's awareness of Chinese cultural symbols

Source: The 3rd survey.

Chinese cultural symbols, and even the Beijing Temple of Heaven, the lowest-ranked symbol, was recognized by 44.8% of interviewees.

The 28 cultural symbols listed in the questionnaire can be classified into five types: (1) token Chinese cultural symbols, such as the Great Wall, the Imperial Palace, the panda, and the Terracotta Warriors; (2) artistic symbols, such as the verses and songs, traditional Chinese painting, Peking Opera, the folk song Jasmine, calligraphy, and blue and white porcelain; (3) symbols of lifestyle, such as the Spring Festival, the Dragon Boat Festival, the Festival of Qingming (Tomb Sweeping Day), Chinese cuisine, TCM, Chinese silk, the Tang suit/cheongsam, Chinese Kongfu, and Fengshui; (4) symbols of philosophical thought, such Confucianism, Taoism, and the concept of Yin and Yang from Tai Chi; and finally (5) educational symbols, such as Peking University and Tsinghua University. Overall, Japanese people have a high awareness of Chinese cultural token symbols and living symbols, most of which enjoy awareness above 90%.

Compared with their high awareness of Chinese cultural symbols, Japanese people have a lower affinity for the symbols as a whole. In the questionnaire, Japanese affinity for cultural symbols was scored on a five-point scale, where 1 represented "Highly Dislike," and 5 represented "Like Very Much." Thus, a higher score indicated greater affinity for a given cultural symbols. As shown in Figure 5.2, the four Chinese cultural symbols Japanese people liked most were Chinese cuisine, the panda, the Great Wall, and Chinese characters. The mean score for Chinese cuisine was 4.28 (between Like and Like Very Much), and remaining symbols scored below

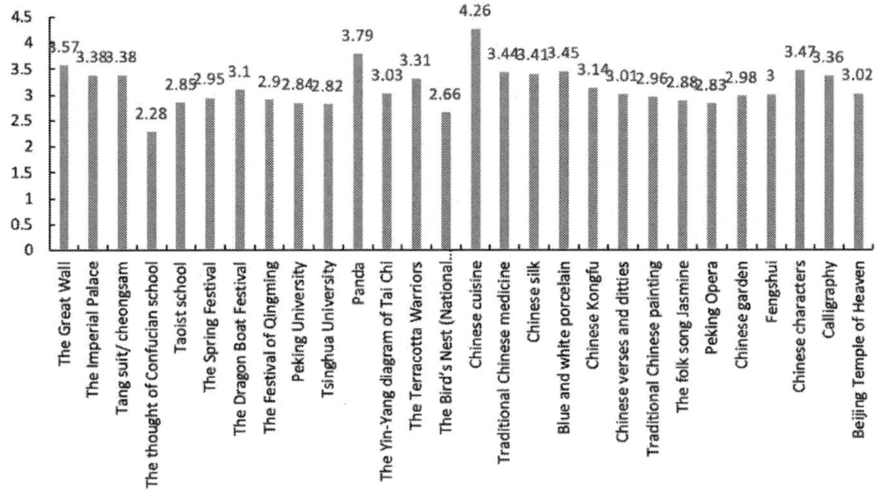

Figure 5.2 Japanese people's affinity for Chinese cultural symbols

Source: The 3rd survey.

4, with most scoring around 3, representing a neutral attitude. The ranking of different types of cultural symbols reveal that Japanese people have a higher affinity for Chinese cultural symbols that can be considered as token symbols, living symbols and educational symbols, while holding a lower affinity for symbols of philosophical thought and artistic symbols. The survey data show that older Japanese people held a greater affinity for Chinese cultural symbols overall.

5.2.2 *Japanese people's interest in and contact with the forms of expression of Chinese culture*

The data from the second survey questionnaire show that Japanese respondents' favorite forms of Chinese culture were Chinese food (56.6%), which matches Japanese people's first impression of China as revealed in the first survey. After Chinese food, Japanese people ranked Chinese history second at 53.3%, then Chinese scenic spots, historic sites, and Chinese Kongfu (23.6%), and then Chinese architecture and gardens (16.1%), Chinese film (15.9%), Chinese characters (15.2%), and Chinese acrobatics (15.0%)—all of which ranged between 10% and 20%. The forms of Chinese culture that Japanese people expressed least interested in were Chinese dance (2.6%) and Chinese drama (4.3%). Additionally, 14% of interviewees expressed no interest in any form Chinese cultural expression listed in Figure 5.3.

Meanwhile, the survey data indicate that the level of the interviewees' interest in Chinese culture is significantly related to their sex, age, and

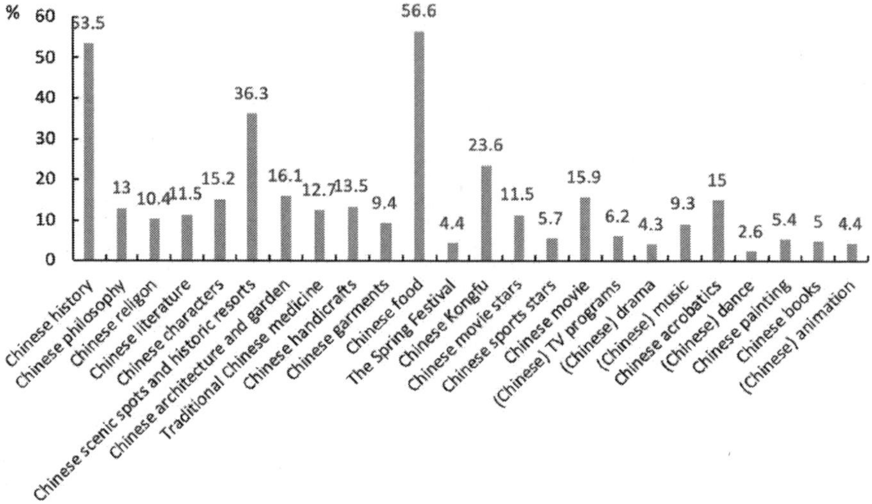

Figure 5.3 Percentage of Japanese people interested in Chinese culture

Source: The 2nd survey.

Chinese language skill. Female interviewees expressed more interest in Chinese culture than male interviewees. Interviewee interest in Chinese culture was positively correlated with age, as well as with spoken Chinese language ability.

Concurrently, the survey questionnaire examined which forms of Chinese culture Japanese people report having contact with in their daily life. Figure 5.4 shows that Chinese food is the form of expression of Chinese culture that Japanese people have greatest contact with, reaching 60.5% of respondents. Chinese history ranked second at 27.9%, followed by Chinese characters (21.5%) and Chinese film (17.4%). For the remaining cultural forms mentioned in the survey, fewer than 10% of Japanese respondents reported contact. Eighteen percent of the interviewees expressed that they had no contact with any of the forms of Chinese cultural expression listed in the questionnaire.

Meanwhile, we surveyed respondents on several aspects of Chinese language, Chinese food, TCM, and Chinese Kongfu to explore how deeply Japanese people had contact with these forms of Chinese cultural expression.

5.2.2.1 *Learning Chinese language*

As shown in Figure 5.5, 14.3% of interviewees expressed that they had studied Chinese language, 21.4% of interviewees expressed the desire to study Chinese in the future, while 64.3% of interviewees expressed that they had not studied and would not study Chinese.

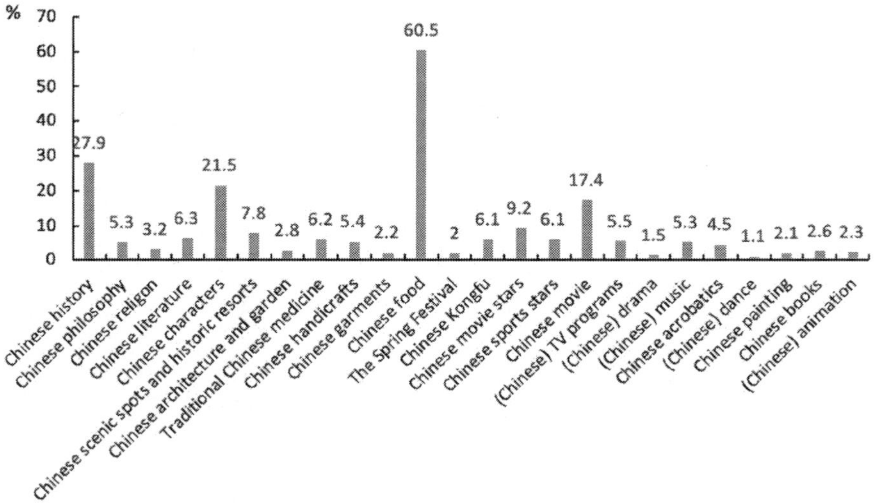

Figure 5.4 Percentage of Japanese people's contact with forms of Chinese culture

Source: The 2nd survey.

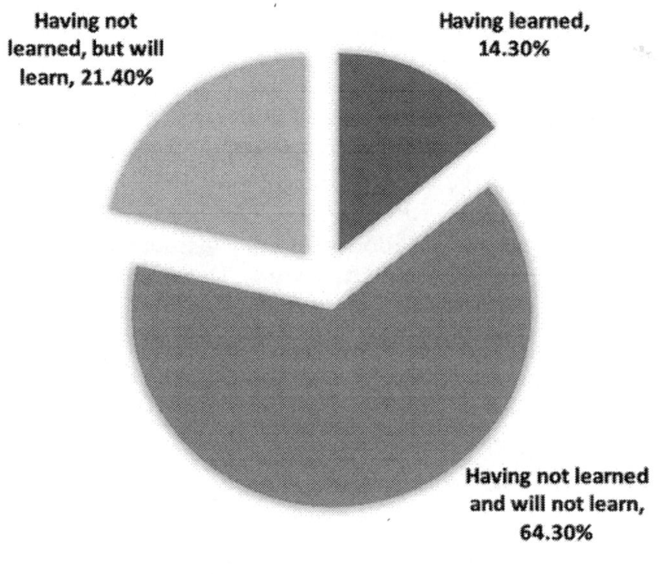

Figure 5.5 Information on learning Chinese language of the interviewees

Source: The 3rd survey.

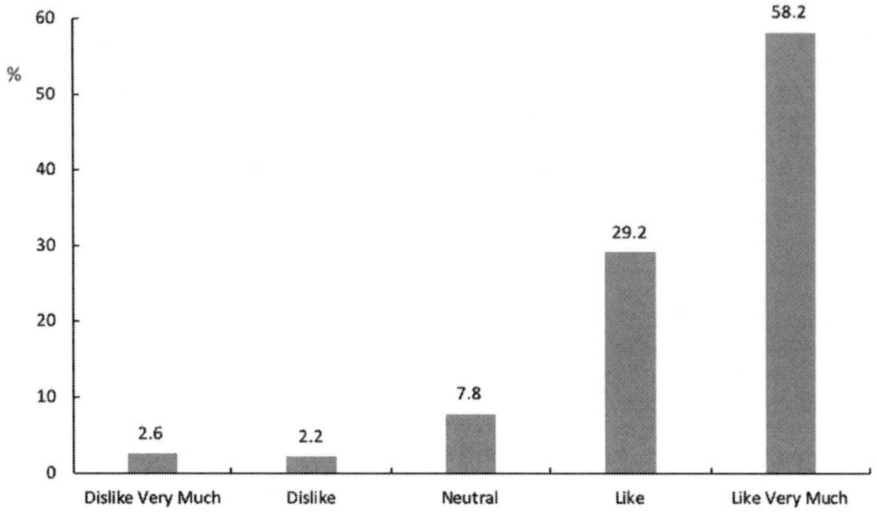

Figure 5.6 Japanese people's affinity for Chinese food

Source: The 3rd survey.

Of the interviewees having studied Chinese language, 71.4% do not use Chinese at all in their daily life, 24% use Chinese language occasionally, and only 4.6% use Chinese language regularly.

5.2.2.2 *Chinese food*

The survey questioned interviewees on how often they ate Chinese food. Over 90% of the interviewees had eaten Chinese food at least once over the past year, and only 8.9% reported not eating Chinese food over the past year. About 72.7% reported eating Chinese food 1 to 5 times per month on an average, while 12.3% ate Chinese food 6 to 11 times per month. About 2.3% reported eating Chinese food over 24 times per month. These data show that Chinese food is very popular with Japanese people.

Not surprisingly, the survey also showed that Japanese people like Chinese food overall. As Figure 5.6 indicates, 87.4% of interviewees reported they either liked or strongly liked Chinese food, and only 4.8% expressed either dislike or strong dislike of Chinese food. According to the five-level scale, affinity for Chinese food among interviewees scored a mean value of 4.38, indicating a strong affinity for Chinese food.

5.2.2.3 *Medical treatment with TCM*

The majority of Japanese respondents agreed that TCM has curative effects. As shown in Figure 5.7, over 60% of the interviewees thought that TCM

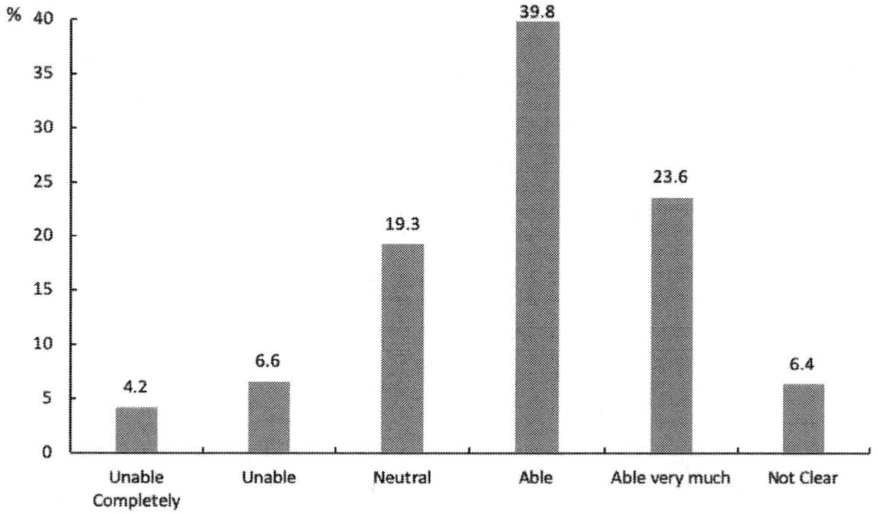

Figure 5.7 Japanese people's views on whether TCM can treat diseases

Source: The 3rd survey.

can treat diseases, only 10.8% disagreed that TCM could treat diseases and 19.3% held a neutral view. In terms of scoring, responses indicating that TCM was "completely unable" to treat disease were assigned the value of 1, and those stating that TCM was "very capable" of treating diseases were assigned a value of 5. Using this five-point scale, the mean response regarding TCM's curative effects was 3.77, indicating that Japanese respondents were in partial agreement that TCM is able to treat diseases.

5.2.2.4 *Chinese Kongfu*

Japanese respondents' affinity for Chinese martial arts was neutral. We assigned 1 to "Strongly Dislike" and 5 to "Like Very Much," and found a mean response value of 3.08 for Chinese martial arts, essentially indicating a neutral attitude on average. Specific data are shown in Figure 5.8. When asked whether they agree with including Chinese martial arts as an event in the Olympic Games, 35.5% of interviewees objected the proposal, 11% agreed, and 43.1% expressed a neutral view. We assigned a value of 1 to "Strongly Object" and 5 to "Strongly Agree," and found a mean response value of 2.58, indicating that on average respondents objected to including Chinese martial arts as an event in the Olympic Games. The questionnaire also surveyed interviewees on their own practice of Chinese martial arts, finding that 97.8% had not practiced Chinese martial arts over the past year.

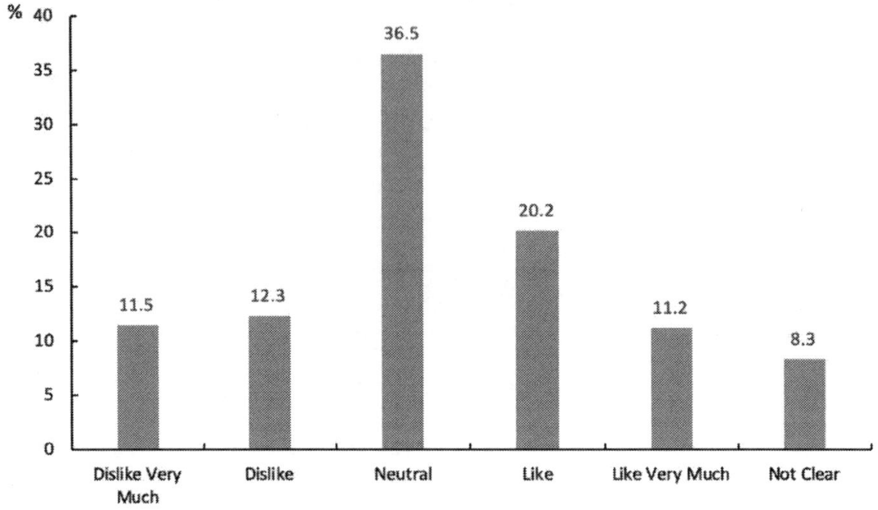

Figure 5.8 Japanese people's attitude toward Chinese Kongfu

Source: The third survey.

5.2.3 *Japanese people's purchase of and affinity for Chinese cultural products*

Regarding consumption of Chinese cultural products, the Japanese respondents reported low levels of consumption and purchase quantity regarding nine types of Chinese cultural products listed in the questionnaire—consisting of, books and periodicals, audio-visual products, music, movies, hand crafts, toys and games, and art works such as calligraphy. However, we noted that there remains significant potential for future Japanese uptake of Chinese cultural products, since each type of product surveyed found support among certain consumer groups represented in the survey. Furthermore, those interviewees who reported purchasing Chinese cultural products also reported purchasing a large quantity on an average, proving that Chinese cultural products are marketable to certain extent in Japan, but efforts should be made to create more opportunities for Japanese people to obtain access to Chinese cultural products and cultivate long-term consumption. Specific data are shown in Table 5.1.

The survey confirmed that one-third of the interviewees had experience with having purchased Chinese cultural products. Of the three buying channels listed in the questionnaire, domestic stores in Japan ranked as the top method, selected by over half of the interviewees, followed by purchases during trips to China and online. Specific data are shown in Figure 5.9.

On the whole, Japanese respondents expressed a low level of desire to buy Chinese cultural products. The survey used a 0–10 scale to quantify

Table 5.1 Japanese people's purchase for Chinese cultural products

Chinese cultural products	*The average purchase of the interviewees as a whole*	*The interviewees with the history of purchase*		
		Number	*Percentage*	*Average purchase*
Chinese books	0.73	185	15.1	4.82
Chinese periodicals	0.38	104	8.5	4.53
Chinese audio-visual products DVD	0.51	143	11.67	4.35
Chinese music products CD	0.52	147	12	4.36
Chinese audio-visual TV program products DVD	0.36	101	8.24	4.42
Chinese artistic handicrafts	0.69	202	16.49	4.19
Chinese animated games	0.31	55	4.49	6.87
Original Chinese toys (such as kite and diabolo)	0.65	192	15.67	4.15
Chinese calligraphy and painting	0.64	178	14.53	4.39

Source: The 3rd survey.

reported level of purchase intention, ranked from low to the high, and obtained a mean value of 2.61, demonstrating a low level of desire to buy Chinese cultural products.

In terms of awareness of Chinese cultural products and brands, the survey showed that Peking Opera and the Palace Museum ranked first and second among respondents, with 65.3% of respondents expressing awareness of Peking Opera, and 53.1% expressing awareness of the Palace Museum in Beijing. These were followed by Beijing Quanjude Roast Duck (36.7%) in third. Over 30% of the interviewees knew the phrase "Happy Spring Festival" and expressed awareness of "Shaolin Glory." The lowest awareness score was for the Year of Chinese Culture, with only 12.2% of respondents aware of this cultural exchange activity. Specific data are shown in Figure 5.10.

The questionnaire also surveyed respondents' like and dislike for these cultural icons and brands. We assigned 1 to "Strongly Dislike" and 5 to

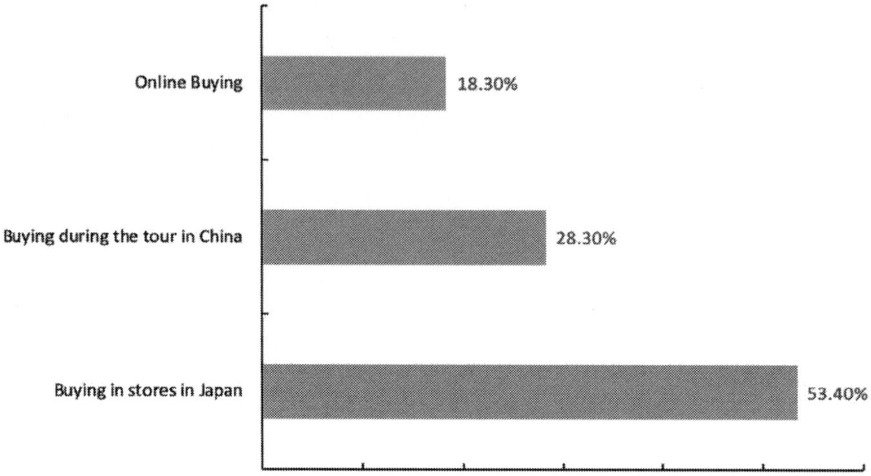

Figure 5.9 Channels through which Japanese people buy Chinese cultural products

Source: The 3rd survey.

"Like Very Much," and found a mean value of Japanese people's affinity for each item surveyed. The higher the mean, the higher the evaluation. Figure 5.11 shows that Japanese people's affinity for each of the listed Chinese cultural products and brands was basically neutral. Though the Palace Museum ranked first in terms of awareness, it scored a mean affinity of 3.52, between being neutral (3) and liking (4). Quanjuede Roast Duck

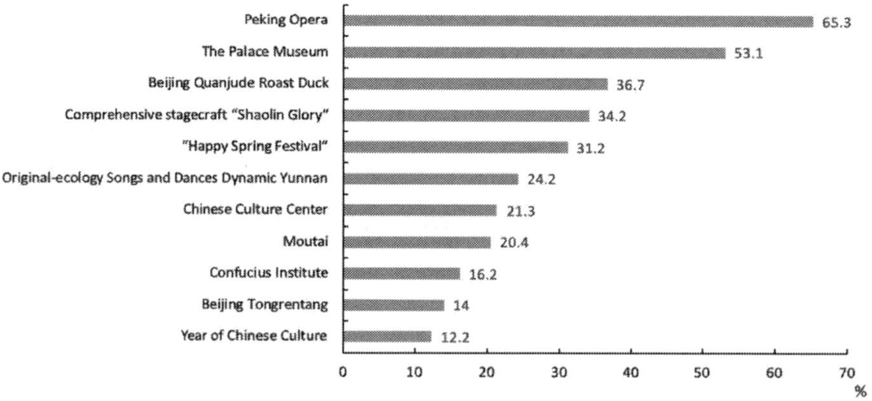

Figure 5.10 Japanese people's awareness of Chinese cultural product and service brands

Source: The 3rd survey.

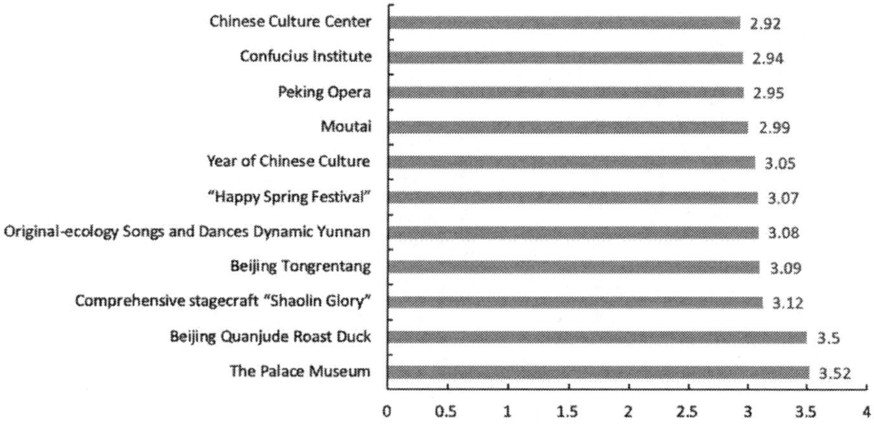

Figure 5.11 Japanese people's affinity for brands of Chinese cultural products

Source: The 3rd survey.

and Shaolin Glory ranked second and third in terms of affinity, while the Chinese Culture Center was given the lowest level of affinity.

5.2.4 *Japanese people's evaluation on Confucius Institute*

The Confucius Institute is a non-profit Sino-foreign cooperative educational organization that conducts Chinese language teaching, popularizes Chinese culture, enhances Sino-foreign cultural exchange and serves as an overall Chinese government vehicle for cultural diplomacy. The first Confucius Institute opened in South Korea by China in November 2004. As of year-end 2014, 475 Confucius Institutes had been established in more than 120 countries and world regions, including 13 in Japan. Figures 5.10 and 5.11 show that Japanese people have a low awareness of the Confucius Institute—only 16.2% reported knowing about the Institute. In addition, respondents' affinity for the Institute is essentially neutral.

To understand influence of the Confucius Institute in Japan, the survey included several questions looking at whether Confucius Institutes could be an effective channel for Japanese people to understand Chinese culture. The data show that among those who did know Confucius Institute, 23% thought that Confucius Institutes helped them understand Chinese culture, and 27% expressed that Confucius Institutes served as an effective channel for Japanese people to understand Chinese culture. Most Japanese people able to speak Chinese have some understanding of Confucius Institutes, and expressed awareness and recognition of the active role of the Institute in teaching the Chinese language and spreading Chinese culture. Therefore, Confucius Institutes do make some contribution to enhancing Japanese

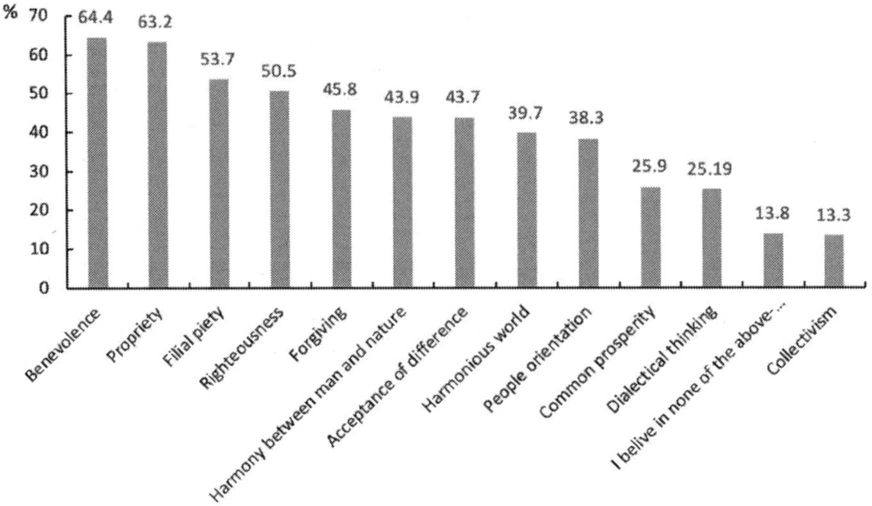

Figure 5.12 Japanese people's identification with Chinese cultural values

Source: The 2nd survey.

understanding of Chinese language and culture, as well as to strengthening educational and cultural exchange and cooperation between China and Japan. On the other hand, the survey shows that the Confucius Institute's influence in Japan remains low, and the Confucius Institute has not become an influential cultural brand or widely demonstrated its ability to spread and popularize Chinese culture.

5.2.5 *Japanese people's identification with Chinese cultural values*

As shown in Figure 5.12, when asking Japanese people's agreement with some Chinese values, over half of respondents expressed agreement with values surveyed as representative of traditional Chinese culture, such as benevolence (64.5% agreement), propriety (62.9%), filial piety (53.5%), and righteousness (50.1%). More than one-third of respondents also expressed support for the values of forgiveness, harmony between man and nature, acceptance of difference, world harmony, and people oriented. Only a low proportion of Japanese expressed support for modern values surveyed such as common prosperity, dialectical thinking, and collectivism. As discussed in Chapter 1, the Japanese respondents expressed high levels of identification with certain Chinese cultural values, but generally think Chinese people have a lower identification with such values than themselves.

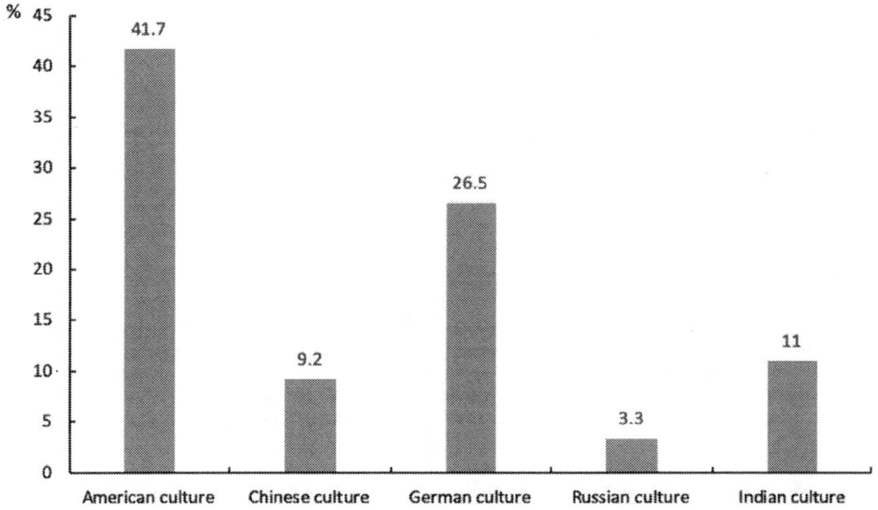

Figure 5.13 Percentage of Japanese people's affinity for Chinese, American, German, Russian, and Indian cultures

Source: The 2nd survey.

5.2.6 *Japanese people's affinity for Chinese culture*

As shown in Figure 5.13, of Chinese, American, German, Russian, and Indian cultures, the survey respondents expressed the highest affinity for American culture, with the proportion higher than 40%, followed by German culture (26.5%), Indian culture (11%), Chinese culture (9.2%), and Russian culture at the lowest with only 3.3%. These proportions reveal that although China and Japan have a long history of cultural exchange, and Japanese culture was deeply influenced by Chinese culture in history, yet since the Westernization policy of Japan, Chinese culture has become less and less attractive to Japanese people, and their affinity for Chinese culture is lower than for European and American cultures of the Western world.

5.3 Chinese institutional culture in the eyes of the Japanese

5.3.1 *Japanese people's understanding of current social system and political party system of China*

The survey also included a question concerning whether the respondents could identify China's current social system. Fewer than one-third of respondents, or 26.9%, provided a definite answer. Excluding those who answered Not Clear, 70% of the interviewees did not know that China

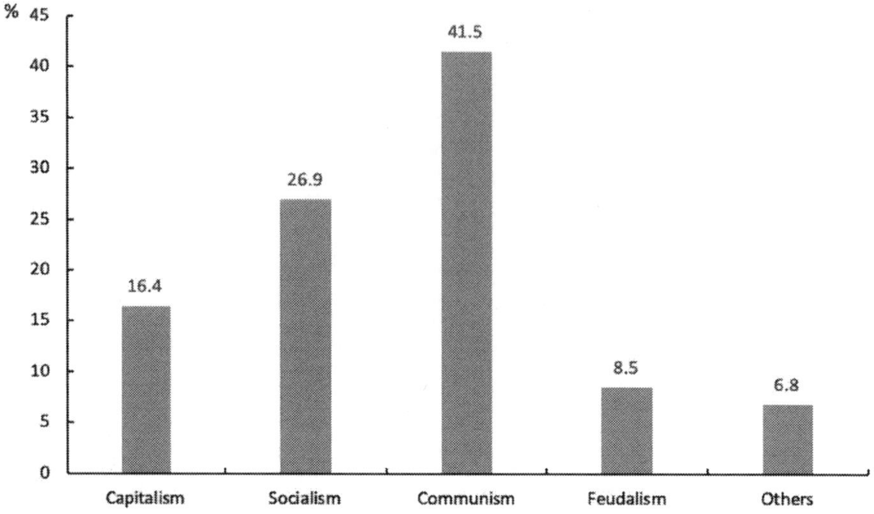

Figure 5.14 Japanese awareness of current social system of China

Source: The 2nd survey.

currently follows a socialist system. About 16.4% of respondents considered China as having a capitalist system. About 41.5% held that China has a communist system, and 8.5% thought that China has a feudalist system. These responses suggest that Japanese people have a limited and one-sided understanding of Chinese society. Specific data are shown in Figure 5.14.

Figure 5.15 shows that only one-fourth of interviewees identified China's current political system as a CPC-led multi-party cooperation system. Excluding those who answered "Not Clear," 66.8% of interviewees expressed the view that China's political party system is a one-party system. Few interviewees thought that China's political party system was a two-party system or a multi-party system. Meanwhile, factors of gender, education level, and Chinese language ability had a significant influence on whether the interviewees recognized China's political party system as a CPC-led multi-party cooperative system—namely, recognition of China as a CPC-led multi-party cooperative system was correlated with male gender, Chinese language ability, and education level.

5.3.2 *Japanese evaluation of China's political system*

As shown in Figure 5.16, one-fourth of Japanese respondents expressed agreement that China's political system promotes China's economic development. Nearly 40% of Japanese people expressed the view that China's political system restrains China's economic development. About 38% responded "Not Clear" or expressed a neutral view. On a five-point scale,

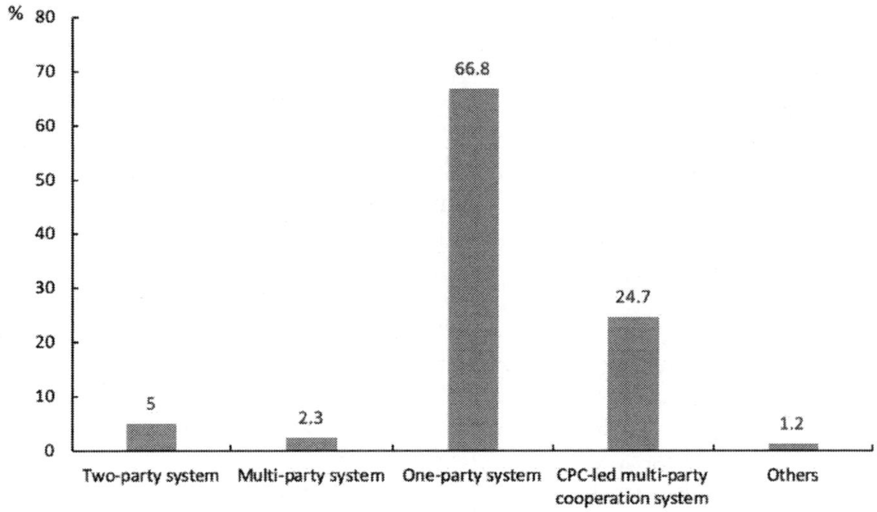

Figure 5.15 Percentage of Japanese people's awareness of the political party system of China

Source: The 2nd survey.

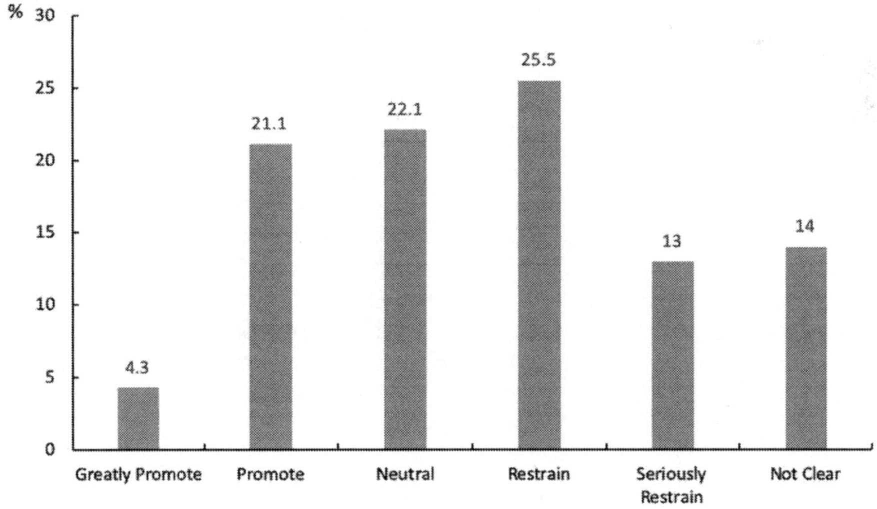

Figure 5.16 Does China's political system promote or restrain the economic development of China

Source: The 2nd survey.

the survey assigned a value of 1 to responses that China's political system "Seriously Restrains" economic development, and a value of 5 to responses that China's political system "Greatly Promotes" economic development, and excluded the response "Not Clear." The mean value of responses was 2.75, showing that Japanese responses indicated that the Chinese political system's influence on its economic development ranged between neutral and negative. This suggests that most Japanese people believe that China's political system restrains China's economic development.

5.4 Survey analysis

The analysis of the survey and interview data reveals that: first, the survey results suggest that Chinese culture has become less attractive to Japanese people. On the whole, Japanese people have high awareness of token Chinese cultural symbols, and have some degree of affinity for those Chinese cultural symbols. Yet we note that identification and affinity focus on the most superficial elements of Chinese culture, such as Chinese food, Chinese characters, the panda, and the Great Wall, and traditional cultural values of benevolence, righteousness, propriety, wisdom, and faith. In contrast, Japanese people have a relatively low identification with institutional Chinese culture and insufficient understanding of China's political and economic systems. Those issues that currently affect Sino-Japanese relations, such as issue of Japan's historical conflicts with China, the Taiwan issue, and territorial disputes, all relate more closely with institutional aspects and values. In particular, we note that when asked to compare the cultures of Western countries such as the United States and Germany with that of China, Japanese consider Chinese culture as less attractive.

Most Japanese journalists and scholars interviewed for this research express strong appreciation for traditional Chinese culture and report frequent contact with certain aspects, such as landscape painting, porcelain, Chinese characters, and Confucianism. However, such elements of traditional Chinese culture have been deeply integrated into Japanese culture for so long that many Japanese do not feel they belong exclusively to Chinese culture. Meanwhile, in contemporary Japan, the value of individualism has grown more prominent while traditional values are weakening. For the younger generation of Japanese, it is hard to accept traditional Chinese values of benevolence, righteousness, propriety, wisdom, and faith, as these values may seem too utopian, as some recent scholarly studies have confirmed. For example, in the interview with Japanese employees of Sony Corporation, Zhang Li found that a very large portion of the interviewees expressed that they are less interested in and do not understand Chinese culture. At the same time, over 40% of the Japanese consider that Chinese and Japanese cultures are inextricably linked, and feel that Chinese culture had provided the basic blocks of Japanese culture. For example, respondents considered that Confucian culture has had a far-reaching influence on

Japan. On the other hand, respondents also felt that Japanese culture has evolved and developed on its own, and grown apart from Chinese culture.[12]

Therefore, although Japanese people remain conscious of traditional Chinese culture and its values due to their historical influence on Japan, but the appeal and influence of Chinese culture have declined among Japanese people due to the development of Japanese society and the influence of other countries. Given this, Chinese culture has a limited role in conveying Chinese soft power in Japan.

The survey also reveals that Japanese people have less contact of Chinese culture as a whole—including through books, films, dances, and television. Today, few Chinese writers and films are household names in Japan. In an interview, one Japanese journalist pointed out: American pop culture is most popular in Japan, and many Japanese people prefer it, particularly young people. This observation agrees with our survey data. The survey also reveals that, when compared with Germany, China, India, and Russia, Japanese people expressed a preference for the United States and American culture. American film, music, and books as well as other cultural products remain popular in Japan. The journalist also mentioned that of Asian countries, South Korean films and TV programs account for the highest market share and are easiest to market in Japan. In particular, after Japan and South Korea jointly hosted the 2002 FIFA World Cup, South Korean film, music, and TV programs became common in Japan. Another journalist mentioned that South Korean TV programs are popular among middle-aged Japanese women. Comparatively, Chinese TV programs are fewer and relatively less popular in Japan, which likely relates to the worsening Sino-Japanese relations to certain extent, but may also relate to the different content of Chinese TV programs, which is less appealing to Japanese audiences.

Many Japanese scholars remain interested in contemporary Chinese culture. One scholar interviewed for this study expressed that he was initially only interested in Chinese history rather than in modern Chinese culture. But after visiting China, he began to enjoy Chinese pop music and TV programs. Faye Wong, a famous Chinese pop singer, was his favorite, and he mentioned buying her CD. During our interview, the Japanese scholar pointed out that he was following the Chinese TV series *The Legend of Wu Mei Niang*. He began watching to study Chinese language, but later grew to like the story. He noted that the story helped him understand how Chinese thinking differs from that of the Japanese. Asked him whether he had any contact with Chinese film or TV programs when in Japan, he replied, "In Japan I have no daily consciousness of contact with Chinese things. The only field I deal with related to China is my field of study itself, namely Chinese politics. Given that I'm from Yokohama, I know that Yokohama has one of Japan's largest Chinatowns. Aside from these two aspects, in Japan I have no contact with Chinese cultural items such as films and performances."

By and large, most Japanese people have little interest in and seldom come into contact with modern Chinese culture. However, when Japanese happen to come across Chinese films, music, or TV, they often find the content appealing. In daily life, however, ordinary Japanese people lack such opportunities, and they report little intention to search for Chinese cultural products. Most Japanese people have little active interest in Chinese cultural products. Therefore, the issue of how to enhance the appeal of Chinese music, film, and TV series is difficult to resolve. China should learn from the experiences of the United States and South Korea, whose music, films, TV series, and other cultural products are popular in Japan—and even in China as well.

The extent to which Japanese lack understanding of China's social, political, and economic system has a major influence on Japanese views of China. The survey data show that less than 30% of Japanese people accurately understand China's current social and political systems. For this reason alone, we believe most Japanese views of China's social and political systems are based on incorrect understanding, which explains why most survey respondents expressed the view that China's current political system hinders the country's economic development. In our interviews, we found that the Japanese scholarly evaluation of China's political system was more objective and accurate. In one interview, a Japanese scholar and expert on China expressed the view that China's political system plays an important role in driving the country's economic development: "Over the past 30 years, China successfully managed the country's macroeconomic development, and this is important to acknowledge."

Another Japanese scholar expressed the view that there is no bad or good system, but only systems that are suitable or unsuitable for each country. China's political system is the choice of the Chinese people, and meets China's development needs. In a country like China with a vast territory and a huge population, power centralization is very necessary. In addition, for China, stability is the top priority. Without national peace and stability, all other issues are meaningless. To ensure stability, the most urgent need has been to develop economically and put food on the table. It should be said that China's current political and economic systems have successfully achieved those goals: China has become the second largest economy in the world and Chinese people enjoy vastly improved living standards versus those of the prior generation. Ordinary Japanese people lack understanding of China, particularly of China's social and political systems, so naturally they view China's political system negatively. From this angle, it is necessary and urgent to enhance mutual understanding between people in China and Japan.

5.5 Policy proposals

Analysis of the survey data reveals that younger Japanese people have relatively lower awareness and affinity for Chinese culture. In both China and Japan, young people will play a decisive role in the future of Sino-Japanese relations. Therefore, in promoting Chinese culture in Japan, China should make full use of social media and online activities such as microblogs, blogs, and video websites preferred by young Japanese, giving them greater access to Chinese music, film, and TV content, and thereby narrowing the gap in cultural access and understanding. China should rely on sporting events, science and technology innovation competitions, and other activities to enhance ties and understanding between students of both countries. Moreover, China can offer government scholarship programs and other types of cooperation educational programs to attract Japanese students to China for study, and thereby create opportunities for communication and exchange with Chinese students and help young Japanese people develop a deeper understanding of Chinese culture and society, and of China's political and economic systems, and enhance mutual understanding and trust. In April 2012, Mr. Cao Qiyong, a famous Hong Kong entrepreneur who studied at the University of Tokyo when he was young made a donation of RMB 20 million to Peking University for establishing the "Sino-Japanese Youth Exchange Center,"[13] with the goals of enhancing exchange and communication between young Chinese and Japanese students, deepening mutual trust and friendship, improving Sino-Japanese relations and promoting stability in East Asia. The program features arrangements for Chinese and Japanese students to live together for greater daily communication, joint recreational activities, and in-depth exchange of thinking. The program is considered a success.

To enhance cultural communication with young Japanese people and enable cultural exchange between Chinese and Japanese youth, China should also expand non-governmental cultural exchange between both countries. The Chinese government has played an important role in past Sino-Japanese cultural exchanges, but in recent years, inter-government cultural exchanges have decreased due to worsening Sino-Japanese relations. Before the normalization of the diplomatic relations between China and Japan, non-governmental exchanges in the economic, trade, and cultural fields help set the stage for improved bilateral relations. Against the backdrop of difficult Sino-Japanese relations today, China should enhance non-governmental cultural exchange and cooperation in order to ease tensions. Historically, China and Japan had many models of informal, non-governmental cultural exchange, which opened the door to improved formal ties. In the early 1970s, Ping Pong Diplomacy help break the cycle of long-term confrontation between China and the United States, and paved the road for official contact between the two governments. In February 2008, more than 250 musicians from the New York Philharmonic visited Pyongyang via Beijing for a historic Tour of North Korea, marking a historic step in cultural exchange between North Korea and the United States. Tension between North Korea and the United States remained, but the cultural exchange undoubtedly helped deepen mutual understanding between the two countries.

Today's Sino-Japanese relations are doubtless much better than those between North Korea and the United States in the present decade, or between China and the United States in the 1970s. Hence people-to-people cultural exchange in all its forms can have a greater benefit on public opinion in both China and Japan, and on improving Sino-Japanese relations. Just as Li Lanqing, former Vice Premier of the State Council of China, said during his visit to France in 2001, "cultural exchange means exchange of thoughts, feelings, and souls." Let the cultural exchange between China and Japan open a new round of communication of thoughts, feelings, and souls between the two countries.

Notes

1. Anholt, Simon. *Competitive Identity: The New Brand Management for Nations, Cities and Regions.* New York: Palgrave Macmillan, 2007.
2. Mark, Simon L. "Rethinking cultural diplomacy: The cultural diplomacy of New Zealand, the Canadian Federation and Quebec." Political Science 62.1(2010): 62–83.
3. Nye, Joseph. *Soft Power: The Means to Success in World Politics.* New York: Public Affairs, 2004.
4. McMurray, Ruth, and Muna Lee. *The Cultural Approach: Another Way in International Relations.* Chapel Hill: University of North Carolina Press, 1947.
5. Iriye, Akira. *Cultural Internationalism and World Order.* Maryland: The Johns Hopkins University Press, 1997.
6. Hu, Wentao. *American Cultural Diplomacy and Its Practice Related to China* [meiguo wenhua waijiao jiqi zai zhongguo de yunyong]. World Affairs Press, 2008.
7. Li, Zhi. *Cultural Diplomacy: An Interpretation Mode of Communication* [wenhuawaijiao: yizhong chuanboxue de jiedu]. Peking University Press, 2005.
8. Peng, Xinliang. *Cultural Diplomacy and China's Soft Power: A Globalized Perspective* [wenhua waijiao yu zhongguo de ruanshili: yizhong quanqiuhua de shijiao]. Foreign Language Teaching and Research Press, 2008.
9. Wang, Xiaode. *American Culture and Diplomacy* [meiguo wenhua yu waijiao]. World Affairs Press, 2008.
10. Jian, Taojie. "American Cultural Diplomacy after the Cold War and Its Influences on Sino-American Relations [lengzhanhou meiguo wenhua waijiao jiqi dui zhongmei guanxi de yingxiang]." Doctoral dissertation of Fudan University (2010): 32–34.
11. Full-text Record of the Forum on How should Chinese Culture Go Abroad. Ifeng.com, Nov. 6, 2011. Retrieved from http://cultule.ifeng.com/huodong/special/zhonghuawenhua/content-3/detail_2011_11/06/104-50871_0.shtml.
12. Zhang, Li. "The Japanese Views of China after the Cold War and the Influencing Factors [lengzhanhou ribenren zhongguoguan jiqi yingxiang yinsu yanjiu]." Master's thesis of East China Normal University (2013).
13. It has been renamed as the Asian Youth Center of Peking University.

6 China's media in the eyes of the Japanese

Mass media, as an important channel of international communications, plays a decisive role in shaping the national image of China. In recent years, with China paying more attention to cultural soft power and its national image abroad, policy makers have attached greater importance to the international communication capability of Chinese media. Mainstream Chinese media outlets, including the Xinhua News Agency, the People's Daily, CCTV, China National Radio, and China Radio International are actively working to improve their international communication capabilities, so as to better propagate Chinese culture, viewpoints, and perspectives and to enhance their international influence. So what role do Chinese media play in cultural communication and information exchange with Japan? How do Japanese people view Chinese media reporting? How do Chinese media influence or shape the image of China in Japan? In this chapter, we explore these questions on the basis of survey questionnaire data, and analyze the relationship between media reports and national image. In addition, based on the in-depth interviews with Japanese journalists, we also analyzed the criteria Japanese media use to select topics for coverage and the reasons journalists employ those criteria.

6.1 Media and national image

As an important information source, how mass media release information and reporting, its accuracy, truth, objectivity, format, topic selection, and quantity all have a major influence on public awareness, opinion, and behavior. Agenda setting and framing in communication theories probe such media effects.

Maxwell McCombs and Donald Shaw first proposed the theory of agenda setting, pointing out that the amount and prominence of media coverage of an event influence the audience's awareness and views about that event or issue, and thereby affect public opinion and individual behavior.[1] A study conducted by Wanta and Hu reveals that the increase of international news media reporting on international conflicts, terrorists, crime, and drug relating to the United States caused increased public concern about these topics.[2] A study by Soroka also finds that in the United States and the United Kingdom, the public's attention to diplomatic events are largely directed by reports in the mass media.[3]

The framing theory further explains the role of mass media in affecting public opinion through "selection and salience," namely "to select some aspects of a perceived reality and make them more salient in a communicating text, in such a way as to promote a particular problem definition, causal interpretation, moral evaluation, and/or treatment recommendation for the item described."[4] In news reporting, journalists or editors often highlight certain implications and opinions, propagating and upholding specific interests or values, and thus influencing the audiences' understanding of and decisions about relevant figures or events. Brewer and other scholars studied how news frames used by media in reporting an event in a country can influence the image of the country through a controlled experiment. The experiment indicated that, when American media's news frame focuses on the Mexican government's efforts in controlling drug and active cooperation with the United States to fight against drug smuggling, American audiences had a positive impression of Mexico; but when the news frame centered on drug abuse in Mexico and its bad influences on the United States, American audiences had a negative impression of Mexico.[5] In addition, combining opinion poll and content analysis data, Wanta, Golan, and Lee studied the correlation between media reporting and public awareness of country image, finding that negative reporting in U.S. media on other countries often causes negative impression of other countries among American audiences.[6]

Some studies show that when the situations allow, most people prefer to make judgments based on their own personal experiences. However, for those with no opportunity for gaining personal experience with an issue or have no access to first-hand information, people have to make judgments mainly through the filter of mass media.[7] Most people have no personal experiences in other countries, so their awareness and evaluation of other countries are mainly based on mass media reporting, making mass media vital to shaping national image.

There exist a number of studies that focus on analysis of the relationship between Japanese media reporting and the image of China in Japan. Liu Linli's *The Image of China in the Mass Media of Japan*, analyzes present-day Japanese newspaper reporting and its influence on China's national image in Japan.[8] Zhan Qi and Liu Yan, through analysis of the reports on China in the *Asahi Shimbun*'s English edition, explore the media image of China in Japan and its inspiration for China's foreign propaganda.[9] Luo Hailong, with reference to international political theory and communication theory, undertakes a macro-analysis of Japanese media reporting on China on the image of China from the perspective of constructivism.[10] Ruan Suqian, by analyzing specific cases of Japanese media reporting related to China, compares the difference of reporting between China and Japan and their influence on the national image of the two countries.[11] Zhao Xinli, considering the various characteristics of Japanese media reports on China, analyzes the image of China displayed in two Japanese documentary films, *Notes on a Trip on China's Railways* and *Dynamic China*, pointing out that objective and accurate reporting in Japanese media on China can help Japanese people understand the real China.[12]

These studies mostly analyze the image of China in Japanese media using content analysis. Fewer studies employ survey questionnaires to understand media influences on national image. In the following paragraphs, we will explore the channels Japanese people use to understand China and their contact with and evaluation of Chinese media—and analyze how media reporting has influenced formation of Japanese views of China.

6.2 Channels for Japanese to understand China and their contact with and evaluation of Chinese media

As noted above, our survey shows that Japanese respondents reported that they rely mainly on Japanese media to understand China and rarely come into contact with or access Chinese media. Japanese people generally express the view that reporting in Chinese media are less objective and accurate, and they have low trust in Chinese media.

6.2.1 *Channels and ways for Japanese to understand China*

In the second survey, questionnaires were distributed to Japanese people residing in Japan. This survey showed that 95% of respondents reported mainly obtaining information on China through domestic Japanese media, and 14% of respondents argued that their understanding of China comes mainly from reporting in Japanese media and that of countries other than China. Only 9% of Japanese respondents said Mainland Chinese media was one of the channels through which they obtained an understanding of China. The data in Figure 6.1 show that Chinese people, Chinese goods, and Chinese restaurants in Japan serve as China's main national image ambassador for exchange between China and Japan, and are the main window for regular Japanese people to understand China. Regrettably, the Confucius Institute, which has been promoted by the Chinese government for propagation of Chinese culture abroad, has almost no influence on Japanese understanding of China.

In our interviews, many respondents frankly informed us that most Japanese people with no knowledge of the Chinese language have little choice other than to rely on Japanese media to understand China. This is normal, since ordinary people usually depend on their domestic media to obtain information. Therefore, how Japanese media report on China has the greatest direct influence on Japanese views of China.

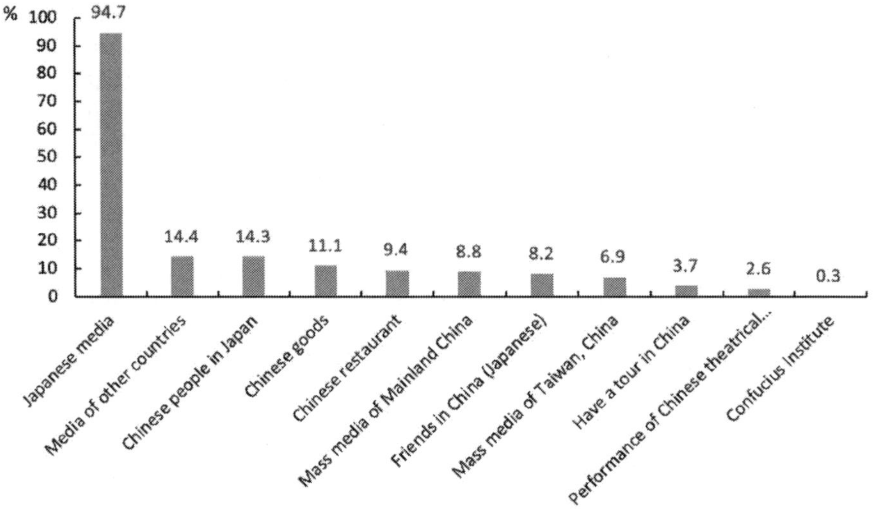

Figure 6.1 Main channels through which Japanese people understand China

Source: The 2nd survey.

In the survey, over 80% of Japanese respondents expressed that TV is their most important communication channel for understanding China, which reflects the immense influence of television media on public opinion. Internet and newspapers are also major information sources, with proportions over 50%, followed by periodicals (18.9%), books (14%), radio (7.5%), film (6.1%), and advertisements (ranked last at only 2.2%) (see Figure 6.2). In the interviews, Japanese journalists and scholars in China also noted that with the development of social media such as microblogs and WeChat, they depend more on the Internet to obtain information for new reports. Due to the lack of opportunities for exchange with Chinese government officials and also a shortage of other information sources, journalists also use domestic Chinese media to understand the intentions of the Chinese government. This includes outlets such as the Xinhua News Agency, People's Daily, CCTV, and Caixin. However, these Japanese journalists also pointed out that they do not trust Chinese media and usually take reports by Chinese media as a reference only, and seek to confirm information they provide.

The development of new media and the Internet greatly improves the efficiency of information exchange, and enables regular people to use tools such as Facebook, microblogs, and Wikipedia to obtain information and data about other countries. The survey data show that the most commonly used online channel for understanding China was Japanese media news websites. As shown in Figure 6.3, over half of respondents mainly rely on such news websites to understand China, showing that traditional media

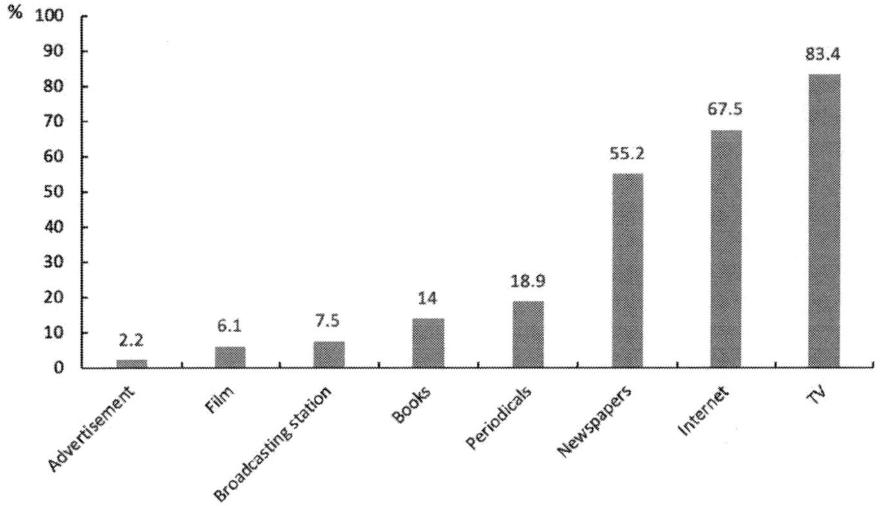

Figure 6.2 Main forms of media by which Japanese people understand China

Source: The 2nd survey.

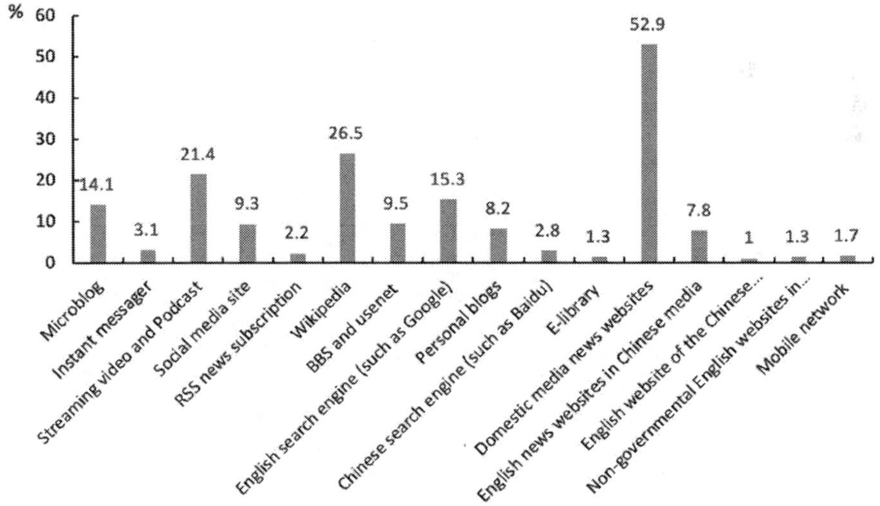

Figure 6.3 Online channels through which Japanese people understand China

Source: The 2nd survey.

retains influence on new media. Nearly 30% of respondents reported that they consult Wikipedia for information on issues and events connected China. In addition, Internet, video, podcasts, blogs, and microblogs were also popular online channels for understanding China. Other online apps are relatively little used.

6.2.2 *Japanese contact with and evaluation on Chinese media*

Over the past year, survey respondents reported the following frequency of contact with Chinese media: Once a while (1–5 times): CCTV English News Channel (10.2%); CCTV Chinese International Channel, People's Daily Overseas Edition, the website of China News Agency, and Xinhuanet.com (all over 5%); and most frequently (6 times and more): www.dbw.cn/Japanese (1.3%), the Japanese channel of People's Daily (1.2%) and CCTV English News Channel (1.1%), respectively (see Figure 6.4). On the whole, Japanese people have little contact with Chinese media.

In the interviews, with the exception of a single Japanese scholar who said he receives a free copy of *People's China* mailed to him by a friend in the publishing house, all other interviewees stated that they had no contact with Chinese media aimed at foreign propaganda, such as the CRI Japanese channel or special Japanese programs of Xinhuanet.com and people.cn. Those Japanese people who speak Chinese prefer to use domestic Chinese media such as the Xinhua News Agency and People's Daily. The one scholar expressed that, during his period of study in China, he most often read the People's Daily, mainly as a way to understand the views of the

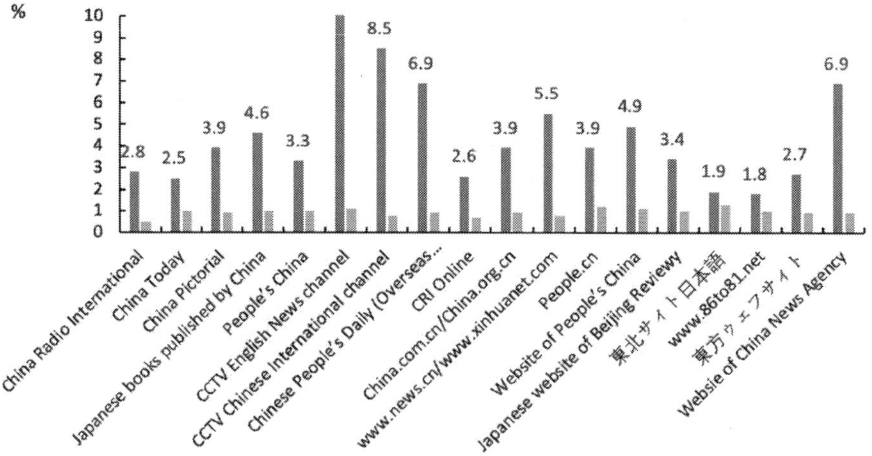

Figure 6.4 Frequency that Japanese people contact Chinese media

Source: The 2nd survey.

Chinese government, and what the government wanted people to know. In addition, he often reads other Chinese media such as Finance & Economics and caixin.com, and Hong Kong media such as Ta Kung Pao. In addition to Chinese media, he stated that personal exchanges with Chinese friends was an important information channel.

There are many explanations for the limited contact Japanese people have with Chinese media, such as language barriers, limited opportunities, different viewing habits, and the relative appeal of different media. Among these, the appeal of different media is the most fundamental and core explanation. In our first survey, in which two thirds of interviewees were Japanese students and corporate employees living in Beijing, most of whom faced no language barrier and could easily access any type of Chinese media. The survey results nevertheless showed that respondents preferred domestic Japanese media and European or American English-language media, and rarely turned to Chinese media—with fewer than 30% reporting that they used Chinese media. In our surveys and interviews, interviewees generally expressed lower trust in Chinese media. Meanwhile, compared with dominant European/American media such as the BBC and CNN, Chinese media are relatively weak in terms of international recognition and influence.

The Japanese public has the highest trust in information from the Internet, Japanese public media, and Reuters. Figure 6.5 lists the degrees of trust reported by Japanese respondents for various kinds of media (excluding responses of "Not Clear"). The results clearly show that the Japanese public places a higher degree of trust in the Internet sources than in news publications and TV stations. The Internet, as a new media for two-way

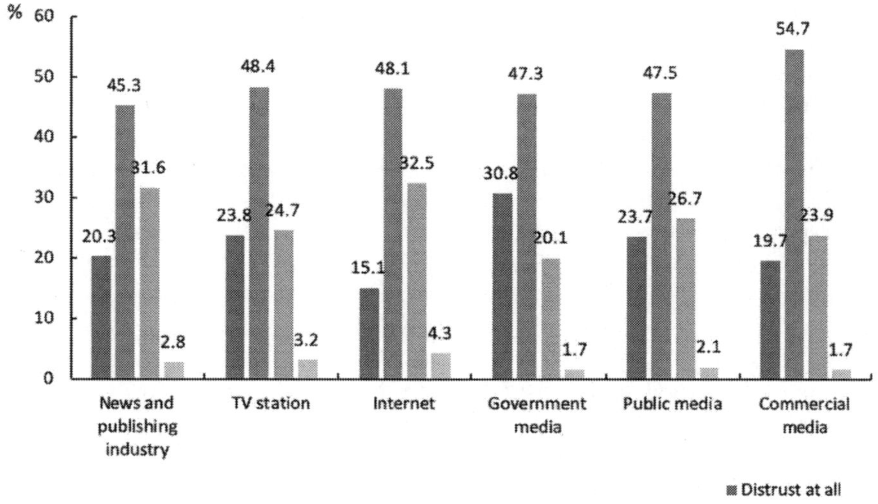

Figure 6.5 Japanese trust in different media

Source: The 2nd survey.

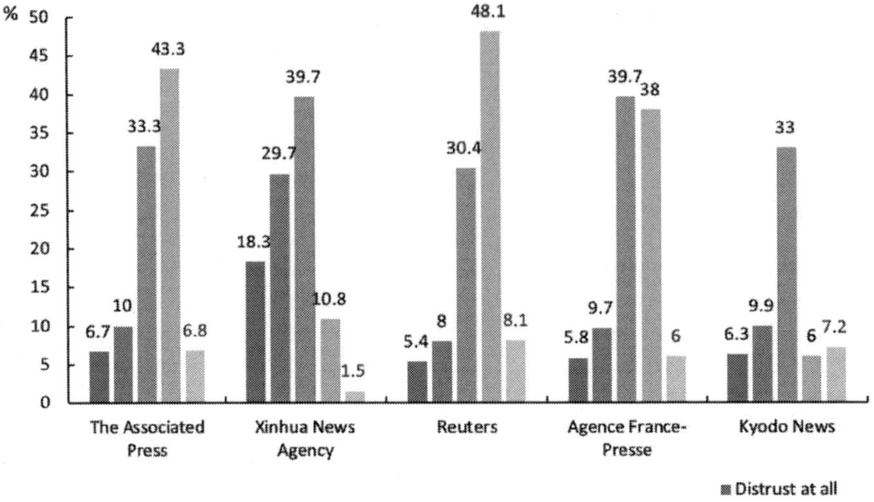

Figure 6.6 Japanese trust in main news agencies

Source: The 2nd survey.

communication that permits users to develop their own original content for widespread dissemination, has replaced the near-monopoly on news-related discourse once held by traditional media and various interest groups. The Internet promotes diversification in both information and discussion. These characteristics may encourage people to place greater trust in information from the Internet. Meanwhile, the Japanese public have a higher trust in public media than in commercial and government media. Of the major international news agencies, the Japanese public trusts Reuters most, followed by Kyodo News Service, the Associated Press, and Agence France-Presse. Ranked last was Xinhua News Agency at only 12.3% (see Figure 6.6).

The Japanese public generally considers reports in Chinese media untrustworthy and inaccurate. The data in Table 6.1 indicate that the Japanese public places an extremely low degree of trust in Chinese media. Only 4% of respondents reported that they either trust or somewhat trust Chinese media. Their impression of Chinese media as a whole is that the reporting is inaccurate and unbalanced, the perspective of the analysis is incomplete, and the news is less timely and readable. This may relate to characteristics of the Chinese media system on the one hand, and to the negative views of the Japanese audiences against China on the other hand. In our interviews, some Japanese scholars expressed the view that reports in Japanese media are also not absolutely accurate and objective, but the Japanese media are free and each media source can adopt its own standpoint, so their reporting angles on China are different. Some media are relatively friendly to China, some not. By reading or viewing more media reports about a subject, one can obtain more objective information. The difference between the Chinese media system and that of Japan, in the eyes of the Japanese audience, is

Table 6.1 Japanese impressions of Chinese media

Chinese media	*Agree*	*Disagree*	*Neutral/not clear*	*Mean (1= disagree, 5 = agree very much)*
Trustworthy	3.8%	67.2%	29.0%	1.99
Timely	10.5%	40.0%	49.1%	2.52
Analysis Perspective Complete	5.3%	58.3%	36.5%	2.17
Accurate	4.0%	64.6%	31.5%	2.04
Just	3.5%	67.3%	29.1%	1.94
Strong readability	7.7%	29.7%	62.6%	2.61

Source: The 2nd survey

that Chinese media reporting is controlled by the government, making its reporting less trustworthy. In fact, some scholarly analysis of Japanese media reporting content has shown that Japanese coverage includes subjective and one-sided reporting. Different Japanese media may have different reporting viewpoints, but people usually prefer to turn to the media outlets that hold the same views as they do. Therefore, the diversity does not necessarily lead to objectivity and accuracy.

6.2.3 *Influences of Chinese media on the Japanese views of China*

When respondents were asked whether Chinese media is helpful for their understanding of China, over half (57%) of respondents answered that it was no help, 30% held a neutral view, and only about 10% replied in the affirmative. These results follow from the other findings of the surveys: Japanese people rarely have contact with Chinese media, and in addition they largely distrust Chinese media. If a person neither uses nor trusts a media source, its information is naturally unhelpful.

How can the Japanese public's contact with and evaluation of Chinese media influence their image of China? To answer the question, we take respondents' opinion on "whether China threatens world peace" as the dependent variable and consider other factors as independent variables—namely, gender; age; Chinese language ability; having visited China; having Chinese friends; having an interest in, contact with, and evaluation of Chinese culture; and contact with and evaluation of Chinese media, to carry out multiple regression analysis. As shown in Table 6.2, the factors such as sex, age, having been to China, and contact with and evaluation of Chinese media have significant influence on respondent's views on "Whether China threatens world peace." That is to say, male respondents, older respondents, those who reported having visited China, those who reported less contact with Chinese media, and those with more negative evaluation of Chinese media tended to express the view that China's development threatens world

Table 6.2 Multiple regression analysis of factors influencing Japanese people's opinion of "whether China threatens world peace" ($N = 1038$)

	Whether China threatens world peace	
Independent variable	*Std. Beta*	*Total R2*
Sex	0.11***	
Age	0.10 ***	
Able to speak Chinese or not	0.02	
Having been to China or not	0.07*	
Having Chinese friends or not	0.02	
Interest in Chinese culture	0.08	
Contact with Chinese culture	–0.06	
Evaluation on Chinese culture	0.02	
Contact with Chinese media	–0.10**	
Evaluation on Chinese media	–0.26 ***	0.12 ***

Note: *$P \le 0.05$, **$P \le 0.01$, ***$P \le 0.001$.

Source: The 2nd survey

peace. Those Japanese people who have more frequent contact with Chinese media and hold a more positive view of Chinese media are more confident in China's peaceful rise.

Similarly, we take respondents' opinions on "whether you like or dislike China" as the dependent variable and consider the same factors from above as independent variables—namely, gender; age; Chinese language ability; having visited China; having Chinese friends; having an interest in, contact with, and evaluation of Chinese culture; and contact with and evaluation of Chinese media, to carry out logic regression analysis and try to identify the factors correlating with affinity for China. The data in Table 6.3 show that male respondents, those reporting more interest in Chinese culture,

Table 6.3 Logic regression analysis of the factors influencing Japanese affinity for China ($N = 1038$)

Independent variable	*Std. Beta*	*Wats*	*Exp (B)*
Sex	0.85*	3.89	2.35
Age	0	0	1
Able to speak Chinese or not	–0.14	0.04	0.87
Having been to China or not	0.27	0.41	1.31
Having Chinese friends or not	0.44	1.5	1.55
Interest in Chinese culture	0.14***	10.85	1.15
Contact with Chinese culture	0.15*	5.88	0.86
Evaluation on Chinese culture	0.41	1.86	1.51
Contact with China's media	0.10**	7.90	1.1
Evaluation on Chinese media	0.16***	12.05	1.18

Note: Chi-square = 70.63, $P \le 0.001$, *$P \le 0.05$, **$P \le 0.01$, ***$P \le 0.001$.

Source: The 2nd survey.

those reporting more contact with Chinese media and having a more positive evaluation of Chinese media also report having a more positive view of China.

The results of the two regression analyses reveal that more contact with Chinese media and a more positive evaluation of Chinese media people causes a more positive image of China, which supports the view that media play a decisive role in shaping the image of a country.

6.3 Survey analysis

6.3.1 *Japanese media report more on China but the topics are mostly negative*

The main purpose of our questionnaire was to understand Japanese people's contact with and evaluation of Chinese media. The survey results show that Japanese respondents mainly depend on domestic Japanese media for information on China. For this reason, in our interviews with Japanese journalists, we particularly asked them for their perspective on how media select topics and trends in reporting about China, to understand the sources for Japanese people's views of China. The journalists expressed the view that aside from media coverage of Sino-Japanese economic development, cultural exchanges, China's development of science and technology—particularly in aerospace and activities of Japanese companies in China—Japanese media also provide coverage of China's growing military strength, environmental problems, rich-poor gap, corruption, food safety issues, and disputes between China and Japan. All such issues are closely linked with Japanese people and are topics of high interest to the Japanese public. For example, Japanese consumers purchase imported Chinese foodstuffs such as vegetables, dumplings, and steamed meat buns, so they are naturally interested in reporting on Chinese food safety concerns. Moreover, the journalists interviewed admitted that Japanese media reports on China occasionally contain exaggerations.

Our survey shows that over half of Japanese respondents considered that Japanese media reporting on China as mainly negative, and consider that reporting has low accuracy and objectivity. This result agrees with several scholarly studies on Japanese media reporting. Zhang Yu analyzed contents of the news reports on China in Asahi Shimbun and Yomiuri Shinbun from 1995 to 2005, and explored the content of media reports and perspectives included nine topic categories of Chinese politics, economy, military, and diplomacy. Zhang's analysis found that Japanese media reports on China mainly ranged from neutral to negative.[13]

In recent years, negative coverage of China has increased in both quantity and proportion. In the 1980s and 1990s, reports on China in Japanese media focused mainly on economic news and remained relatively objective. In the past decade, given changes in Sino-Japanese relations, reporting on China has shifted focus toward China's military, environmental quality, and food safety. In our interviews, several journalists pointed out that before 2000, reporting on China's military strength or other negative and threatening aspects accounted for a very low number and proportion of their reports on China. But after 2000, reporting on these fields began to increase rapidly, and this likely had a powerful influence on Japanese public opinion, increasing public awareness of China as a potential threat compared to other issues.

6.3.2 *Negative reports in Japanese media and Japanese public opinion*

In one interview, a Japanese scholar expressed the view that there exists a vicious cycle between negative Japanese media reporting on China and Japanese public opinion. Negative reporting on China in Japanese media has increased in volume. Particularly after the 2010 ship collision incident, Japanese media have been filled with reporting expressing doubts about China's intentions, exacerbating any existing Japanese dislike of China. In addition, to cater to audience sentiment of dislike for China, Japanese media may deliberately highlight negative events connected to China, exaggerate them, and thereby intensify the negative influence on public opinion. Ultimately, this can lead to an increasing cycle of negative reporting and negative sentiment toward China among the Japanese public. Negative reporting on China in Japanese media can cause Japanese public to have negative views of China—this effect has been well demonstrated through the framework theory of communication. Namely the media's ways of reporting about an event, including the selection of facts and viewpoints, and the choice of reporting format, can influence the audience's awareness of and attitude toward the event. Why do the media outlets seek to cater to the audience's existing views and relentlessly provide news coverage that gratifies or confirms existing opinions? This can be explained in part by the fact that Japanese media are mostly commercial and independent. Independent media in Japan serve as a fourth estate alongside the country's legislative, executive, and judicial branches, and seek to play an oversight role of public affairs. In this role, media depend on public support. If the public opt not to subscribe to a newspaper or decline to watch a TV news programs, the newspaper, or TV outlet may not survive. In this media environment, once journalists discover which type of news coverage the public prefers, they have an incentive to intensify reporting on such news to attract the audience. Worsening Sino-Japanese relations and ongoing conflict over the Diaoyu Islands issue have themselves further worsened negative Japanese public sentiment toward China, so negative events relating to China have become hotspots in media coverage.

6.3.3 *Reports in Chinese media and Japan are influenced by Sino-Japanese relations and media's selective policy causes information asymmetry*

It is impossible for media to offer completely objective reports. Particularly, reports in Chinese media and Japanese media on the respective counterpart are inevitably influenced by the general climate of Sino-Japanese relations and include some nationalist or patriotic content, which influences public's ability to evaluate events objectively. When Sino-Japanese relations have been smooth, media's focus is more on bilateral cooperation and complementary advantages. When bilateral relations worsen, media always turn to more negative reporting, and provide different coverage of events. As one Japanese scholar studying Chinese politics noted, when China and Japan experience good relations, the character and image of Doraemon rises in popularity in China and serves as a symbol of friendly cultural exchange between China and Japan. When bilateral relations are bad, the same symbol can be interpreted in China as an unacceptable form of Japanese cultural invasion.

In a similar fashion, media in each country typically prefer to report information favorable for that country while ignoring views that they perceive as unfavorable. This is striking about reporting in China and Japan, and leads to serious information asymmetry for audiences. As noted above, Japanese media reporting on China focuses on negative news. Chinese media similarly highlight some information but ignore other information.

A Japanese scholar noted in one interview that information asymmetry between China and Japan is the main factor that explains worsening Sino-Japanese relations. The scholar provided the example of how Chinese media dislike Japanese Prime Minister Shinzo Abe, and often pay more attention to negative information on him, but give no attention to his speeches expressing hope for friendly Sino-Japanese relations. For example, in his address at the Diet of Japan in September 2014, Abe said, "Japan and China are inseparable from each other. China's peaceful development is a great opportunity for Japan. I hope that China and Japan, shouldering the heavy task of peace and prosperity in the region, can hold a summit as early as possible to establish stable and friendly relations, and further develop a 'strategic mutual-benefit relationship' through dialogue." Chinese media did not report on the address. Similarly, on November 10, 2014, at the Sino-Japanese Summit, Abe gave a statement saying, "I want to explore Sino-Japanese relations for the 21st century with President Xi from the general situation and the long-term perspective. I feel that it is very important to conduct multi-level cooperation between both countries centering on four aspects of: enhancing people-to-people understanding, deepening economic relations, cooperating in the East China Sea, and stabilizing the security environment in East Asia." Unfortunately, Chinese media also failed to report on these remarks.

Similarly, President Xi Jinping addressed the National Memorial Day for the Victims of the Nanjing Massacre, stating that, "The National Memorial Day for Victims of the Nanjing Massacre is designed to arouse every kind-hearted person's yearning for and insistence on peace, rather than prolonging hatred. The Chinese people and the Japanese people should be friends from one generation to the next, take history as a mirror, and face the future to make contributions to human peace. We should not be hostile to a nation just because few militarists in the nation started an aggressive war. It is the few militarists rather than the people who should bear responsibility for the crime of the war." Japanese media did report on President Xi's address, but the coverage failed to focus on China's wish for friendly relations lasting through generations, and rather paid more attention to the ongoing differences between China and Japan.

When ordinary people in China and Japan lack comprehensive information on their counterparts, their opinions will be one-sided. Therefore, it is very important for China and Japan to conduct dialogue, maintain a free mind, and keep information public.

6.4 Policy proposals

6.4.1 *Improve international communication capacity of Chinese media*

Both the survey and interview data show that those Japanese with more Chinese media exposure and more positive views of Chinese media can play a positive role in promoting positive Japanese public opinion on China. Unfortunately, most Japanese people distrust Chinese media, and have little exposure to it—either to traditional media or online media—for the important reason that they do not identify with China's media system and consider it unfree, controlled by the government, and excessively political. This view originates from Japanese people's prejudice against Chinese media, but is also related to reporting practices of Chinese media. For example, one interviewee mentioned that Chinese media reports often lack key information about sources, and other interviewees considered that reports in Chinese media contained emotional elements. Therefore, Chinese media should change the current patterns of news reporting, taking into account the expectations and preferences of international audiences. This can help Chinese media provide coverage that international audiences would accept, and enable them to build internationally influential media brands and media outlets, sharpening their influence versus competing international media outlets.

In recent years, the Chinese government has actively encouraged Chinese media to go abroad, and adopted various programs to improve their international communication. The key in improving Chinese media reporting abroad is authoritative international discourse. The influence of internationally dominant media such as BBC and CNN are based on their authoritative discourse power. Therefore, Chinese media, particularly those devoted to foreign propaganda and international communication, should properly identify their position, transform as soon as possible, and make efforts to build powerful brands with international influence, to better transmit China's image and voice to people around the world, including Japanese people.

6.4.2 *Guide Japanese media to report on China more accurately and objectively*

Both the survey and interview data show that Japanese media reporting on China lacks accuracy and objectivity, and is mainly negative. This tendency is both influenced by worsening Sino-Japanese relations and is closely related to the difficulty Japanese journalists have acquiring information on China. Japanese journalists lack sources, have lower understanding of China's history and national situation, and rarely interact with Chinese journalists. In our interviews, several Japanese journalists expressed concerns about having limited opportunity to talk to Chinese officials, especially leaders, and noted it was difficult to conduct interviews on important events. This is different from Japan, where journalists can stop a senator for an interview at any time. Given the difficulty obtaining first-hand information sources, journalists can only repeat or interpret reports from Chinese media. Meanwhile, some Japanese journalists have little understanding of China prior to coming to China on assignment, and expressed the view that Chinese issues were difficult for them to understand, making it hard to report on China accurately and objectively. Other Japanese journalists expressed the similar view that lack of exchange between Chinese and Japanese journalists is a reason for mutual distrust between them. If there were enhanced exchanges and ways of working and discussing issues together among journalists of both countries, this could help guide Japanese media to report on China more accurately and objectively.

Objective and accurate Japanese media coverage on the real China would greatly help the Japanese public to understand China and awareness of issues facing China. In this regard, the 2007 NHK documentary film *Notes on a Trip on China's Railways* provides a useful example. The film records the entire journey taken by Japanese artist Tomohiro Sekiguchi went around China by train. His trip had no pre-arranged itinerary, but was rather an account of a backpacker train trip accompanied by views of Chinese landscapes seen from the train, views of urban transit, and scenes of talking, eating, and working with ordinary Chinese people. The film faithfully recorded his experiences on the trip, portraying real views of China and the Chinese people. The film achieved high viewership, and viewers sent the program a large number of messages expressing that the film helped them develop a deeper understanding of China. Japanese audiences were attracted by the film's showing of China's magnificent waters and mountains, and were moved by the enthusiastic and simple ordinary Chinese people, and were surprised at the difference between their own prior understanding of China versus the reality shown in the film. A 28-year-old female Japanese audience wrote, "My brother and his family will work in Guangzhou next April. Thinking of how my young nephew will go to China, which he knows nothing about, I was initially full of worry. However, after watching Tomohiro's tour in China, my impression of China changed completely. After seeing the many warm faces and thoughtful behavior of Chinese people in the film, I now think my nephew will gain valuable life experience in China."[14] A 56-year-old Japanese wrote, "I often go to China for business, and I am always attracted by Chinese people, who are full of human interest and are never shy with strangers. So I began to like China and Chinese people unconsciously. However, returning to Japan, I never knew how to convey the charm of Chinese people to the Japanese people around me. After watching the program, I said to my wife: 'Great! That is the real China what I've wanted to tell others about.'"[15]

The audiences' messages suggest that for audiences who are not prejudiced by first impressions from negative Japanese media coverage, if all media can record the real China and Chinese people, the Japanese public would have less misunderstanding and obtain deeper awareness of China. Today, there are many reports on China, but news items are rarely portrayed without subjectivity. Therefore, if media journalists of both countries can exchange with and understand each other, and work to objectively and accurately report on the other country, this will play a decisive role in improving bilateral relations.

Notes

1. McCombs, Maxwell, and Donald L. Shaw. "The Agenda-setting Function of Mass Media." Public Opinion Quarterly 36.2(1972): 176–187.
2. Wanta, Wayne, and Yu-wei Hu. "The Agenda-setting Effect of International News Coverage: An Examination of Differing News Frames." International Journal of Public Opinion Research 5.3(1993): 250–264.
3. Soroka, Stuart. "Media, Public Opinion, and Foreign Policy." Harvard International Journal of Press/Politics 8.1(2003): 27–48.
4. Entman, Robert. "Framing: Toward Clarification of a Fractured Paradigm." Journal of Communication 43.4 (1993): 52.
5. Brewer, Paul, Joseph Graf, and Lar Willnat. "Priming or Framing: Media Influence on Attitudes Toward Foreign Countries." Gazette: The International Journal for Communication Studies 65.6(2003): 493–508.
6. Wanta, Wayne, Guy Golan, and Clseolhan Lee. "Agenda Setting and International News: Media Influence on Public Perceptions of Foreign Nations." Journalism and Mass Communication Quarterly 81.2(2004): 364–377.
7. Mutz, Diana. "Mass Media and the Depoliticization of Personal Experience." American Journal of Political Science 36.2(1992): 483–508.
8. Liu, Linli. *The Image of China in Japanese Mass Media* [riben dazhong meitizhong de zhongguo xingxiang]. Communication University of China Press, 2007.

9. Zhan, Qi, and Yan Liu. "On the Building of the National Image Based on the Reports on China in Major Newspapers of Japan [cong riben zhuyao baozhi shehuabaodao kan guojia xingxiang de shuli]." International Communication 9(2008): 59–60.
10. Luo, Hailong. "Constructive Analysis of the Reports on China in Japanese Mass Media [riben dazhong chuanmei duihuabaodao de jiangouzhuyi fenxi]." Master's thesis of Hebei University, 2008.
11. Ruan, Suqian. "Study on China-Japan Mutual Reporting and the National Image of the Two Countries [zhongri xianghu baodao yu liangguo xingxiang yanjiu]." Master's thesis of Nanchang University, 2007.
12. Zhao, Xinli. "The Image of China in Japanese Documentaries [riben jilupianzhong de zhongguo xingxing]." Youth Journalist 10.1(2009): 15–17.
13. Zhang, Yu. "A Study on the National Image of China in Japanese Newspapers (1995–2005)—Taking Asahi Shimbun and Yomiuri Shinbun as Examples [riben baozhizhong de zhongguo guojia xingxiang yanjiu (1995–2005): yi zhaorixinwen he dumaixinwen weili]." Journalism & Communication 4(2007): 75–83.
14. Zhao, Xinli. *Chinese and Japanese Communication and Public Diplomacy* [zhongri chuanbo yu gonggong waijiao]. China: Social Sciences Academic Press, 2012: 147.
15. Zhao, Xinli. *Chinese and Japanese Communication and Public Diplomacy* [zhongri chuanbo yu gonggong waijiao]. China: Social Sciences Academic Press, 2012: 149.

7 Chinese people in the eyes of the Japanese

National image is closely related with the spiritual outlook, civilization level, and morality demonstrated by the nationals of the country.[1] Japanese media frequently reports on crimes by Chinese people in Japan, on various incidents of inappropriate behavior of Chinese tourists in Japan, and on cases in which Chinese nationals had unfair business dealings with Japanese people. What image of Chinese people do Japanese people hold? How can the image of Chinese people among Japanese be improved? How does the image of Chinese people shape the national image of China in Japan? In this chapter, we will discuss these questions through survey and interview data.

7.1 The Image of a country's citizens and of nation

Most studies on the image of a country's people define it as the "abstract whole of citizens' quality, behavior, morality, idea and spiritual pursuit,"[2] and mainly emphasize aspects of citizens' quality and morality. Scholars including Xie Xiaoyan propose that the temperament of citizens is also a part of the national image of a country, and point out that efforts to shape the image of China as a major power should "highlight awareness of human rights, rule of law, justice, responsibility, ecology and benevolence."[3]

The daily life and travel of a country's ordinary people embodies the image of their country, and is an effective way to convey and improve the image of a country. Simon Anholt, the nation branding expert, points out that most countries have six channels for improving their national image, one of which is addressing how the public deals with problems, conducts itself, and conceives of public morality.[4] Lu Ziwen argues that compared with government-led national image-shaping activities, the ways in which the public engages in people-to-people contacts can have a greater effect on national image, because communication undertaken by individuals or the public as a whole is more colorful, specific, true, and sometimes more heart wrenching.[5]

In shaping the national image of a country, the image of a country's citizens represented by celebrities and by ordinary people is equally important. First, a country's celebrities, such as athletes, film stars, TV stars, and well-known writers, both disseminate a national image while shaping their own individual images for the sake of their own international exposure. For China, the top representative abroad may be Yao Ming, a basketball star. During the eight years from when he joined the National Basketball Association (NBA) in 2002 to 2010 when he retired from professional basketball, Yao Ming served as a unique symbol of China in the United States. His athletic performance, hard work, modesty, kindheartedness, dedication, humor, and maturity represented values accepted in Asia and America, helping make him a bridge and cultural ambassador between Chinese and American cultures.[6] In "Yao Ming: NBA's towering presence looks to his future," published in July 2011, just before Yao Ming's retirement, the CNN Bureau Chief Jaime Florcruz wrote: "Next to the giant panda perhaps, Yao is the most recognizable—and likable—Chinese face … Often described as the 'Smiling Giant,' his wholesome image helped change some of the stereotypical images of China overseas … Admirers say Yao has done more for improving China's image overseas than any modern-day politician or diplomat."

In Yao Ming, they could see not only outstanding athletic performance of a Chinese basketball star, but more importantly "the kindheartedness, wisdom, and adaptability to modern industrial society of an ancient Asia country. Yao Ming has definitely uplifted the national image of China in the U.S., and is a subtle symbol and influence in Sino-American political relations. In 2006, when Chinese President Hu Jintao made an official visit to the U.S., President George W. Bush and his wife Laura hosted a grand welcome luncheon including Yao Ming on the guest list prepared personally by President Bush and his wife."[7] These reports indicate the importance of stars like Yao Ming in shaping the national image of China.

Second, the morality, etiquette, and spirituality of ordinary people can demonstrate the accomplishment of its nationals and increase the country's appeal in tourism and business. In studying the relationship between global sporting events and the shaping of national images, Wang Xiuli and Jia Zhemin point out: compared with common political and economic events, large-scale sports events such as the FIFA World Cup and the Olympic Games are more able to attract ordinary people to participate, and hence can demonstrate a more comprehensive image of a country's nationals. For example, during the Beijing Olympic Games, the volunteers offered warm, thoughtful and careful services, and regular citizens demonstrated the friendliness, warmth, and modesty, making a deep impression on visitors from around the world and shaping the image of China as a warm, responsible, ceremonious, and modern country.[8]

Similarly, the nationals of a country who attend sporting events as audience members can also demonstrate the national image: and their clothing, slogans, and fervor can reflect an energetic and united spirit. For instance, during the FIFA World Cup 2002 Korea/Japan, more than 10,000 Korean spectators established the cheerleading group known as "Red Devils," and popularized the cheering slogan, "Let Dreams Come True," to encourage the Korean team. They were passionate but orderly, and the images from the event had a powerful appeal for audiences, improving the national image of South Korea.[9]

The role of ordinary citizens in improving the national image is particularly important for China, given how its system and culture differ from those of Western countries. When people interact with and derive their understanding of China mainly through media and similar channels, they may conceptualize China abstractly through its political system and ideology, and "view China as a cultural image relatively independent from Western countries in terms of ideas, values, faith and feeling,"[10] leading people to make simplistic and demonizing judgments. Routine contact with ordinary people from a country can produce a more accurate, specific, and diverse image of China and dispel misunderstandings caused by media reporting.

The image of a country's citizens not only shapes the national image, but it can also influence the country's diplomatic policy. In today's high-information society, citizens of all countries increasingly participate in diplomatic affairs, so no government can afford to ignore the feelings of its own citizens when considering its relationships with other countries. Over the past decade or more, ordinary Chinese and Japanese people experienced a decline in good-feeling for their counterparts. This worrisome trend has been mainly caused by issues in overall Sino-Japanese relations, but worsening feelings between the nationals of the two countries can act as a restraint preventing an improvement in relations. For example, the Japanese men's football team was booed in an Asian Cup guest match in China, and there were audible outbursts during the playing of the Japanese national anthem. This, along with other anti-Japanese incidents such as the burning the Japanese flag, provoked hostility toward China among Japanese people and worsened Sino-Japanese relations.

After two years of diplomatic standoff after the Diaoyu Islands dispute, Sino-Japanese bilateral relations finally turned warmer during the Asia-Pacific Economic Cooperation (APEC) Summit in November 2014. The summit between both countries was driven by national interests, but due to lack of good feeling among the general public, leaders of both countries engaged in "facial expression diplomacy"—that is, using facial expressions to give the impression of meeting unwillingly and only out of necessity. International media have delighted in this new phase of tension. Friendly relations and mutual trust between the nationals of China and Japan are an important foundation for improving Sino-Japanese relations.

7.2 Chinese people in the eyes of the Japanese

7.2.1 *Values identification of the Chinese in the eyes of the Japanese*

Traditional Chinese values include benevolence, righteousness, propriety, filial piety, harmony between humanity and nature, and public service. Figure 7.1 shows the extent to which Japanese survey respondents associated

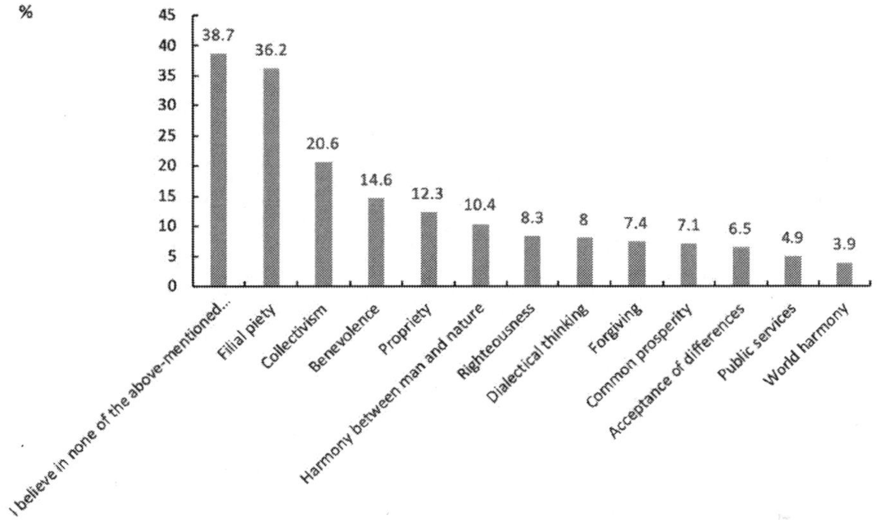

Figure 7.1 Japanese people's identification with traditional Chinese values

Source: The 2nd survey.

these values with China. Respondents think Chinese people identify with filial piety most, with 36% identifying this value with China, followed by collectivism, benevolence, propriety, and harmony between humanity and nature, all with responses higher than 10%. Other values such as righteousness, forgiving, dialectic thinking, common prosperity, acceptance of differences, public service, and world harmony, all had response rates lower than 10%. Nearly 40% of respondents felt that the Chinese do not identify with any traditional values.

The data in Figure 7.1 indicate that Japanese people consider Chinese as indifferent to traditional values, particularly compared with Japanese people's evaluation of their own identification with these values. In our survey, respondents generally reported having a higher identification with these traditional values. As shown in Figure 7.2, over half of respondents reported identifying with the values of benevolence, righteousness, propriety, and filial party. Over 30% of respondents identified with the values of forgiveness, harmony between humanity and nature, acceptance of differences, world harmony, and public service. Over 10% identified with the values of common prosperity and dialectic thinking, far higher than the proportion who considered that Chinese people identify with such values. That is to say, Japanese people think Chinese people do not identify with traditional Chinese values.

7.2.2 *The Japanese general impression of Chinese people*

The survey data show that about half of respondents consider Chinese people hard working. About 30% of respondents considered Chinese

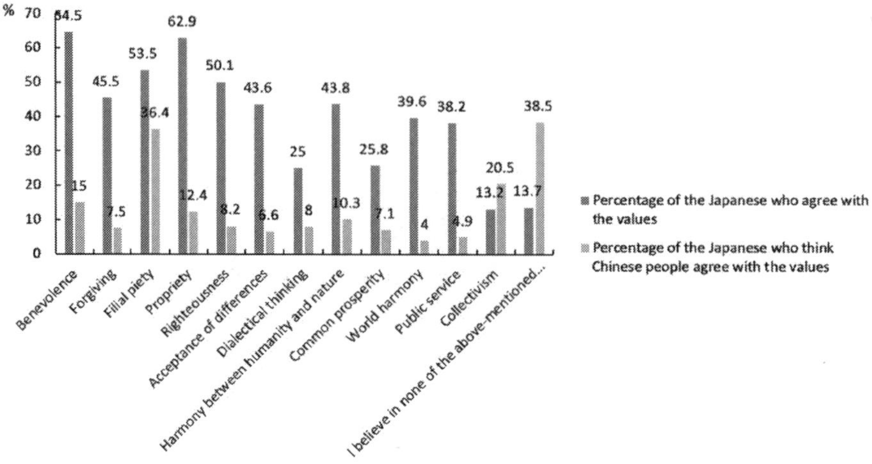

Figure 7.2 Comparison between Japanese people's identification with traditional Chinese values and their viewpoint of Chinese people's identification with the values

Source: The 2nd survey.

people creative and sensitive. Less than one-fifth of respondents considered Chinese people as cultured and orderly. Only about a tenth of interviewees considered Chinese people friendly and honest. (For specific data, see Figure 7.3.) T-tests of independent survey samples show that those Japanese people who had visited China had a more positive and active evaluation of Chinese people than those who had never been to China. Those who had visited China and those with higher levels of education mainly considered Chinese people creative and hard working. Overall, Japanese people have a negative impression of Chinese people, but those with direct contact with Chinese people have a more active and positive evaluation of Chinese people.

Interviews generally corroborated the results of the surveys on the general Japanese impression of Chinese people. In our interviews, several Japanese journalists and scholars expressed the view that Chinese people are diligent, intelligent, innovative, spirited, and dynamic. However, interviewees pointed to problems of Chinese students and tourists in Japan showing discourtesy—for example, by not observing public order or causing noisy disturbances. One Japanese scholar said, "Some Chinese students have left messes in bathrooms or have thrown refuse into public toilets, leading to complaints from school sanitation workers. Some Chinese tourists are in the habit of talking loudly in public places such as subways, supermarkets, and bathrooms, whereas Japanese culture favors quiet in public spaces … Such behavior directly influences Japanese views of the image of China." These differences in life habits and daily behavior need to be improved to

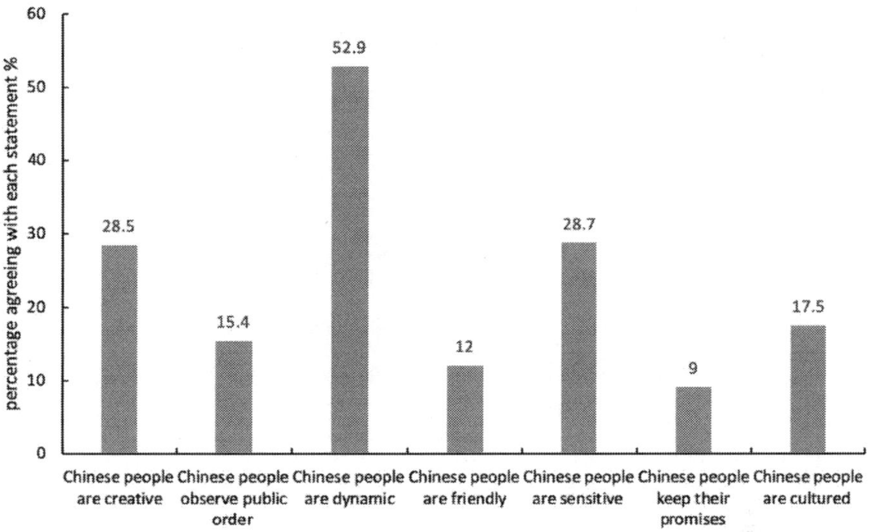

Figure 7.3 Japanese people's overall impression of Chinese people

Source: The 2nd survey.

some extent both in Japan and in China. "If they [Chinese visitors to Japan] can address such issues, the Japanese image of Chinese people and of China will improve." On the other hand, the scholar also pointed out: "These habits and behaviors are in fact minor problems rather than major ones. Japanese tourists abroad also cause various problems. It is a slow process to improve." In another interview, one Japanese scholar pointed out the perception among Japanese that Chinese people worship money or put money ahead of people, but he also argued that this is not a problem an individual could resolve, but rather arises from China's stage of social development and the general attitude toward money of society as a whole. With time, as China's economy and social development improve, spiritual pursuits will rise accordingly.

In terms of honesty, in his book *China in the Eyes of the Japanese*, Professor Satoshi Amako mentions his "painful experiences in dealings with some Chinese people."[11] On two occasions, he helped Chinese students and visiting research fellows apply for faculty positions, but later learned they had gone to a better school despite his successful reference. He considers this as opportunism, and thinks that "there are many opportunistic Chinese people … due to social pressures, people think that survival depends on being opportunistic." Japanese people, living in an environment with strong social trust, always feel that they should trust people's word and do what they can to help, but neglect the fact that many Chinese people come from a relatively harsher or cutthroat environment, and usually keep something in reserve.[12]

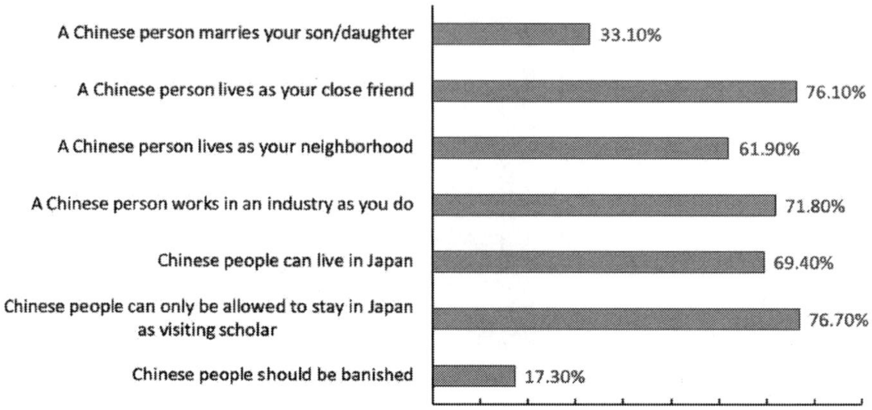

Figure 7.4 Japanese willingness to experience social proximity with the Chinese

Source: The 3rd survey.

7.2.3 *Japanese people's social affinity for Chinese people*

In the survey, we listed seven choices regarding how willing respondents felt about social proximity with Chinese people. Ranked in order of declining social affinity, the choices were: whether the respondent is willing to let a Chinese person marry their son or daughter, be their closest friend, be their neighbor, and so on. The survey results show that most Japanese people hold a friendly attitude toward and a strong willingness to interact with Chinese people. About 70% of Japanese people expressed that they are willing to have Chinese people as their closest friends and work together with them or welcome their living in Japan. Over 60% of respondents were willing to have Chinese people as their neighbors, and over 30% expressed willingness to let their son or daughter marry a Chinese person. (For specific data, see Figure 7.4.)

The survey data show that Japanese people have a strong willingness to interact socially with Chinese people, which was also corroborated in our interviews. All the interviewees expressed a very strong sense of willingness to interact with Chinese people, and reported having many Chinese friends and getting along well with them. The interviewed visiting Japanese scholar in China expressed that he has many Chinese friends in Japan and gets along well with them, and that "Chinese people who have lived in Japan for a long time integrate well into the Japanese society, and they enjoy a very stable life there."

7.2.4 *Quantity of Chinese friends of Japanese people*

To understand the contacts and exchanges between Japanese people and Chinese people, we asked the respondents of the quantity of their Chinese

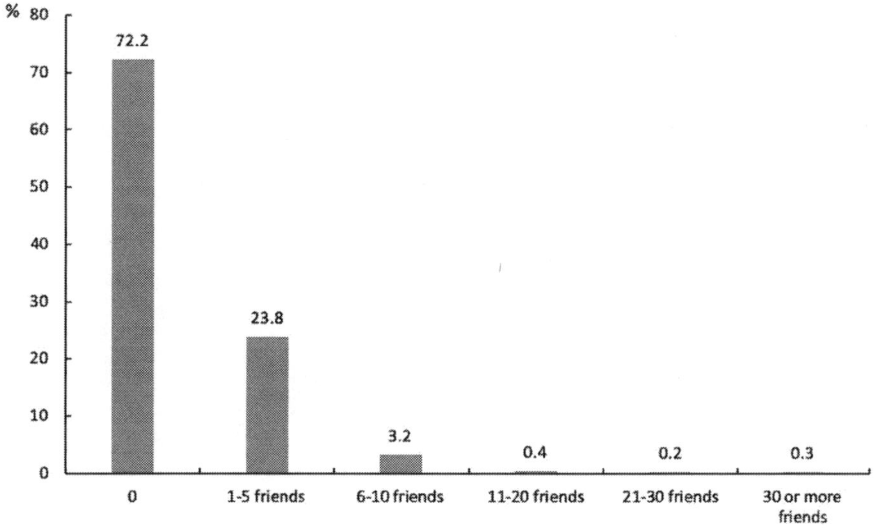

Figure 7.5 Number of Japanese people's Chinese friends

Source: The 3rd survey.

friends. Of the 1,225 respondents, 72.2% (884) reported having no Chinese friends, and 15% have one Chinese friend. We grouped responses into six categories or buckets: 0 Chinese friends, 1–5, 6–10, 11–20, 21–30, and 31 and more. Most responses were below 15, with several peaks at 1 friend, 10 friends, and 15 friends. Data in Figure 7.5 clearly show that Japanese people have little contact with Chinese people and most have no Chinese friends.

7.2.5 *Awareness and reputation of Chinese celebrities among Japanese people*

The survey revealed that of the Chinese celebrities listed in the questionnaire, the movie star Jackie Chan ranked first with the awareness rate of 97.5%. Among those with high recognition scores, he was followed in rank order by political leader Mao Zedong, the ancient philosophers Confucius and Lao-Tsu, the political leader Deng Xiaoping, the ancient poet Li Bai, the political leader Sun Yat-sen, and the movie star Zhang Ziyi. As shown in Figure 7.6, respondents had a lower awareness of Chinese entrepreneurs, astronauts, and scientists. For example, only 17.4% of respondents recognized rice expert Yuan Longping. Overall, Japanese people have a higher awareness of ancient Chinese philosophers and poets, as well as of modern movie stars.

Based on the awareness scores for the celebrities listed above, we also surveyed respondents on their reputation, assigning a value of 1 for "strongly dislike" and 5 to "like a lot." Higher mean response values for a celebrity

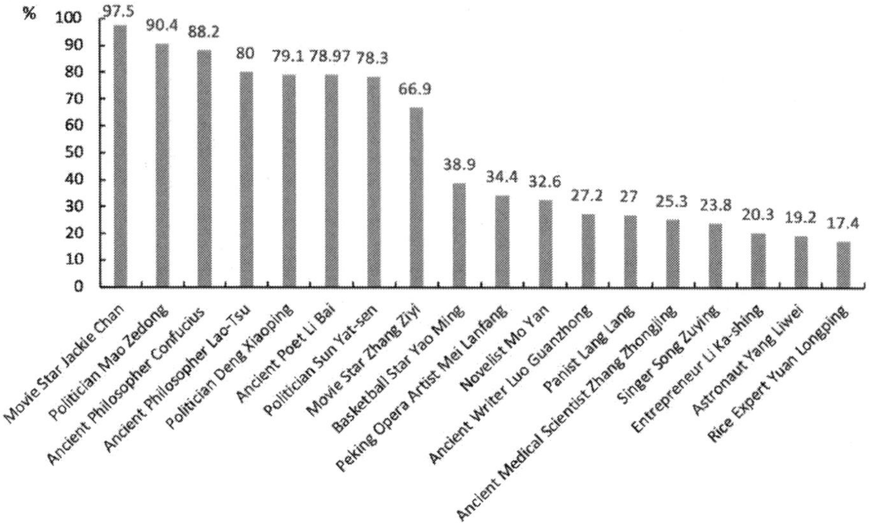

Figure 7.6 Percentage of Japanese people's awareness of Chinese celebrities

Source: The 3rd survey.

indicate greater fondness among interviewees. As shown in Figure 7.7, movie stars Jackie Chan and Zhang Ziyi were the favorites of the interviewees. Secondly, Japanese people also like ancient Chinese cultural celebrities such as the philosophers Confucius and Lao-Tsu, poet Li Bai, writer Luo Guanzhong, and medical scientist Zhang Zhongjing. Respondents were neutral about contemporary artists such as Mei Lanfang, Song Zuying,

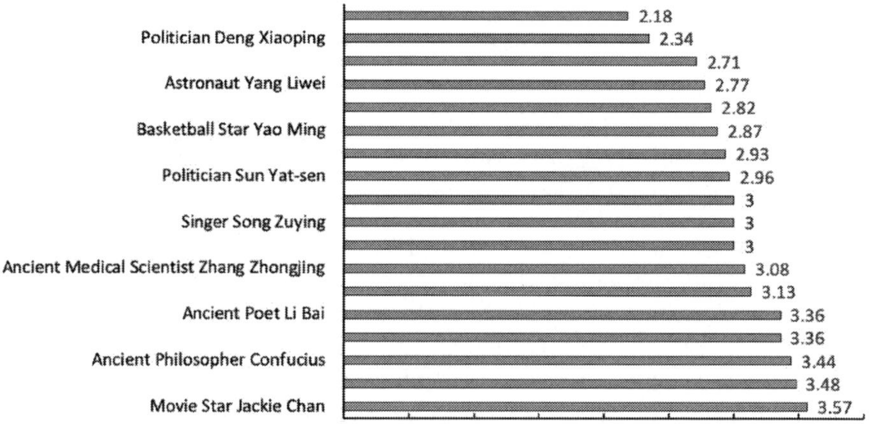

Figure 7.7 Japanese people's fondness for Chinese celebrities

Source: The 3rd survey.

and Lang. The two famous Chinese figures with the lowest popularity score among respondents were the political figures Mao Zedong and Deng Xiaoping.

From the perspective of reputation, Japanese people have mostly negative views of Chinese politicians, which was also corroborated in our interviews. Several journalists and scholars we interviewed expressed the view that after experiencing World War II, Japanese people have developed an attitude of distrusting and disliking political leaders, such as the leaders of countries, political party leaders, and other political figures—disliking not only Chinese politicians, but also Japanese ones.

In contrast, Japanese people showed a high affinity for movie stars Jackie Chan and Zhang Ziyi, tied to their positions in Asian movie world. Jackie Chan has starred in over 60 films shown in Japan over the years, with total box-office take of more than JPY 50 billion, and Jackie Chan was named most popular artist for several consecutive years. Several films starred by Zhang Ziyi have been shown in Japan, particularly the popular film Memoirs of a Geisha. Therefore, it is no wonder that the two movie stars enjoy a high regard in Japan. Meanwhile, Japanese fondness for ancient Chinese philosophers and writers such as Confucius, Lao-Tsu, Li Bai, and Luo Guanzhong is closely related with wide dissemination and strong influence of Chinese culture throughout Japanese history.

7.3 Survey analysis

7.3.1 *Analysis of the reasons for the source of Japanese people's impression of Chinese people*

Differences in life habits and values can explain the negative impression held by Japanese people toward Chinese people. Japanese people hold a negative impression of Chinese behavior, particularly in terms of hygienic habits and the observance of public order and rules. These differences in behavior in turn relate to different habits of daily life and educational difference between Chinese people and Japanese people. From a young age, Japanese people are instructed not to bother others, and particularly not to make noise in public places—and to observe collective rules and not disturb others. These traditions have led Japanese to adopt the good habit of keeping quiet in public places. Comparatively, some Chinese people pay little attention to those around them, and have little regard for whether others are bothered by their behavior, contrasting with Japanese habits and likely to cause discomfort among Japanese strangers.

In his book *China in the Eyes of the Japanese*, Professor Satoshi Amako compares and contrasts the values held by Chinese and Japanese people, and summarizes the following two points: first, whereas Chinese society features severe mutual distrust, Japanese society features high or absolute levels of mutual trust. This is manifested by a highly cautious mentality among Chinese people in their daily contacts with others, and sometimes by failure to keep promises. Second, whereas Chinese people take an extremely self-centered approach to life, Japanese generally hold an interdependent outlook on life. Given a relatively self-centered outlook, Chinese people have developed the habit of belittling laws, rules, and regulations, sometimes ignoring traffic lights and not queuing when waiting for the bus or subway. According to an old Chinese phrase, "policies from on high say one thing, the people below do the other."[13]

7.3.2 *Japanese people deal with Chinese friends and regular Chinese people in different ways*

In our interviews, we found an interesting but reasonable pattern concerning the distinction interviewees gave between their Chinese friends versus their regard for other Chinese people. Almost all interviewees highly esteemed their Chinese friends, but held some reservations for other ordinary Chinese people. One Japanese journalist who had studied in China for four years during the 1990s mentioned that since then he had had many Chinese friends and gotten along well with them; he remained in contact with his friends and exchanged visits with them either in China or Japan. He expressed the view that his Chinese friends attach high importance to keeping promises and staying loyal to friends, and preserving a harmonious relationship with him and his family. As for ordinary Chinese people aside from his friends, "Some Chinese people should improve their character. The [recent] case of an airline passenger opening the emergency exit of an airplane on the ground is a typical example of not observing rules."[14] He considered that, given current social development stage of China, the character of many Chinese people is still below what would be expected given China's economic development.

Another journalist expressed that he considered Chinese people as very cordial, and he felt a strong degree of social warmth when among Chinese people. But for those without Chinese friends, he said, Chinese social circles seem very different from an external perspective. After coming to China, he made Chinese friends and found Chinese people very reasonable, easy to get along with, and very obliging. This differed from the feeling he had for Chinese people before he came to China: he had considered Chinese people as arrogant and unreasonable.

Overall, Japanese opinions about ordinary Chinese people shows a high degree of the Third-Person Effect[15]: Japanese held a higher opinion of Chinese people with closer social distance than of those with greater social distance. Japanese people considered their own Chinese friends as polite, friendly, and morally upright, and felt their friends to be special versus other Chinese people, whom they considered relatively less aware of social rules and having relatively lower character. Could it be true that the Chinese friends of these Japanese people really have better character than Chinese strangers? Of course not. The impression can be explained by the feelings of understanding and trust caused by friendship, which weakens Japanese prejudice and stereotypes of Chinese people, and make respondents view Chinese friends in a more tolerant and open-minded manner. This further demonstrates the importance of people-to-people contact between China and Japan.

In our interviews, one interviewee asserted that negative news about Chinese people as reported in Japanese newspapers should be considered as applying only to the individuals mentioned, and not applied to all Chinese people. China has a huge population, vast territory, and wide differences between regions and among levels of education. Thus Chinese people exhibit wide differences in social habits and behavior. Comparatively, Japanese society is relatively uniform, and society is homogenous. The interviewee also considered that more Japanese people should acknowledge this difference between China and Japan.

7.4 Policy proposals

The survey and interview data show that among Japanese people with more contacts with Chinese people, respondents tend to have a more positive evaluation of Chinese people. Similarly, respondents and interviewees have a more favorable evaluation of familiar Chinese friends than that of Chinese people they don't know. It follows that strengthening contacts and exchanges between the Chinese and Japanese people in various fields and at various levels will enhance mutual understanding between China and Japan and hence improve the image of China in Japan. Almost all interviewees expressed that when national relations between China and Japan are strained, people-to-people relations are more important. "Government-to-government relations are different from people-to-people relations, and should not influence the latter," one interviewed scholar said. "If exchanges between Chinese and Japanese people are closer and more frequent, mutual understanding between them will be deepened, and more friendships will be made. With the passage of time, government-to-government relations will improve in consequence.

In late May 2015, Toshihiro Nikai, Chairman of the General Council of the ruling Liberal Democratic Party of Japan, led a 3,000-member delegation to China for sightseeing and cultural exchanges, and were received warmly. Such a large-scale mission aimed at people-to-people contact, taking place against the backdrop of still strained Sino-Japanese relations, was hardly easy, and marked a significant step in improving Sino-Japanese relations. It is true that problems remain in the Sino-Japanese relationship, and this makes it even more necessary to push ahead with people-to-people contacts between both countries. Such exchanges play an important role in improving strained bilateral relations. Regular and friendly non-governmental exchanges are an unavoidable necessity in this situation, and can lay a foundation for normal development of the relations between both countries.

Therefore, no matter how government-to-government relations are going, people-to-people relations should not be equated with the government-to-government political relations, and should serve as a calming factor rather than as a exacerbating factor in international relations. Similarly, people-to-people relations between China and Japan can play the role of improving rather than worsening bilateral relations, just as took place prior to the diplomatic normalization between China and Japan in 1972, when China and Japan either lacked official diplomatic ties or had hostile relations. In this case, civilian diplomacy between the nationals of the two countries helped maintain people-to-people contacts and became the main channel for mutual communication and understanding, preparing the social foundation for what evolved into the re-establishment of official diplomatic relations.

In recent years, during the week-long holidays of the annual Spring Festival, the May 1 International Workers' Day, and China's October 1 National Day, hundreds of millions of Chinese tourists have traveled to Japan for sightseeing and shopping. Though this type of everyday people-to-people contact may have only a minor impact on the Japanese society, it can still help foster mutual understanding and good feelings between the nationals of the two countries, as long as tourist and shopping travelers abide by local norms and customs.

In view of the current tense diplomatic situation, non-governmental relations between China and Japan remain fragile, and are inevitably colored by the existing political tensions. However, the 3,000-person Japanese delegation that visited China for sightseeing and cultural exchanges created an encouraging precedent, upholding the notion that people-to-people contacts should continue even when bilateral relations are troubled, and indeed should be facilitated. No matter how political relations between the two countries develop, relations between the two peoples need to be cultivated with good will, and kept free from hatred. While it's true that individual attitudes are hard to improve, but very easy to damage. Once feelings are damaged, it is more difficult to restore good will. We hope that people-to-people contacts between Chinese and Japanese nationals are no longer interrupted in response to any political turmoil or event, and both parties will strive to gradually enhance good will through such exchanges, making people-to-people relations a solid foundation and hope for improving bilateral political relations and safeguarding peace and tranquility.

Notes

1. Anholt, Simon. *Competitive Identity: The New Brand Management for Nations, Cities and Regions*. New York: Palgrave Macmillan, 2007.
2. Liu, Xiaoyan. "On Building National Civilization Image from the Perspective of Communication of Nationals Image [cong guomin xingxing chuanbo kan guojia wenmin xingxiang de goujian]." Chinese Journal of Journalism & Communication 3(2007): 17–21.

3. Xie, Xiaoyan, and Xiaoyan Yang. "On Chinese Temperament in Shaping the Image of China as a Power [lun zhongguo daguo xingxiang suzaozhong de guomin qizhi]." Journal of Lanzhou University (Social Sciences) 4(2012): 48–54.
4. The other five channels as mentioned by Simon Anholt are: tourism promotion, government policy, foreign investment, brand of exports, and cultural exchange activities.
5. Lu, Ziwen. "Nationals-based Foreign Publicity: the Effective Way through which Nationals' Cross-cultural Ability Promotes Building of National Image [guomin waixuan: guomin kuawenhua nengli cujin guojia xingxiang jianshe de youxiao lujing]." Tribune of Study 5(2012): 49–53.
6. Jaime Florcruz. "Yao Ming: NBA's towering presence looks to his future," CNN, July 15, 2011. Retrieved from http://edition.cnn.com/2011/WORLD/asiapcf/07/15/nba.yao.ming/index.html.
7. "Yao Ming Phenomenon and the Image of China [yaoming xianxiang yu zhongguo xingxiang]." People's Daily—People's Tribune. Retrieved from http://news.xinhuanet.com/ politics/2010-06/01/c_12166755.htm.
8. Wang, Xiuli, and Zhemin Jia. "Global Sports Events and the Shaping of National Image [quanqiu tiyu saishi yu guojia xingxiang suzao]." Journal of China University of Geosciences 2(2011): 97–101.
9. Ibid.
10. Chen, Xiaowei. "Star Symbol and the Building of National Image [mingxing fuhao yu guojiaxingxiang de jiangou]." Dongyue Tribune 1(2012): 65–68.
11. Satoshi, Amako. *China in the Eyes of the Japanese* (Trans. Fan Li). Social Sciences Academic Press, 2006: 68.
12. Satoshi, Amako. *China in the Eyes of the Japanese* (Trans. Fan Li). Social Sciences Academic Press, 2006: 69.
13. Satoshi Amako. *China in the Eyes of the Japanese* (Trans. Fan Li). Social Sciences Academic Press, 2006: 85.
14. The emergency exit incident mentioned by the journalist took place in 2015. For more information, see "Passenger opens emergency exit due to dissatisfaction over flight delay." Retrieved from http://china.cnr.cn/news/20150111/t20150111_517378629.shtml.
15. The Third-Person Effect was first put forward by American scholar Davidson in a 1983 article, *The Role of The Third-Person Effect in Communication*, and states that people generally assume that some information from the media has a greater influence on others than on themselves. Later studies by other scholars have revealed that social distance is one of the factors that influences the Third-Person Effect. People think that the influences of negative information are lower on their own group (family members, friends) at a closer social distance than those on those at a greater social distance.

8 Sino-Japanese relations in the eyes of the Japanese

China and Japan are two most important countries in East Asia, and their relationship undoubtedly is one of China's most important foreign relationships. However, since the mid-to-late-1990s, structural changes in Sino-Japanese relations took place, including reduced need for strategic cooperation and lessened economic complementarity. The two countries experienced frictions and disputes over a series of issues such as recognition of Japan's military history in Asia, the Diaoyu Islands, maritime border delimitation and energy development in the East China Sea, the American-Japanese Alliance, and Taiwan. Some of these disputes led to perception of a security dilemma between both countries. Both parties lack mutual trust, and competition has overwhelmed cooperation in their relationship.

Given these changes, the mutual sense of affinity between the nationals of China and Japan decreased, and particularly Japanese affinity toward and of trust of China has declined steadily. Today, with China's national strength increasing, how do Japanese people view the current Sino-Japanese relationship? Which factors most restrain the development of positive Sino-Japanese relations? How can the countries improve their relationship? Such issues not only influence the development of the bilateral relationship, but also hold significance for whether China can develop peacefully.

8.1 Japanese people's evaluations on current situations of Sino-Japanese relations

The Sino-Japanese relationship in recent years has loosely been characterized as "cold politics, hot economy," and this phrase reflects the basic characteristics of Sino-Japanese relations in the present era. The "cold politics, hot economy" phase began in the mid-1990s, and refers to the rapid growth in economic ties even as political relations fluctuated sharply. Economic and trade data show an increasing trend lasting nearly 20 years, but without a concomitant improvement in political relations. On the contrary, the cold politics and political tensions has actually had a deleterious effect on economic relations, and could even be said to threaten the advent of

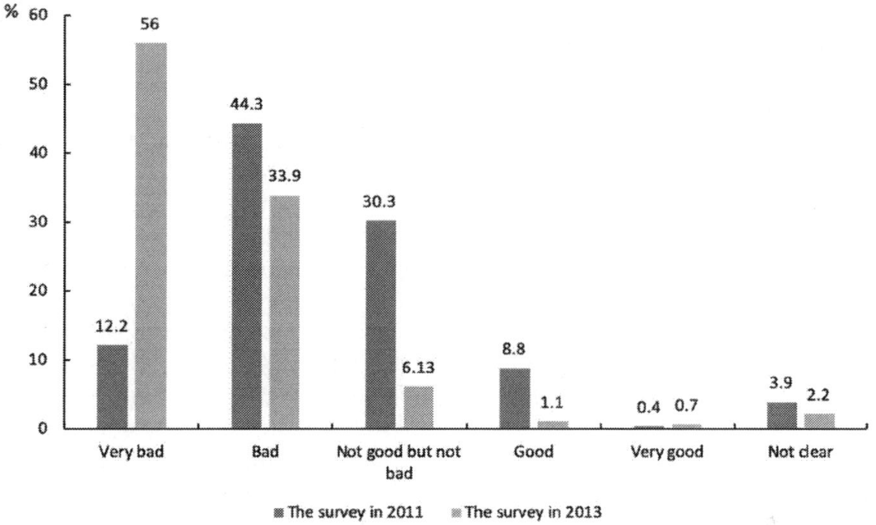

Figure 8.1 Japanese public opinion on the current state of Sino-Japanese relations

Source: The 2nd and the 3rd surveys.

a "cold economy." However, considering world economic developments, structural changes in Sino-Japanese economic and trade relations, and the potential for further economic and trade cooperation between China and Japan, given warmer political relations and increased economic exchanges between China and Japan since 2014, we believe the prospects for closer Sino-Japanese relations are hopeful.

8.1.1 *Sino-Japanese political relations*

In recent years, Japanese public opinion about Sino-Japanese political relations has declined steadily. Figure 8.1 displays survey data on Japanese views about Sino-Japanese relations at year-end 2011 and 2013. According to the 2011 survey, 56.5% of respondents considered Sino-Japanese relations as either "very bad" or "bad." At the end of 2013, this had increased to 90% of respondents. In 2011, 9.2% of respondents considered Sino-Japanese relations "very good" or "good", but this proportion below 2% in 2013. In 2011, 30% of respondents considered Sino-Japanese relations as neither good nor bad, and this proportion fell to just 6% in 2013.

We assigned values to responses, ranging from 1 for "very bad" and 5 for "very good," and ignored responses of "unclear." The mean for the 2011 survey was 2.38, the mean indicating that respondents considered Sino-Japanese relations as "bad" on average. This figure dropped to 1.53 in 2013, midway between "bad" and "very bad." The decline in the two years from 2011 to 2013 can be attributed mainly to the Diaoyu Islands dispute, large anti-Japanese demonstrations in China, and incidents of public smashing of Japanese goods at demonstrations in several large Chinese cities in 2012.

Through regression analysis, we found that the income level and ability to understand Chinese significantly influenced respondents' evaluation of Sino-Japanese relations. Those interviewees who understood Chinese tended to rate Sino-Japanese as better, on average, while higher income tended to correlate with a lower assessment of Sino-Japanese relations.

On the whole, the interviews with Japanese scholars and journalists tended to confirm the results of the questionnaire survey. All interviewees unsurprisingly confirmed that the period was seeing the worst Sino-Japanese relations since normalization of diplomatic relations, and considered that this was reflected in both worsening of inter-government relations as well as decreasing people-to-people contact. One Japanese journalist expressed a pessimistic view of Sino-Japanese relations, stating that the worsening of Sino-Japanese relations was "directly [caused] by the Diaoyu Islands dispute, and closely related to the domestic situation in both countries. For example, both China and Japan are augmenting their military strength on the grounds of the Diaoyu Islands issue." The interviewee expressed the view that it would be difficult to reconcile competing territorial claims in a way both countries found satisfactory.

Some Japanese journalists were more optimistic, and considered that the worsening of Sino-Japanese relations would be temporary, and the common interests of the countries would leave room for future cooperation. Similarly, some interviewees felt that, through negotiation and compromise between both parties, the relationship could once again improve. Similarly, one interviewee compared the disputes to conflict among old friends: "Sino-Japanese relations are like two friends with differences—sometimes they quarrel, sometimes they reconcile. This alternating pattern has been repeated several times since the normalization of diplomatic relations in 1972."

One Japanese scholar and China expert gave the following frank assessment: "It is really terrible. Sino-Japanese relations should not be like this. We should emphasize cooperation." Later, he mentioned that "Sino-Japanese" relations consist of two aspects: resilience and fragility. But over the past year [2014], both countries focused on aspects where their relations were fragile, though there remained many aspects of resilience. For example, China and Japan maintained cooperation in many unconventional security fields. Both countries should focus more on cooperation, including economic exchange and cultural exchange. They should intensify cooperation in areas of strength and resilience, and control aspects where relations remain fragile. This should serve as our common goal.

8.1.2 *Sino-Japanese economic relations*

In contrast to the worsening political relationship, Sino-Japanese economic relations have developed steadily since the establishment of the diplomatic relations, and witnessed progress in trade, investment, and economic cooperation. In 2014, the bilateral trade volume reached US$312.3 billion, accounting for 7.3% of China's total foreign trade. Japanese investment in China totaled US$4.33 billion, ranking fourth among foreign investment volume in China, though the 2014 figure was lower than the US$7.06 billion recorded in 2013 and US$7.38 billion in 2012. By the end of September 2015, the cumulative Japanese investment in China reached US$101.15 billion. Meanwhile, Chinese investment in Japan increased rapidly, reaching US$434 million in 2013, doubling the investment of US$210 million in 2012.[1]

Chinese tourist visits to Japan have also steadily increased in recent years. In 2015, China became the largest source of tourist visits to Japan. Japanese Tourism Agency data from January to October 2015 show that foreign tourist visits to Japan reached 16.3 million, up 48.2% from the prior year, of which tourists from Mainland China reached 4.3 million, ranking first, and accounting for one-fourth of all tourist visits. Chinese tourists were notable for strong consumption patterns. Chinese tourist spent an average of JPY 280,000 (about RMB 14,870) in 2015, up 19% from the prior year, and representing total spending in Japan of approximately RMB 75 billion.[2] Several Japanese journalists we interviewed expressed the view that Chinese tourists had made a significant contribution to Japan's economic recovery, and hoped that Chinese tourism in Japan would continue to increase, thus enhancing mutual understanding between the countries their peoples.

The recent tensions in Sino-Japanese political relations has also hurt bilateral economic ties, but all interviewees emphasized that economic cooperation was a necessity for both, given their complementarity and long-term ties. Interviewees considered that the potential for increased economic and trade cooperation remained high. The complementarity in economic development between the countries, and their different needs, would motivate continuous development of bilateral economic cooperation. In the 1970s, during the period of diplomatic normalization, the economic development gap between China and Japan provided immense potential for bilateral economic cooperation and complementarity. Through its rapid development in the 1950s and 1960s, Japan had experienced a startling economic rise, but the impact of the oil crisis and pressure difficult trade disputes with the United States over iron and steel and color TVs had made Japan eager to diversify energy sources and open new export markets. Against this backdrop, China, with its rich coal resources, huge market, and large labor pool, and located just across a narrow sea from Japan, seemed an ideal partner. On the other hand, due to China's worsening relations with the Soviet Union, China also needed a new source of capital and technology support to enable its own economic development. Hence, due to their specific and highly complementary economic development needs, Japan and China enjoyed 30 years of fruitful bilateral economic relations.

Now that its economy has grown immensely since the 1980s, making China the second largest economy in the world, do the economic needs of Japan and China still complement each other? At a November 2015 dialogue for Chinese and Japanese entrepreneurs co-sponsored by the China Council for the Promotion of International Trade (CCPIT) and the Japan-China Economic Association, Chinese and Japanese economic leaders expressed a positive view. Jiang Zengwei, then Director of CCPIT, stated, "China and Japan are at different stages of development, and their economic complementarity is far greater than their competition."[3] Japan leads in intelligent manufacturing, medical services, energy efficiency, and the environmental protection industry, and has advantages in R&D, technology, and talent. China has rich labor resources, is accelerating new industries, digitization, urbanization, and agricultural modernization, while building the vision of an ecological civilization. China has a particular need for Japan's advanced technologies and management experiences.

China and Japan "are pursuing structural economic reform, giving companies new opportunities for cooperation," said Jiang.[4] Japanese business leaders at the dialogue agreed. Kokubo Kenichi, Managing Director of Hitachi, in his speech expressed the view that Hitachi, as an established electronics and equipment company, would like to offer technology and expertise, and work with Chinese companies to build out the supply chain, and help contribute to the structural transformation of the Chinese manufacturing sector.[5]

During the dialogue, economic figures from both countries expressed the wishes to expand economic cooperation, and, beyond that, work together to promote economic development throughout Asia and the world. Nobuo Kuroyanagi, Special Advisor to MSB Tokyo UFJ Bank, pointed out that in terms of Asian infrastructure, "China and Japan each have special expertise that can support the sustainable development of other Asian countries through coordination and competition." Shi Jiyang, President of the China-Africa Development Fund, said that China and Japan can expand third-party market cooperation in Africa: "Japanese enterprises are experienced in African project development, building technology, project quality, and risk management. Our Fund would also like to explore cooperation with Japanese enterprises in non-agricultural, manufacturing, and connectivity infrastructure with an open-minded attitude, through equal cooperation and on the basis of mutual benefit, based on relevant agreements on cooperation in Africa."[6]

Although the Sino-Japanese political relationship has yet to recover, and public opinion in the two countries toward the other remains poor, there still remain immense opportunities for bilateral economic cooperation. Given their deep economic ties, both countries can work together to gradually shift from the present situation of "cold politics, hot economy," toward a new pattern of "warm politics, hot economy."

8.2 Important factors influencing Sino-Japanese relations

What has caused the dramatic changes in Sino-Japanese relations in recent years? The question is doubtless very complex. We can explore the reasons both from the history of Sino-Japanese relations and the change in the international environment after the Cold War, and from changes in Japan itself and its national character, or from China's growing national strength and changing political environment.

8.2.1 *Historical issue*

Of the interviewees, several journalists identified the core issue with the greatest negative influence on Sino-Japanese relations is the general dispute about the history of Japanese military involvement in Asia, which has been exacerbated by official Japanese visits to the Yasukuni Shrine, revisions to history textbooks, and the lack of Japanese compensation to civilian war victims.

Since the mid-1980s, when the first reports appeared in world media of visits by Japanese political leaders to the Yasukuni Shrine, these visits have always resulted in strong protests by the Chinese government, as well as opposition by ordinary Chinese people. Official Japanese visits to the shrine, where Class-A war criminals are entombed and worshipped have ulterior motives and are designed to revert to aspects of Japan's militarist tradition. Japanese media reports on the protests against the Yasukuni visits have in turn provoked negative reactions among the Japanese public.

The focus on visits by Japanese political leaders to the Yasukuni Shrine closely relates to historical changes at the shrine. The shrine emerged from the Tokyo Shokonsha, established on August 8, 1869, in memory of the more than 3,500 warriors sacrificed for recovering the power of Emperor Meiji in the 1868 Boshin War, a Japanese civil war. In 1879, Emperor Meiji ordered the shrine renamed as the Yasukuni Shrine: the word "Yasukuni" is taken from the phrase "by which I want to stabilize our nation" in 4th Century BCE Chronicles of Zuo (Zuo Zhuan), meaning "Pacifying the Country." Since its construction, the shrine became a focal point for sacrifice by state leaders. After the Meiji Reform, Japan began its foreign expansion, and the Yasukuni Shrine began to consecrate the soldiers who died fighting for Japan in wars including the Sino-Japanese War of 1894–1895, the Russo-Japanese War, and World War II. (Family members were also entombed there.) At that time, only the Yasukuni Shrine was controlled by the military system while the other 52 shrines around Japan were administered by Japan's cabinet office.

After Japan's defeat in World War II, in December 1945, the military occupation authorities issued the "Shinto Order," ending the special relation between the Yasukuni Shrine and the government. Article 20 of Japan's peaceful constitution formulated in September 1952 contained articles related to the separation of church and state, and stipulated that the government cannot intervene in any religious matters. As a result, the Yasukuni Shrine become a non-governmental independent religious legal person.

In October 1978, Nagayoshi Matsudaira, who then managed the shrine, moved the remains of 14 Class-A war criminals, including Hideki Tōjō, to the Shrine for consecration in the name of "Showa Martyrs," fundamentally changing the nature of the Yasukuni Shrine.[7] After this decision, Emperor Hirohito stopped paying official visits to the Yasukuni Shrine, whereas he had visited annually from the end of the war right up to 1978.

The 1978 historical change at the Yasukuni Shrine indicates that the Yasukuni Shrine has come to symbolize the way that the Japanese government recognizes and deals with its history of invasion of foreign countries—both within Japan, and among the people of Asian countries that suffered invasion by Japanese militarists. For many people in Asia, the official visits raise concern about the direction of Japan's future development, and this explains why reports on visits by Japanese leaders to the Yasukuni Shrine have triggered protests by Asian countries, including China. In Japan as well the visits have led to conflict: the descendants of Japanese war veterans as well as the right wing political forces view the shrine as a spiritual symbol, and uphold the idea that the shrine should be re-nationalized, viewing visits by national leaders as a sign of support for this cause. In contrast, many among the Japanese public consider official visits to the shrine as a violation of the constitution, and contrary to the constitutional principle of separation between church and state. Others in Japan have argued that the shrine is an ordinary temple, only serving as a place for sacrifice to relatives and prayers for peace—that it has no connection to restoration of wartime militarism. Whatever the case, however, Japanese leaders should consider public opinion in Japan and the rest of Asia, which was deeply hurt by the actions of Japanese militarists, and stop paying any form of visit to the Yasukuni Shrine.

The issue of changes to Japan's historical textbooks represents the collision between different historical narratives in Japan, and has caused continuous friction between Japan and the countries it invaded in Asian, including China. After the normalization of diplomatic relations between China and Japan, school textbook material on the history of Japan's imperial invasions of Asian countries was revised by the right wing in 1982, and in 1986 these revisions were examined and approved by Japan's Ministry of Culture. Later, in the mid-1990s and through the early part of the 21st century, Japanese official history textbooks underwent several further revisions, weakening their accounts of Japanese imperial aggressions, and even putting a positive interpretation on them. The edition of the history textbook created by the New History Textbook Compiling Center, established by Nishio Kanji, a professor at the University of Electronic Communications, Nobukatsu Fujioka, professor at the University of Tokyo, Kobayashi Yoshinor, a right-wing cartoonist, and Takahashi Shiro, professor at Meisei University, represents the history of Japanese invasions abroad in a positive light, and puts a favorable spin on Japanese militarism. China and Japan have undergone years of contention about these textbook portrayals of historical Japanese aggression and militarism, and the textbook changes have contributed to the steady worsening of Sino-Japanese relations.

In addition to the disputes over the Yasukuni Shrine visits and Japanese history textbook contents, the issue of civilian compensation has also led to deterioration in Sino-Japanese relations. The issue relates particularly to Japan's refusal to compensate groups and individuals affected by remains of chemical weapons used in the war, victims of military enslavement and rape of "comfort women," and victims of forced labor. In 1972, the Chinese government waived any government claim against Japan for war compensation, but since the 1980s, individuals and groups in China have organized to seek compensation and redress, though these efforts have largely failed. The issue of Japan's denial of compensation to civilians for wartime atrocities and crimes has had a negative influence on public opinion within both countries, and of course directly affects the Chinese victims themselves.

These historical disputes have increasingly become a large barrier to communication between ordinary Chinese and Japanese people, and have seriously affected Sino-Japanese relations. As one Japanese journalist noted, "The Chinese detest Japan due to Japan's aggression against China, whereas many Japanese people in return think China merely uses these historical issues as a handle against it. Chinese people feel that Japan has whitewashed the history of Japanese aggression, and that Japan lacks repentance, so they detest Japanese people more strongly. Correspondingly, this leads Japanese people to further dislike Chinese people. It is a vicious cycle."

In his book *China in the Eyes of the Japanese*, Professor Satoshi Amako mentions that many Japanese people feel that no matter how deeply Japan apologizes for its historical aggressions, China still requires Japan to repeatedly "reflect" and "apologize," to the point of obsession. This causes Japanese people to tire of such demands, gradually leading to aversion, and statements such as, "China should not go too far," or, "Will the apology never end?" For many Japanese people, China too frequently plays the "history card," and making historical issues into just another diplomatic bargaining chip to achieve other foreign policy aims.[8]

In his article *Should Japan Fear the Rise of China?*, Fujihira Shinju writes that many Japanese people feel that Japan has already apologized for its wartime aggressions, and made repeated apologies over time, leading to "Apology Fatigue." Similarly, he believes China's practice of seizing on

Japan's past faults is a case of playing the "history card," and does not simply represent a demand for further apology.[9]

He also argues that during 2005 demonstrations in China against Japan's request for status as a permanent member of the United Nations Security Council, Chinese police took no measures to protect the Japanese embassy or assets of Japanese people in China. This further intensified the sense of "Apology Fatigue" in Japan and aggravated Japanese weariness with Chinese protests and dissatisfaction with China. Many in the Japanese public came to view Chinese hostility to Japan as having been incited by Chinese media and China's educational system rather than as a response to Japan actions.[10]

While historical disputes are among the reasons for the worsening of Sino-Japanese relations, they are not necessarily fundamental. In the 1980s, disputes over historical matters existed, but did not have a major influence on Sino-Japanese relations. Why? In any era, real and concrete national interests outweigh any historical dispute. The interpretation of historical issues is based on weighing real interest. When two countries share interests, they tend to interpret historical issues more favorably; when their current national interests come into conflict, historical disputes become a further contradiction between them. Therefore, historical issues are not the fundamental reason for the worsening of Sino-Japanese relations, but rather the weighing of real interests by the governments of China and Japan.

8.2.2 *Disputes over territory and maritime delimitation*

In our interviews, one Japanese scholar said that disputes over real national interests, including administration of the Diaoyu Islands and conflict over maritime borders in the East China Sea represent the most important factors influencing Sino-Japanese relations. Regarding the Diaoyu Islands dispute, China claims that the Diaoyu Islands have been Chinese territory since ancient times, while Japan holds that the Diaoyu Islands constituted terra nullius—unoccupied territory—and that the Japanese first found the Islands and placed them under the jurisdiction of Okinawa County in January 1895. In recent years, the Japanese and Chinese governments and public have argued fiercely over the sovereignty of the islands, without any solution. In September 2012, the Japanese government announced the "nationalization" of the Diaoyu Islands, triggering huge anti-Japanese demonstrations around China and further worsening Sino-Japanese relations.

In the late 1990s, China and Japan fell into the dispute over the delimitation of the continental shelf of the East China Sea. In 1996, Japan adopted a new Law on the Exclusive Economic Zone and Continental Shelf. In 1998, China issued the Law on the Exclusive Economic Zone and Continental Shelf of the People's Republic of China. The laws contained different delimitations of the East China Sea continental shelf. Japan proposed delimiting the continental shelf and the exclusive economic zone on the principle of the center line, while China insisted on the continental shelf principle as stipulated in international law. Given the contradictory positions, China argued for the fairness principle, but both parties understood the concept of fairness differently: China has taken the position that since China has a long coastline and larger population, it should have a bigger share, while Japan holds that fairness implies delimitation on an even split. In 2008, China and Japan concluded an agreement over the issue of how to develop oil and gas fields in the East China Sea, and delimited an "Area for Common Development" near the center line. However, after a 2010 incident where two ships collided in the East China Sea, both parties postponed further negotiation, leaving the East China Sea issue unresolved.

At present, territorial disputes concerning sovereignty over the Diaoyu Islands and oil and gas resources in the continental shelf of the East China Sea represent conflicts over real national interests, and are the most significant and most difficult aspects to resolve. Resolution requires Chinese and Japanese leaders and people to jointly explore solutions acceptable to both parties, which in turn needs political wisdom and open-mindedness.

8.2.3 *China's rise and "China Threat"*

In our interviews, Japanese scholars and journalists all mentioned the influence of China's rapid development on Sino-Japanese relations. Given China's rapid development, in contrast to Japan's recent economic stagnation, the concept of the China Threat has grown in Japan. Many Japanese scholars and people think that China's rise constitutes a threat to Japan. China has focused on economic development over the recent two decades, but that has also led to rapid changes in China's political, foreign, military, and social aspects. Those changes have altered Japanese views of China. Moreover, China's hard strengths, such as rapid progress and improvement in its economic, technological, and military capabilities, have made it possible for China to take tougher positions internationally, enhancing China's fight for supremacy of Asia.[11]

In 2010, China's GDP surpassed that of Japan and China became the world's second largest economy. China also made strides in strengthening its scientific and technological development, as represented by its manned space program and leadership in certain high-end technologies. Its construction of a new aircraft carrier and buildup of its blue-water navy have also attracted worldwide attention. These developments have demonstrated China's power and enhanced Chinese national pride, but also caused fear and suspicion among Western countries and Japan. In turn, these have altered Japanese impressions of China and caused concerns over the China Threat, and in turn made China's rising economic strength and relative international position a structural factor influencing Sino-Japanese relations.

China has continued to peacefully modernize its military, but this modernization makes Japan worry that China will use its growing economic and military power to expand its influence in, and control over, East Asia. The report, "A New Chapter in Sino-Japanese Relations: Going Beyond Historical Issues and Moving Towards Co-existence and Common Development," by the Japanese Institute of International Affairs, notes that China's military expenditure has increasing by double-digit percentage points for twenty consecutive years, and there is little transparency over these expenditures and the intentions behind them. Moreover, China has rapidly enhanced its naval and air forces. PLA Navy ships have entered areas that Japan considers its territorial waters, and China has successfully tested anti-satellite missiles—all of which have caused concern among Japan and other countries in East Asia.

In our interviews, a Japanese journalist summarized the fundamental reason for worsening relations as follows: "Superficially, the worsening of Sino-Japanese relations is due to disputes over historical reasons or the differences in their political systems. In fact, however, the sudden rise of China is the basic reason for worsening relations. With its increasing military power, and demands for expanded boundaries, a stronger China intensifies the sense of alarm felt by many Japanese. Chinese people may not feel the change, but Japanese people have really felt it. Like a child who has grown from age 10 to an adult at age 20, his capabilities have changed more than he may think, while others experience a huge difference. This feeling exists not only among Japanese people, but also in Southeast Asian countries. Today, Southeast Asian countries generally fear China, as China has become stronger."

As for the intention of the Japanese government in hyping and exaggerating China Threat, a few scholars and Japan experts we interviewed considered that Japanese leaders mainly rely on the China Threat as a pretext to suppress domestic opposition, strengthen the Japanese military, and increase the support for Japan's new security law among American and East Asian countries.[12] Japan's intentions require people of all countries in Asia, including China, to remain vigilant.

8.2.4 *Strengthening of the Japan-US alliance*

In our interviews, one Japanese scholar noted that the strengthening of the Japan–U.S. Alliance is also one of the key factors influencing Sino-Japanese relations, and has vital importance for the security situation in East Asia. The Alliance was established at the beginning of the Cold War on the basis of the Treaty of Mutual Cooperation and Security Between the United States and Japan. At its core was the U.S. security guarantee of Japan. According to the treaty, if Japan is attacked, the U.S. should offer military protection to Japan.

The Alliance had different targets at different stages. During the Cold War, the alliance was mainly aimed at socialist countries such the Soviet Union, China, and North Korea. In 1996, after the end of the Cold War, the treaty was redefined and expanded from mainly defending Japan's security to safeguarding the leading position of Japan and the U.S. in maintaining the security of the whole Asia-Pacific region. At that time, American policy on China featured a mixture of engagement and containment, and the Japan–U.S. Alliance was part of a strategic defense against China. After the September 11 attacks, the role of the alliance was further expanded, and affected other major issues around the Asia-Pacific region, including issues related to Taiwan and Korea, maritime security disputes in the Asia-Pacific region, issues connected to Russia, the Middle East, Southeast Asia, and the fight against terrorism. The extent of the cooperation makes Japan a decisive player in the U.S. strategy for the Eastern Hemisphere.[13]

The strengthening of the Japan–U.S. Alliance is to a large extent aimed at China, and therefore prevents the resolution of Asia-Pacific security issues, and poses a strategic threat to China. Therefore, the Japan–U.S. Alliance is also an important factor influencing the relationship between China and Japan. In 2005, Japan and the United States held talks—known as two-plus-two, due to the participation of the two countries' top defense and foreign policy officials—to discuss the security situation in the Asia-Pacific region, including the Taiwan issue. In November 2012, the U.S. Senate voted to add an additional article in the annual defense authorization to stipulate that Article 5 of the Treaty of Mutual Cooperation and Security Between the United States and Japan covers the Diaoyu Islands, effectively intervening in the dispute.

Aside the four reasons already mentioned that have negatively influenced Sino-Japanese relations, some journalists and scholars we interviewed also mentioned the differences in Chinese and Japanese political systems and the influences of demonizing media reporting in both countries. It is undeniable that the difference in systems and negative media reporting have both influenced the trend of Sino-Japanese relations, but these are not fundamental explanations. The difference in political systems existed at the when diplomatic relations were normalized, and this did not influence Sino-Japanese relations at that time. Media reports are influenced by national interests, policies, and by public opinion. Some negative reporting in Chinese and Japanese media relate mainly to the political conflicts between both countries and conflicting national interests. For this reason, the change in national interests due to the change of relative national strengths between China and Japan is the fundamental factor influencing Sino-Japanese relations. All issues, regardless of the territorial dispute over the Diaoyu Islands, the strengthening of the Japan–U.S. Alliance, or China's rise and the increase of China's military strength, are closely tied with the national interests of both countries.

8.3 The ways to improve Sino-Japanese relations

Naturally, China's development is based on its own demands and path. China should not, and could not, simply follow the wishes of the people of Japan or other countries. However, in the era of globalization and peaceful development, international competition and conflict through hard strength is unfortunate and untimely. On the contrary, only by conforming to the general trend of the world and integrating into the international community can a country fully realize its national interests and development goals. As major countries in East Asia, China and Japan would find any direct conflict unbearable. Under the current worsening trend in Sino-Japanese relations, finding ways to improve relations is of vital importance not only for the development of China and Japan, but for peace and development in East Asia and the whole world.

8.3.1 *Enhancing people-to-people contacts*

During our interviews, all Japanese scholars and journalists agreed with the view that the most important way to improve Sino-Japanese relations is to enhance exchange and cooperation between the two countries. As one scholar noted, "Both China and Japan should remember their history of cooperation after the normalization of diplomatic relations. Cooperation creates mutual benefit. One main feature of the current situations is that China and Japan are going through a period of insufficient people-to-people contact and cooperation, insufficient military cooperation, and even less exchange among political leaders. Dialogues and exchange at various levels between China and Japan are seriously lacking and should be enhanced. Japanese leaders make decisions based on the will of the people. If people-to-people contacts between both countries were increased, this would help improve inter-government relations. More Chinese tourist visits to Japan will also promote better Sino-Japanese relations."

Speaking about improving Sino-Japanese relations, one journalist interviewed said, "No one can really think of a good solution at present. The most important thing right now is to avoid conflict between China and Japan, and from there to enhance economic and trade cooperation and people-to-people contact."

According to our survey data, Japanese people who have been to China, have Chinese friends, or have experience and contact with China generally exhibit greater understanding of China more and a more positive view of China. Therefore, enhancing exchanges and cooperation between China and Japan in political, economic, educational, and cultural fields, and particularly promoting people-to-people contacts between the countries, are important ways to help Japanese people understand Chinese society, improve the image of China, increase the sense of affinity for China, and thereby improve Sino-Japanese relations.

Both China and Japan are culturally East Asian, share similar cultural values, and attach importance to interpersonal relations, so such exchanges can help ordinary people in China and Japan develop greater mutual understanding. In addition, the interpersonal relations established through such exchanges can also help them develop mutual trust and affinity.

Currently, there remain some exchanges and visits between Japanese and Chinese government officials, companies, colleges and universities, individuals, cultural groups, and non-governmental organizations, but the scope and size are insufficient. Efforts should be made to further enhance exchanges between China and Japan in politics, economy, culture, and education, and thereby help Japanese people personally understand Chinese culture, and recognize what Chinese society is really like.

To be sure, more contact does not necessarily lead to mutual understanding and friendship in each case, but without exchange, surely there will be no understanding or friendship. The key lies in paying attention to the quality of interactions while expanding the number and amount of interactions. Focusing on people-to-people contact will make it easier to develop communication between the people of China and Japan. For example, in July 2003, Chinese band Twelve Girls presented a traditional Chinese cultural performance using modern music, a successful example of non-governmental cultural exchange that can help improve Japanese affinity and awareness of Chinese culture and China.

8.3.2 *Enhancing inter-government dialogue and cooperation*

The phrase "cold politics, hot economies" has been used to summarize Sino-Japanese relations in recent years. Political disagreements or differences had little influence on the relationship between the two countries in the years after diplomatic normalization, but have come to have a major impact on the economic relations and non-governmental exchanges as bilateral political relations have steadily worsened in recent years. The intensification of the Diaoyu Islands dispute and the fight over oil and gas resources in the East China Sea have aggravated the tense atmosphere at the governmental and non-governmental levels between China and Japan. If the governments of the two countries can address the disputes over politics, territory, and security matters through dialogue and cooperation, they will be able to not only eliminate any foundation for any propaganda in Japan portraying the China Threat, but improve Japanese opinion about China and thus promote overall improvement of Sino-Japanese relations.

In one interview, one Japanese scholar said, "If the Chinese government can modify some of its behaviors, for example, stopping provocatively sending naval vessels to sail close to the Diaoyu Islands about twice weekly, this would certainly change the Japanese public opinion on China, and more Japanese people will want to visit China." The Japanese scholar's opinion is from the Japanese viewpoint. From the Chinese viewpoint, if Japanese government officials cease visits to the Yasukuni Shrine, reverse the nationalization of the Diaoyu Islands, and stop other provocations, this will improve Chinese public opinion on Japan. Therefore, if Chinese and Japanese political leaders can explore substantive solutions to their disputes, and cooperate more actively, this will not only ease the tense political atmosphere, but also enhance mutual affinity among the general public in each country.

8.3.3 *Enhancing cooperation in economic and trade fields, particularly in environmental protection and technology*

In one of our interviews, a scholar noted that the economic complementarity between China and Japan has decreased compared with 20 years ago, but both countries still have ample room for mutually beneficial economic cooperation in the fields of environmental protection and advanced technology. Some problems facing China, such as environmental pollution and food safety, not only seriously influence public health and quality of life in China, but also discourage Japanese tourism and study in China. Comparatively speaking, Japan not only has advanced technologies but also has decades of experience in environmental protection and ensuring food safety.

The close geographical positions of China and Japan environmental protection have a shared interest, and hence cooperation in this field has increased in recent years. The cross-border aspect of environmental problems inevitably leads to shared environmental benefits or negative consequences of actions taken within one country. From problem in agricultural product quality caused by environmental pollution in China, to Japan's problems of seasonal pollen allergies, and the Fukushima nuclear disaster, environmental problems may directly or indirectly influence the economic interests and health of people in both countries. Therefore, China and Japan need to cooperate, and have the ability to cooperate, on environmental protection. As one Japanese scholar said in an interview, "There is ample room for cooperation on environmental protection between China and Japan, and such cooperation can have major significance for realizing a strategic relationship of mutual benefit between the two countries."

Besides environmental cooperation, China and Japan also have room for cooperation in advanced technology. China has witnessed rapid development in science and technology over the past several decades, and has made remarkable achievements in several fields, but Japan remains most technologically developed economy in Asia. Japan has advanced science and technology, high quality management practices and international business operations, and world-leading technologies in many fields. These include superconducting materials, communications, new energy, energy efficiency, environmental protection, electronics, precision instruments, and high-end equipment manufacturing. Relative to Japan, China has a larger market, faster economic growth, a larger national infrastructure and industrial base, and advantages of labor quality and quantity. For this reason, China and Japan still have economic complementarity and good potential for technical cooperation.

In the years following diplomatic normalization, China and Japan cooperated in multiple fields including technology, and this cooperation played a decisive role in the improvement in Sino-Japanese relations. In recent years, however, political tensions have slowed such cooperation. In the future, China and Japan should deepen their cooperation in technology and further intensify their economic relationship, laying the foundation for improvement in political relations.

At the Beijing-Tokyo Forum 2011, Zhang Xiaoqiang, Vice Director of China's National Development and Reform Commission delivered remarks emphasizing the need for China and Japan to deepen bilateral economic and technical cooperation. In April 2015, the Sino-Japanese Economic and Technical Cooperation Platform was officially launched in Beijing. The platform aims to pair technologies developed by Japanese industries and research institutions with the emerging industries in China, enabling technology transfer in the industrial fields of energy conservation, environmental protection, pharmaceuticals, and food processing.[14]

Facing each other across a narrow sea, both China and Japan are major world powers. Their relationship is now at a new historical low, but visionary experts in each country remain optimistic about the future of the relationship. At present, Sino-Japanese economic exchanges and people-to-people contacts are gradually recovering, and Chinese tourists have helped in Japan's recent economic turnaround. If both countries further enhance people-to-people contacts, expand political dialogue, and deepen economic cooperation in the environmental and technical fields, it will enhance mutual understanding and trust and create new opportunities for improving bilateral relations.

Notes

1. Data source: China National Bureau of Statistics. Retrieved from http://data.stats.gov.cn/easyquery.htm?cn= C01.
2. Chinese Tourists Present Crazy Buy in Japan and Double Soaringly in the First Ten Months This Year. Website of The Paper.cn, Nov. 30, 2015. Retrieved from http://www.thepaper.cn/newsDetail_forward_1403158.
3. Warmer Economic and Trade Relation between China and Japan, a New Opportunity for Cross-Border E-Commerce and Third-Party Market. Website of the 21st Century Business Herald, Nov. 3, 2015. Retrieved from: http://epaper.21jingji.com/html/2015-11/03/content_25094.htm.
4. Warmer Economic and Trade Relation between China and Japan, a New Opportunity for Cross-Border E-Commerce and Third-Party Market. Website of the 21st Century Business Herald, Nov. 3, 2015. Retrieved from: http://epaper.21jingji. com/html/2015-11/03/content_25094.htm.
5. Ibid.
6. Ibid.
7. Yasukuni Shrine—the Soul-Calling Poster for Japanese Militarists, www.xinhuanet.com. Retrieved from http://news.xinhuanet.com/2015-04/29/c_127743358.htm.
8. Satoshi Amako. *China in the Eyes of the Japanese* (Translated by Fan Li). Social Sciences Academic Press, 2006: 23.
9. Shinju, Fujihira. "Should Japan Fear the Rise of China?" (Translated by Zhang Ling). *Foreign Theoretical Trends* 10 (2008): 57–61.
10. Ibid.

11. Xie, Xiaoguang, and Peng Yue. "Structural Factors Influencing Sino-Japanese Relations after the Cold War [lengzhanhou yingxiang zhongri guanxi de jiegouxing yinsu jianyan]." Japanese Research 3(2013): 28–33.
12. Zhao, Yue, and Honghui Shen. "Japan has Ulterior Motives in Hyping 'China Threat' [riben chaozuo zhongguo weixielun bieyouyongxin]." Retrieved from http://news.163.com/15/0723/07/AV6BQ9JG00014Q4P. html.
13. Pang, Zhongying. "On American Factors in Sino-Japanese Relations [lun zhongri guanxizhong de meiguo yinsu]." International Economic Review 3(2002).
14. "The Sino-Japanese Economic and Technological Cooperation Platform" is Launched after the Agreement was Concluded Officially. Website of the Central People's Government of the People's Republic of China, April 16, 2015. Retrieved from: http://www.gov.cn/xinwen/2015-04/16/content_2848049.htm.

Conclusions

With the general trend of peace, globalization, and democratization since the end of the Cold War, countries have become more and more interdependent. Besides the traditional factors that inhibit friendly international relations, such as differing political ideologies, military security guarantees, and economic frictions, culture is becoming an increasingly important determinant of international relations—namely, cultural soft power plays a growing role in forming the national image, enabling a country to occupy the commanding height of morality and justice, winning the respect of the international community, and improving relations with other countries. To be sure, here culture in a broad sense refers to all aspects of traditional culture, mass culture, and political culture. Cultural soft power refers to cultural content that can attract and influence the behavior and culture of ordinary people in other countries.

In the over 40 years since diplomatic normalization, China and Japan have greatly expanded their exchanges in various fields, and people-to-people contacts have also increased, but mutual understanding between ordinary people in both countries remains lacking. It even seems that ordinary people in the two countries have grown more and more estranged, and their relationship has evolved into one featuring geographical proximity paired with social distance. As recent public opinion surveys in China and Japan show, positive views of the public for those of the other country have steadily declined. It is undeniable that main reasons for this decline are the political and security disputes between the countries that have taken place since the mid-1990s, but the lack of understanding or cultural misunderstandings between their publics also plays a role. In other words, differences or discrepancies in how each party views their counterpart due to changes in the international situation, and the alteration in China's relative strength compared to Japan since the end of the Cold War have influenced Sino-Japanese political and security relations.

With its rapid economic growth and expanding involvement in international affairs, China's influence in the world is far greater than in past decades. However, how other countries including Japan interpret China's growing influence and their willingness to accept China's development and rise, depend on China's cultural soft power and national image. Namely, acceptance depends on whether China's development is perceived as bringing benefits, and whether China's influence can generate attraction and appeal for those in other countries. Only by enhancing soft power while sharpening hard power in economics, science and technology, and the military can China fully realize its grand strategic goal of peaceful rise.

To this end, we selected Japan as a window to understand China's cultural soft power, relying on survey questionnaires and in-depth interviews to gather data and analyze how Chinese culture is being communicated and perceived in Japan, and on how Japanese views toward China, Chinese culture, Chinese media, Chinese people, and Sino-Japanese relations are changing. We conducted three questionnaire surveys among the Japanese general public through directly conducting questionnaire surveys and via survey companies in 2010, 2011, and 2013. The first survey was conducted by directly distributing questionnaires to Japanese students and employees in Beijing and Tokyo. The second and third surveys were conducted in Japan by professional Japanese Internet survey firms. The content of the surveys related to respondents views of China and their impressions of Chinese people, interests in and knowledge of various aspects of Chinese culture, identification with traditional and modern Chinese values, knowledge of China's political and social systems, degree and form of contact with China, trust in Chinese media, and evaluation of Sino-Japanese relations. To supplement the questionnaire results and analyze the deeper reasons behind Japanese impressions of China, in the second half of 2014, we carried out in-depth interviews with Japanese journalists and scholars working, visiting, and studying in China.

Our analysis of the survey and interview data reveals that Japanese people do identify with some Chinese values, history, and life habits. For example, Japanese identify with Chinese values of benevolence, righteousness, propriety, and filial piety, appreciate ancient Chinese culture and history, and enjoy Chinese cuisine. Our study shows Japanese have a limited identification with modern Chinese mass culture, and even have a negative view of China's modern institutional culture, considering that China's political and economic systems and their development are not in line with the interests of Japan and the world. What's more, many Japanese hold the view that although Chinese people still believe in shared, traditional values, their opinion of Chinese people is basically negative. Japanese people have little contact with Chinese media and do not trust it, considering Chinese media reporting as inaccurate, unfair, incomplete, untimely, and difficult to watch or read. Japanese people have the highest affinity for American and German cultures, and fewer than 10% of respondents preferred China and Chinese culture over others.

It is clear that ordinary Japanese people accept and like traditional Chinese culture, ancient Chinese history, and some traditional Chinese values. Japanese culture contains similar cultural aspects, and Japanese appreciation and enjoyment of traditional Chinese culture is limited to those shared aspects, and hardly goes beyond this appreciation. For this reason, China's traditional culture has weak soft power for the outside world. Japanese people partially identify with modern Chinese mass culture, such as modern Chinese films, movie stars, pop songs, and musicians, but the influence of these symbols of Chinese culture remains inferior to those of Western or Japanese cultures. Though many Japanese people identify with aspects of traditional Chinese culture, they mainly focus on appreciation and entertainment, which provide only weak soft power. Japanese people find it hard to accept China's modern political culture, and even expression rejection of it. Most Japanese people think China's system and development are not in line with their interests and values, and that China even poses a threat or brings uncertainty to the world. Correspondingly, these views may weaken China's soft power. On the whole, Chinese culture has little attraction and influence in Japanese society, and its cultural soft power is lacking.

To be sure, China's development does not depend on whether Japanese people like it. According to our survey and analysis, however, we can develop a dispassionate view of China's current cultural soft power in Japan, and take measures to improve the content and methods of communicating China's cultural soft power in Japan, so as to enhance China's soft power in foreign countries. Addressing the existing problems identified in this analysis, we make the following policy proposals:

1 China should attach greater importance to the content of communications, focusing on non-political news or emphasizing social life as far as possible. Traditional Chinese culture is popular among the Japanese public, but we should pay attention to modernizing Japanese views of traditional Chinese culture. That is to say, we should add modern elements to the forms of traditional Chinese culture, as since traditional culture with more modern expressions is most acceptable. Examples of such modernization efforts include the 2004 visit of China's Twelve Girls Band, the 2010 Spring Festival performance in Japan of "Cultural China, Spring for All" organized by the China Association of Overseas Chinese, as well as other programs combining modern forms with traditional musical content.
2 China should improve the image of Chinese media, namely changing its image from serving as the mouthpiece of the government, and reducing its stiffness and rigidity, and instead developing an image of independence, fairness, justice, and supervision, thus enhancing its trustworthiness among viewers.
3 China should seek to change the style and manner of communication with foreign publics, from one of preachiness, aggression, and self-serving utilitarianism, to one involving greater attention to softer interactions with the audience, based on unforced cultural psychology of the Japanese society.

4 China should expand people-to-people contacts between China and Japan at various levels and in various fields, since those Japanese with experience of contact with China and those with Chinese language ability have better views of China obviously than those without. Moreover, efforts should be made to enhance exchanges and interactions between young Chinese and Japanese people, since young people are the future. Our surveys reveal that Japanese interest in Chinese culture and positive opinion of China are inversely proportional to age.

The above-mentioned countermeasures are basically technical. Enhancing China's cultural soft power in the outside world and improving the image of China in the eyes of Japanese people fundamentally depend on China's concerted efforts. Namely, enhancing soft power will require continuing political reform; building a virtuous society based on prosperity, justice, and sustainable development; and improving the overall character of the Chinese people. Only by realizing such social changes can China's cultural soft power be strengthened and the image of China be improved, so as to help China gradually increase its appeal and influence around the world, and fully achieve the goals of peaceful development and becoming a respectable member of the international community.

The completion of this book takes place just as China celebrates the 70th anniversary of victory in Chinese People's Counter-Japanese War and the World Anti-Fascist War. We hope that the governments and people of China and Japan can start anew in the common interests in development of both countries, bury previous resentments, let go of historical burdens and look to the future, seek common ground while reserving differences, and increase their understanding of and trust in each other, so as to create a virtuous cycle in Sino-Japanese relations. If events develop in line with this hope, this will be a blessing for the Chinese and Japanese people, and for Asia and the world.

Postscript

It took us 5 years to complete the first draft of this book, starting in 2010 with the design of the questionnaires, up through May 2015. During this period, Sino-Japanese relations experienced ups and downs, and witnessed complex changes. The period saw the naval collision between Chinese and Japanese ships near the Diaoyu Islands waters in 2010, and the worsening of bilateral political and security relations after the so-called "nationalization" of the Diaoyu Islands in 2012. The period also experienced the course of the four points of consensus and the summit in 2014 and an improving relationship thereafter. In terms of future change and development, we predict that bilateral relations will be basically smooth, but with some fluctuations. We anticipate the two countries will not experience a repeat of serious conflict like the Diaoyu Islands crisis in 2012, but will nevertheless face ongoing contradictions. They will not experience any quick improvement of their relations, and the current momentum of better relations will continue.

This opinion is based on the following considerations: both China and Japan have been affected by the process of globalization. Although there remain many contradictions between China and Japan, and potential sources of crises in East Asia, the general international situation will not allow any major conflict between powers such as China and Japan. Their global economic ties make the two countries more and more interdependent, unless the leaders of one decides to pay any cost to achieve some goal. In fact, each country has its strong points and is equally matched with the other. If any conflict happens, neither is certain to win, and, on the contrary, could face a catastrophic outcome. Therefore, in the view of their fundamental interests, both countries will likely manage to avoid the occurrence of any crisis, and if one arises, they will likely deal with it in a peaceful way.

At the beginning of 2016, in his administration's speech to the Diet, Prime Minister Abe Shinzo noted his diplomatic goal of improving Sino-Japanese relations, and stated that his administration's focus on revitalizing Japan's domestic economy would require greater cooperation with China. Similarly, China also needs stable Sino-Japanese relations, and would not like to see any tensions over disputes related to the South China Sea, Taiwan Straits, or the DPRK nuclear issue. In 2016, top leaders of China and Japan will have several opportunities to meet each other: China-Japan-ROK Tripartite Leaders' Meeting will be held in Japan, and China will host the G20 Hangzhou Summit, where President Xi will meet the Japanese Prime Minister. In addition, it is expected that the high-level economic dialogue between China and Japan will be restarted in 2016 after having been shelved for many years. These activities have the potential to improve Sino-Japanese relations, or at least will not worsen them.

It is undeniable that: structural contradictions in Sino-Japanese relations still exist; their disputes over recognition of the history and territorial issues and the mutual distrust regarding security matters remain; and the opinions held by nationals of both countries toward their counterparts are still very low. Though such problems remain, Sino-Japanese relations have the potential to improve or at least remain stable—as long as the two governments want to improve the relations and are willing to take measures to do so, such as to restrain crises, to expand bilateral economic and cultural exchanges, and to enhance people-to-people exchanges. In recent years, Chinese tourist visits to Japan have continued to increase. In 2015, China became Japan's top source of incoming tourists. It is hoped that more Japanese will travel to China for tourism, study, and work, which will help enhance mutual understanding among regular people in both countries, and thereby improve bilateral relations. In the days to come, we will continue to monitor Sino-Japanese relations and the communication of Chinese cultural soft power in Japan, and share further research findings.

We hereby express our gratitude to many people, who made their contributions to smooth publication of this book. Our thanks go first to professor Guan Shijie at the School of Journalism and Communication, Peking University, who made great efforts in organizing the project group to carry out questionnaire design, data analysis, and manuscript writing. We also want to thank our coworkers for their encouragement and help in project implementation and draft writing. Our special thanks are hereby extended to associate professor Xu Jincan at Peking University, who provided the assessment and survey data about the influences of Chinese culture in Japan chaired by her as the supplement to and contrast with the data from previous two surveys, to help writing of this book. Several journalists with Japanese media and two Japanese scholars studying in China took the time to answer our interviews and expressed their sincere wishes for better Sino-Japanese relations, for which we thank them.

Our heartfelt gratitude goes to all others who made their contributions to this book, including professor Wang Jisi with Peking University, who, despite a tight agenda, read the manuscript and wrote a foreword to the book, and made many valuable suggestions on revision and perfection of the manuscript; professor Li Yu with Peking University, research fellow Cui Shiguang with the Institute of Japanese Studies, CASS, Mr. Motozawa Ichiro, former newscaster with NHK, who read and made recommendation of this book, and editor Xu Shaoyan with the Peking University Publishing

House, who offered many suggestions on contents, structure, and standardization of this book.

This book is the research result under the major NSSFC programs "Research on External Communication of Chinese Cultural Soft Power" (08&ZD057) and "In-depth Research on Enhancing External Communication of Chinese Cultural Soft Power" (14ZDA053). At the end, we express our thanks to NSSFC and Beijing Program for Youth Talents for their supports concerned.

Wang Xiuli

Beijing, Feb. 2016

References

Anholt, Simon. *Competitive Identity: The New Brand Management for Nations, Cities and Regions*. New York: Palgrave Macmillan, 2007.

Bai, Shifan. "Second Revolution to Build a Socialist Country." Chuokoron Shinsha, Extra urgent edition 4(1967).

Brewer, Paul, Joseph Graf, and Lar Willnat. "Priming or Framing: Media Influence on Attitudes toward Foreign Countries." Gazette: The International Journal for Communication Studies 65.6(2003): 493–508.

Chen, Xiaowei. "Star Symbol and the Building of National Image [mingxing fuhao yu guojia xingxiang de jiangou]." Dongyue Tribune 1(2012): 65–68.

Cheng, Manli. "On Nation Image Building and Mass Communication [dazhong-chuanbo yu guojia xingxiang suzao]." Chinese Journal of Journalism & Communication 3(2007): 5–10.

Eisenstadt, S. N. *Japanese Civilization: A Comparative View* (Translated by Wang Xiaoshan, et al.). The Commercial Press, 2008.

Entman, Robert. "Framing: Toward Clarification of a Fractured Paradigm." Journal of Communication 43.4(1993): 51–58.

Fan, Wenlan. *The Modern History of China* [zhongguo jindai shi], Vol. 1 of Book I. People's Publishing House, 1951.

Fukuzawa, Yukichi. Datsu-A-Ron, Vol. 10, The Complete Works of Fukuzawa Yukichi. Iwanami Shoten, 1962.

Guan, Wenhu (Ed.). *On National Image* [guojia xing xiang lun]. University of Electronic Science and Technology of China Press, 2000.

He, Hui, and et al. *Construction and Communication of National Image in New Media Environment* [xinmeiti huanjingzhong guojia xingxiang de goujian yu chuanbo]. Foreign Languages Press, 2008.

Hikotaro, Ando, Muramatsu Akira, and Takeuchi Minoru. "Is the Cultural Revolution Destruction or Construction?" Chuokoron Shinsha 11(1966).

Hu, Wentao. *American Cultural Diplomacy and Its Practice Related to China* [meiguo wenhua waijiao jiqi zai zhongguo de yunyong]. World Affairs Press, 2008.

Huang, Qing. "International Consciousness and National Image in External Publicity [duiwai xuanchuanzhong de guoji yishi yu guojia xingxiang]." Chinese Journalist 9 (1998): 54.

Huntington, Samuel. *The Clash of Civilizations and the Remaking of World Order* (Translated by Zhou Qi, et al.). Xinhua Publishing House, 2002.

Ikutaro, Shimizu. "Peaceful coexistence between Japan and China." Top Travel 11(1959).

Iriye, Akira. *Cultural Internationalism and World Order*. Maryland: The Johns Hopkins University Press, 1997.

Jian, Taojie. "American Cultural Diplomacy after the Cold War and its Influences on Sino-American Relations [lengzhanhou meiguo wenhua waijiao jiqi dui zhongmeiguanxi de yingxiang]." Doctoral dissertation of Fudan University in 2010.

Kanji, Nishio, et al. *New History Textbook*. Fusosha Publishing Company, 2001(6): 219.

Kato, Shuichi. *The 21st Century and Chinese Culture* (Translated by Peng Jiahong). Zhonghua Book Company, 2007.

Katsu, Kaishū. *The Origin of Japan, Vol. 2 of the Complete Works of Katsu Kaishū*. Kodansha, 1973.

Kotobuki, Kuwahara. "The Aftereffects of the Cultural Revolution." Chuokoron Shinsha, Extra urgent edition 4(1967).

Kozai, Yoshishige, Shiro Nohara, and Nomura Koichi. "Discussion on 'What is Mao Zedong Thought on the Proletarian Cultural Revolution.'" Top Travel 11(1966).

Kunczik, Michael. *Images of Nations and International Public Relations*. Mahwah: Lawrence Erlbaum, 1997.

Kyouichi, Saionji, and Matsumoto Shunichi. "'China? Japan? Asia.'" Chuokoron Shinsha 10(1970).

Li, Yannan. "The 'Image of China' in Modern Japanese Literature [jindai riben wenxuezhong de zhongguo xingxiang]." Doctoral dissertation of Jinan University, May 2005.

Li, Yu, et al. *Sino-Japanese Relations under the Perspective of Civilization* [wenming shijiaoxia de zhongri guanxi]. Hong Kong Social Sciences Press, 2006.

Li, Zhengguo. "Crisis Communication, Role of the Media and Restoration of State Image [weiji gongguan, meiti juese yu guojia xingxiang de xiufu]." China Radio & TV Academic Journal 3(2006): 25–27.

Li, Zhi. *Cultural Diplomacy: An Interpretation Mode of Communication* [wenhua waijiao: yizhong chuanboxue de jiedu]. Peking University Press, 2005.

Liu, Jiaxin. *How Japanese Modern Intellectuals View China* [riben jindai zhishi fenzi de zhongguoguan]. Nankai University Press, 2007.

Liu, Jinan, Hui He, et al. *Image of China in World Mainstream Media* [jingxiang zhongguo: shijie zhuliu meitizhong de zhongguo xingxiang]. Communication University of China Press, 2006.

Liu, Linli. *The Image of China in Japanese Mass Media* [riben dazhongmeitizohng de zhongguo xingxiang]. Communication University of China Press, 2007.

Liu, Xiaoyan. "On Building National Civilization Image from the Perspective of Communication of Nationals Image [cong guomin xingxiang chuanbo kan guojia wenmin xingxiang de goujian]." Chinese Journal of Journalism & Communication 3(2007): 17–21.

Liu, Xiaoyan. "Thinking on Shaping of State Images by the Media [guanyu chuanmei suzao guojia xingxiang de sikao]." Chinese Journal of Journalism & Communication 2(2002): 61–66.

Lu, Ziwen. "Nationals-based Foreign Publicity: The Effective Way Through Which Nationals' Cross-cultural Ability Promotes Building of National Image [guomin waixuan: guomin kuawenhua nengli cujin guojia xingxiang jianshe de youxiao lujing]." Tribune of Study 5(2012): 49–53.

Luo, Hailong. "Constructive Analysis of the Reports on China in Japanese Mass Media [riben dazhong chuanmei duihua baodao de jiangou zhuyi fenxi]." Master's thesis of Hebei University, 2008.
Mark, Simon L. "Rethinking Cultural Diplomacy: The Cultural Diplomacy of New Zealand, the Canadian Federation and Quebec." Political Science 62.1(2010): 62–83.
Masahide, Bito, et al. *New Japanese History A*. Suken-tosho, 1995: 11.
Masahiro, Fujima. *Formation of the Modern East Asia World*. Nippon Bunka Publishing, 1977.
McCombs, Maxwell, and Donald L. Shaw. "The Agenda-setting Function of Mass Media." Public Opinion Quarterly 36.2(1972): 176–187.
McMurray, Ruth, and Muna Lee. *The Cultural Approach: Another Way in International Relations*. Chapel Hill: University of North Carolina Press, 1947.
Morley, Michael. How to Manage Your Global Reputation: A Guide to the Dynamics of International Public Relations. New York: New York University Press, 1998.
Mutz, Diana. "Mass Media and the Depoliticization of Personal Experience." American Journal of Political Science 36: 483–508.
Nomura, Koichi. *Comprehension of China in Modern Japan* (Translated by Zhang Xuefeng). Central Compilation & Translation Press, 1999.
Nye, Joseph. *Soft Power: The Means to Success in World Politics*. New York: Public Affairs, 2004.
Pang, Zhongying. "On American Factors in Sino-Japanese Relations [lun zhongri guanxizhong de meiguo yinsu]." *International Economic Review* 3(2002): 48–51.
Peng, Xinliang. *Cultural Diplomacy and China's Soft Power: A Globalized Perspective* [wenhuawaijiao yu zhongguo de ruanshili: yizhong quanqiuhua de shijiao]. Foreign Language Teaching and Research Press, 2008.
Ruan, Beiqian. "Study on China-Japan Mutual Reporting and the National Image of the Two Countries [zhongri xianghu baodao yu liangguo xingxiang yanjiu]." Master's thesis of Nanchang University, 2007.
Sakuzo, Yoshino. *On Sino-Japanese Relations, Vol. 6 of Works of Dr. Sakuzo Yoshino on Democracy*. Shinkigensha. 1947.
Satoshi, Amako. *China in the Eyes of the Japanese* (Translated by Fan Li). Social Sciences Academic Press, 2006.
Shen, Haitao. "Japan's Perception of China and the September 18 Incident [riben de zhongguo renshi yu jiuyiba shibian]." Northeast China History and Geography 4(2011): 10–15.
Shinju, Fujihira. "Should Japan Fear the Rise of China?" (Translated by Zhang Ling), Foreign Theoretical Trends 10(2008): 57–61.
Song, Chengyou. *A New Modern History of Japan* [xinbian riben jindaishi]. Peking University Press, 2006.
Soroka, Stuart. "*Media, Public Opinion, and Foreign Policy*." The Harvard International Journal of Press/Politics 8.1(2003): 27–48.
Sun, Youzhong. "*Connotation and Functions of National Image* [guojia xingxiang de neihan jiqi gongneng]." International Forum 3(2002): 14–21.
Takasugi, Shinsaku. *Records of the Tour Around the Qing-ruled China, The Posthumous Work* of Mr. Takasugi Shinsaku by the Committee in Memory of the 50th Anniversary of Mr. Takasugi Shinsaku. Kotobank, 1961.
Tan, Jianchuan. *The Image of China in Japanese Textbooks* [riben jiaokeshu de zhongguo xingxiang yanjiu]. Peking University Press, 2014.

Tarou, Sakamoto. The History of Japan (Translated by Wang Xiangrong, et al.). China Social Sciences Press, 2008.

Teng, Jun, et al. (Eds.) The *History of Sino-Japanese Cultural Exchanges* [zhongri wenhua jiaoliushi]. Peking University Press, 2011.

Tomoji, Abe. "Culture and Society." Top Travel 1(1955).

Tu, Guangjin, and He Gong. "Agenda Building in Beijing Olympics and National Image Communication [Beijing aoyun yu guojia xingxiang chuanbozhong de yicheng]." China Radio & TV Academic Journal 7(2008): 5–7.

Uchiyama, Kanzo. "Returning from China." Top Travel 5(1953).

Wang, Xiaode. *American Culture and Diplomacy* [meiguo wenhua yu waijiao]. World Affairs Press, 2008.

Wang, Xiuli, and Zhemin Jia. "Global Sports Events and the Shaping of National Image [quanqiu tiyu saishi yu guojia xingxiang suzao]." Journal of China University of Geosciences 2(2011): 97–101.

Wanta, Wayne, Guy Golan, and Clseolhan Lee. "Agenda Setting and International News: Media Influence on Public Perceptions of Foreign Nations." Journalism and Mass Communication Quarterly 81.2(2004): 364–377.

Wanta, Wayne, and Yu-wei Hu. "The Agenda-setting Effect of International News Coverage: An Examination of Differing News Frames." International Journal of Public Opinion Research 5.3(1993): 250–264.

Wu, Guanghui. *The Image of China in Japan* [riben de zhongguo xingxiang]. People's Publishing House, 2010.

Wu, Guanghui. "Research on Japanese Images of China—Exploration of Theories and Methods [riben de zhongguo xingxiang yanjiu: lilun yu fangfa de tansuo]." Japanese Language Education and Japanese Studies 1(2011): 146–152.

Wu, Wenxue, et al. *Contemporary Sino-Japanese Relations* [dangdai zhongri guanxi]. Current Affairs Press, 1995.

Wu, Youfu. *The Building and Communication of China's National Image* [zhongguo guojia xingxiang de suzao he chuanbo]. Fudan University Press, 2009.

Xie, Xiaoguang, and Peng Yue. "Structural Factors Influencing Sino-Japanese Relations after the Cold War [lengzhanhou yingxiang zhongri guanxi de jiegouxing yinsu jianyan]." Japanese Research 3(2013): 28–33.

Xie, Xiaoyan, and Xiaoyan Yang. "On Chinese Temperament in Shaping the Image of China as a Power [lun zhonguo daguo xingxiang suzaozhong de guomin qizhi]." Journal of Lanzhou University (Social Sciences) 4(2012): 48–54.

Xu, Tianxin, et al. *The General History of the World* (Modern Times) [shijie tongshi (xiandaijuan)]. People's Publishing House, 1997.

Xu, Xiaoge. "On National Image in International News Communication [guoji xinwen chuanbo Zhong de guojia xingxiang wenti]." Journalism & Communication 2(1996): 36–46.

Yan, Shaodang. "The Japanese View on China in the 20th Century [20shiji ribenren de zhongguoguan]." Daizong Journal of the Journal of Taian Institute of Education 2(1999): 37–46.

Yan, Shaodang. "The Japanese View on China in the Post-War 60 Years [zhanhou 60nian ribenren de zhongguoguan]." Japan Studies 3(2005): 1–11.

Yang, Dongliang (Ed.). *Japan's View on China since Modern Times* [jindai yilai riben de zhongguoguan]. Jiangsu People's Publishing House, 2012.

Zhan, Qi, and Yan Liu. "On the Establishment of the National Image Based on the Reports on China in Major Newspapers of Japan [cong riben zhuyao baozhi shehua baodao kan guojia xingxiang de shuli]." Foreign Communication 9(2008): 59–60.

Zhang, Kun, and Qiong Xu. "On the Inscape of the Nation Image [guojia xingxiang chuyi]." Chinese Journal of Journalism & Communication 3(2007): 11–16.

Zhang, Li. "The Japanese Views of China after the Cold War and the Influencing Factors [lengzhan hou ribenren zhongguoguan jiqi yingxiang yinsu yanjiu]." Master's thesis of East China Normal University. 2013.

Zhang, Ning. *China in Japanese Media: Reporting Framework and National Image* [riben meitishang de zhongguo: baodao kuangjia yu guojia xingxiang]. Jilin People's Publishing House, 2006.

Zhang, Yajing. "The Japanese View on China: during the Period of the Cultural Revolution in China [ribenren de zhongguoguan: yi wenhua dageming shiqi wei zhongxin]." Historical Journal of Fu Jen Catholic University 12(2001).

Zhang, Yu. "A Study on the National Image of China in Japanese Newspapers (1995–2005)—Taking Asahi Shimbun and Yomiuri Shinbun as Examples [riben baozhizhong de zhongguo guojia xingxiang yanjiu (1995–2005)—yi zhaorixinwen he dumaixinwen weili]." Journalism & Communication 4(2007): 75–83.

Zhang, Yuqiang. "Shallow Views on National Image [guojia xingxiang chuyi]." Modern Communication 2(2002): 27–31

Zhao, Xinli. "The Image of China in Japanese Documentaries [riben jilupianzhong de zhongguo xingxiang]." Youth Journalist 10-1(2009): 15–17.

Zhao, Xinli. *Chinese and Japanese Communication and Public Diplomacy* [zhongri chuanbo yu gonggong waijiao]. Social Sciences Academic Press (China), 2012.

Zhou, Ning. "'A Giant Other': 'China' in Japan's Modernity Self-Imagination [juda de tazhe—riben xiandaixing ziwo xiangxiangzhong de zhonguo]." Tianjin Social Sciences 5(2011): 101.

Index